ULENDO

ULENDO

TRAVELS
of a Naturalist In and Out of
AFRICA

by

ARCHIE CARR
1909—1987

Foreword by George Schaller
Preface by and Letters to Marjorie Harris Carr

UNIVERSITY PRESS OF FLORIDA
Gainesville   Tallahassee   Tampa   Boca Raton
Pensacola   Orlando   Miami   Jacksonville

Library of Congress Cataloging-in-Publication Data

Carr, Archie Fairly, 1909– 1987
 Ulendo: travels of a naturalist in and out of Africa / Archie
Carr; with preface by and letters to Marjorie Harris Carr.
  p. cm.
 Originally published: New York: Knopf, 1964.
 Includes index.
 ISBN 0-8130-1179-5 (acid-free paper)
  1. Zoology—Africa. 2. Natural history—Africa. 3. Africa—
Description and travel—1951–1976. 4. Carr, Archie Fairly, 1909–
—Correspondence. I. Title.
QL336.C37   1992   92-34453
591.96—dc20   CIP

Originally published by Alfred A. Knopf, Inc.
Copyright 1964 by Archie Carr
Copyright 1993 by the Board of Regents of the State of Florida
Printed in the United States of America on acid-free paper ∞
All rights reserved

The University Press of Florida is the scholarly publishing agency for the State University System of Florida, comprised of Florida A & M University, Florida Atlantic University, Florida International University, Florida State University, University of Central Florida, University of Florida, University of North Florida, University of South Florida, and University of West Florida.

Orders for books should be addressed to
University Press of Florida
15 Northwest 15th Street
Gainesville, FL 32611

TO

*Margie, Mimi, Chuck, Steve,
Tom, and David*

Contents

List of Plates	viii
Foreword by George Schaller	xi
Preface to the *1993* Edition by Marjorie Harris Carr	xv
Preface to the *1964* Edition	xvii
Sixteen-Mile Safari	3
Portuguese East	14
Nyasa	60
Kungu	79
Chambo	105
The Snake	140
The Bird and the Behemoth	159
The Lion Song	226
1993 Preface to the *1952* Letters	259
Letters from Archie to Marjorie Carr, *1952*	260
1993 Preface to the *1963* Letters	292
Letters from Archie to Marjorie Carr, *1963*	293
Index	299

List of Plates

FOLLOWING PAGE 104

All photographs are by the author,
except where otherwise specified

PLATE
- I Archie Carr and Wilson.
  (PHOTO BY LEWIS BERNER)
  Kikuyu village in Kenya.
- II Hippopotamus yawning.
  Vultures on the body of a young elephant.
- III Elephants in a dense forest.
  The *Piri Piri* on the Zambezi.
  (PHOTO BY LEWIS BERNER)
- IV Zebras.
  Cheetahs.
- V Elephants winding.
  Rhinoceros with cattle egrets.
- VI Giraffe at Ol Tukai.
- VII Elephant in village, Murchison Falls National Park.
  Thomson's gazelles.
- VIII Vultures waiting.
  Ankole cattle.

List of Plates

PLATE

IX Crocodile.
    Young lion.

X   Lioness keeping an eye out.
    Wildebeests.

XI Oribi, a small African antelope.
    Hippopotamus irked at photographer.

XII Cattle heron on elephant in grass.

XIII Waterbucks.

XIV Elephants and egrets.

XV Fish eagle.
    Cattle egrets and snowy egrets with cows.

XVI Giraffes at Ol Tukai.

MAP   xxii–xxiii

Foreword

MOST VISITORS come to Africa to bear witness to the last days of Eden. For fleeting moments they step back into other centuries and resurrect the past as they observe elephants glide among yellow-barked fever trees, the last great gathering of wildebeest in the Serengeti, and a cheetah in elegant pursuit of a gazelle. Long ago I studied mountain gorillas and lions, both magical creatures in which biology and myth combine. I have memories of a male mountain gorilla massively at rest on a forested slope, his silver back sparkling like morning frost, and of lion roars throbbing in the stillness of night. But such memories now resonate with sadness. It is the terrible fate of this generation to understand the full magnitude of destruction of Africa's wildlife, a renunciation of our beginnings. We know just enough about these large animals to mourn their disappearance. We cannot look at a black rhinoceros, or even the photograph of one, without guilt, without comprehending the wasteland of future memories.

I read *Ulendo: Travels of a Naturalist In and Out of Africa* more than a quarter of a century ago, and only dimly remembered its contents. But I looked forward to rereading an Archie Carr book. His passion for and appreciation of the natural world is always transmitted in a prose that is elegant, witty, warm, and perceptive. He was that rare professional naturalist whose books hold a place in literature. Like William Beebe, Aldo Leopold, and Frank Fraser Darling, he eloquently bridged the gap between science and the public. Yet I rather shied away from rereading *Ulendo*, expecting a book mostly about the demise of elephants, lions, and other wilderness totems. Every day another creation crumbles. The many books on the subject seem almost like memorials. Ironically, they somehow begin to lessen the intensity of our sorrow; capacity for concern is finite. But I need not have worried. Archie Carr came to Nyasaland in 1952, now called Malawi, to collect snails and mosquitoes.

Ulendo probes the lives of creatures that others skip in their compulsive search for charismatic animals. Full of curiosity and wonder, Archie Carr describes in vibrant prose whatever intrigues him. On encountering an Egyptian cobra, he notes that "the noise of a prowling snake is like no other animal sound I know." He puzzles over how evolution and ecology combine to produce an adaptive radiation of two hundred species of endemic cichlid fish in Lake Nyasa. He marvels at the huge, tornado-like spouts of midges over the same lake. Cakes made from these midges do not, he discovers, have an engaging flavor, but at least his guests at a Florida cocktail party did not complain when they unknowingly ate them, served on crackers. Along the Shire River in Mozambique most wildlife was gone. "There, where David Livingstone saw elephants, lions, and buffaloes, there were only cattle for egrets to stand with," the birds waiting for the hooves to stir up grasshoppers and other insects. This melancholy sight leads to a rumination about snowy egrets in Florida. There they also accompany cattle, but once they had spectacular companions including mammoths, camels, giant ground sloths, and glyptodonts. Do "the genes of the bird remember" the lost hosts?

Foreword

Archie Carr was a scientist, the world expert on sea turtles, but his perspective was that of a humanist. Whether writing about the behavior of jumping spiders or the joys of marimba music, he longed to obliterate the borders between himself and his surroundings. He conveys a sense of unknown possibilities and an intense appreciation of the harmonious order in nature, even among the most humble creatures. He could have made a backyard safari exciting. Although it was written three decades ago, take *Ulendo* on your next African trip: it is even more timely now than when it was first published. It is not what we see in a landscape but how much we see in it, and Archie Carr was the ultimate thinking traveler.

Ulendo is prophetic with the insights of a superb ecologist. A search for "a bit of old Africa" yielded maize fields, cars around a lion pride, and the gift of a bloody elephant tail. All around was the depressing silence of a wilderness from which the wildlife had gone. A healthy environment is perhaps the most basic of all human rights. "Some day, to exist in the world coming, every big game wilderness will lie behind fences—real varmint-stopping fences, leopard tight and eland high." And the biologist's job will be to manage such wilderness, not just protect it. "How much land, for instance, is the right amount to make a permanent preserve?" How do you manage lions? How much do savannahs owe to burning? What is the role of commercial wildlife cropping outside reserves?

When Archie Carr asked these questions they were prophecy. That future is here. Maize fields have grown ever more extensive as Africa's population has doubled and will soon double again; in reserves, tourist vehicles surround lions like clouds of gnats; and such species as the rhinoceros depend for survival increasingly on fenced areas that must be guarded to keep out varmints armed with automatic rifles. Conservation biologists continue to debate the best shape and size of reserves, and they ponder how to maintain a heterogeneous environment, the greatest diversity of species, both inside and outside them. It is now known that natural extinction rates of species on islands of habitat, such as reserves, are extraordinarily high. Furthermore, through inbreeding small populations lose their genetic variability and with it possibly their adaptability to changing circumstances. The problems of protecting and managing the earth's passing wilderness are enormous. The sad fact is that human economies are now part of almost all natural systems, even most so-called national parks and reserves.

"The way things are moving in Africa, the time will soon be past when even a good fight can save anything more than scraps," wrote Archie Carr as he recorded the growing emptiness around him. "To help awake regrets of this is a hope of mine." However, doubts and worry are the earmarks of the devout, not the pessimist. Without romantic illusions he exhorted humankind to protect the future. And he knew that a trend is not destiny. Indeed he lived until 1987 and saw that Africa had then more reserves than in the 1950s and had retained them in spite of crushing social needs. *Ulendo* expresses Carr's loyalty to the earth, and like religion it offers hope and evokes unremitting devotion to the natural world.

George Schaller
Wildlife Conservation International

Preface to the 1993 Edition

ONE OF Archie's goals in writing *Ulendo* thirty years ago was to "make a few more people feel sure that something is being ignominiously lost when we let African wilderness go into a pure stand of mankind." He did just that. Archie and other vibrant writers, natural history films, and an increasing number of visitors to Africa have defined and given dimensions to the extraordinary values of the wild landscapes—complete with hard to manage great and small beasts.

Even before Archie died in 1987 the business of ecotourism had developed. Since then it has burgeoned and in many developing countries it is the source of substantial national income. Thoreau was prophetic in a way he perhaps never dreamed of when he wrote "in wildness is the preservation of the world." Around the world and here at home governments are scrambling to preserve the natural landscapes and arrange for people to view them without loving them to death. The public, in increasing numbers, wants to visit wild areas, see them, smell them, listen to them. What the public wants the public will get if it asks for it loudly enough.

The public has always prized the natural world but has considered it limitless—the sun and rain, the wheel of the seasons, the return of the birds in the spring, and the nesting of sea turtles in the summer. These good things would never end, or so they thought. When they ceased or when they showed signs of great damage, the public became *conservationists*.

The passage of the Endangered Species Act in 1973 brought great comfort to Archie. When he realized how wide was support for the act, he realized for the first time there was hope for saving Africa—and the rest of the world as well. When he realized that the average citizen, the telephone operator, the gas station attendant, the bank teller, was vehement and strong in his desire not to lose *any species* of life on earth, he knew there was a chance for Eden. The general public did not want the world to be bereft of leopards or snail darters or whales or spotted owls or crocodiles or bears or elephants or rhinoceroses or louseworts—yes, louseworts. Man's joy in these species was not limited to protein or hunting or even biodiversity. He just wanted them around in his world. They were part of his inalienable right in "the pursuit of happiness" guaranteed in the Constitution.

The delights of the natural world are a multitude. They far outstrip those made by man although some of those are pretty fancy. Archie's ability to put his delight of the African landscape in writing makes *Ulendo* especially appealing in the light of the increased awareness of the lovely but endangered world around us.

This new edition includes the letters Archie wrote home while he was on *ulendo*. His enthusiasm for Africa is evident. I wish I could have been with him on those trips. The next best thing is rereading *Ulendo*.

Marjorie Harris Carr
Gainesville, Florida

Preface to the 1964 Edition

ULENDO means journey in Chinyanja, a language spoken in Nyasaland. I once spent three months in Nyasaland, *on ulendo*, as one says there. The book I have written started out to be the story of that trip, a tale of pythons, fly spouts, and our curious man Wilson—of incidents, animals, and people of sorts not prevalent in the spate of books on Africa the past decade has seen. And mainly that is the way *Ulendo* still is. But a long time passed while it was being written. The world changed fast. I went back to Africa three times. Each time I came home and worked on the manuscript again, ideas crept in that I never expected at all. One of these was that the wilderness of Africa, like all the original earth, is being lost at a sickening rate before the racing spread of man. No cures for that are suggested in the book—there may not be any. But I hope *Ulendo*, simply by the slants and shadings of my own personal joy in the Africa I saw, may make a few more people feel sure that something is being ignominiously lost when we let African wilderness go into a pure stand of mankind. That may be the main theme of the book, if a theme has to be named.

My first visit to Africa was a hunting trip. We went to hunt snails and mosquitoes. Lewis Berner, a colleague of mine at the University of Florida, had distinguished himself by his work in malaria control in Africa during the Second World War. Lewis was asked by Sir William Halcrow and Partners, a London engineering firm, to make a survey of medically important animals of the Shire Valley of Nyasaland. The Halcrow engineers had undertaken a huge drainage, irrigation, and flood-control program in the valley of the Shire River. They wanted to know what animal-borne diseases might be expected if the valley were settled by Europeans and by Africans from other regions. Lewis invited me to work with him on the survey, and, having always thought of Africa as the ultimate earthly reward of right-living naturalists, I happily did.

Our main official concern was to take censuses of, and determine means for controlling, malarial mosquitoes and the snails that are the intermediate hosts for the disease known as bilharziasis or schistosomiasis, which in many Nyasaland villages afflicted nearly every living soul. We were also to look out for filiariasis and its mosquito vector, and for black-flies that carry a tiny worm that can cause blindness when transferred to man by the bite of the fly. Besides those specific concerns we were charged with learning something of the ecology of Shire-side habitats, as a basis for predicting changes when water levels along the course of the river would be manipulated. Those were our assigned duties. My own secret aim, not revealed in correspondence with Sir William Halcrow and Partners, was to see my dream of Africa unfold.

Later on, my interest in sea turtles took me back to Africa to try to find out what kinds of turtles live along the coasts, and where their nesting and feeding grounds and routes of migration are. One outcome of this travel was a step toward solving the mystery of the ridley turtle, which I made such a fuss over in *The Windward Road*. Another was the setting up of a tagging project out at

Preface to the 1964 Edition xix

Ascension Island, halfway between Africa and Brazil. This brought the first proof that green turtles cross oceans in their migrations and make pinpoint landfalls after hundreds of miles of open-sea travel.

But the most stirring thing I learned in Africa was how fast its classic landscapes are being lost. Others had begun to see this long before; but like most people, I had thought of Africa as inexhaustible. Now, however, I am not able to get rid of the thought of its waning. It comes repeatedly into the *Ulendo* story, and has modified somewhat the tone of blithe irresponsibility I was aiming for at the start.

A little while ago, looking idly through a friend's library, I pulled out Aldo Leopold's *Game Management*, attracted by the solid sense and good taste of that surprising man, to leaf through his book again. The book opened at the preface, and my eye fell upon a cryptic query dimly penciled in the margin. It said:

What will pleasant be in 3000?

The words made no sense to me, out there by themselves like that. But I read down through the text to the level of the note, and found this comment there:

Are we too poor in purse or spirit . . . to keep the land pleasant to see and good to live in?

I stopped there and thought, and after a while I saw the meaning of the marginal scribble. It meant that the way the world is changing, how do we know what will seem pleasant to people a thousand years from now? It meant that the earth is being remade by our one race and that we are already being brainwashed into a state of mind that will accept any artificial life that may be in store for us. From there it went on to imply—regretfully, I think, but resignedly—that saving old landscapes and wild creatures makes no sense in the long run because our descendants will see no good in them.

And it could be so. Our race is frighteningly malleable. *Adaptable* we would rather call it. Already masses of people have been conditioned to processed cheese, to bread that I think is made of plastic foam, and to gaudy fruits from which all taste has been jettisoned for the sake of durability in shipment. The other day I heard a television interview with seamen on an atomic submarine. The interviewer asked them if they didn't get pretty bored, cooped up inside a machine for weeks and months. One boy said he did; he missed the green of trees and grass and he loved to grow things in a garden. But another boy just shrugged and said he never had it so good, good food and movies every night and all, and it seemed all right to him to be in there. His point of view was the one the man who wrote in Leopold's book had in mind. People can be made not just to live shoulder-to-shoulder in tiers, but to enjoy living that way.

So while most of *Ulendo* is still pretty lighthearted, I want to make it clear here that even in that part a cold thought is implicit. It is that Africa, the cradle of humanity and the habitat of the most exciting assemblage of living beings that remain on earth—the last asylum of the Grand Savanna Life of the Pleistocene—is magic and pleasant for only the little time left before men ruin it. To help awaken regrets of this is a hope of mine. Otherwise, my book is a rambling ulendo.

In wildness is the preservation of the world.

THOREAU

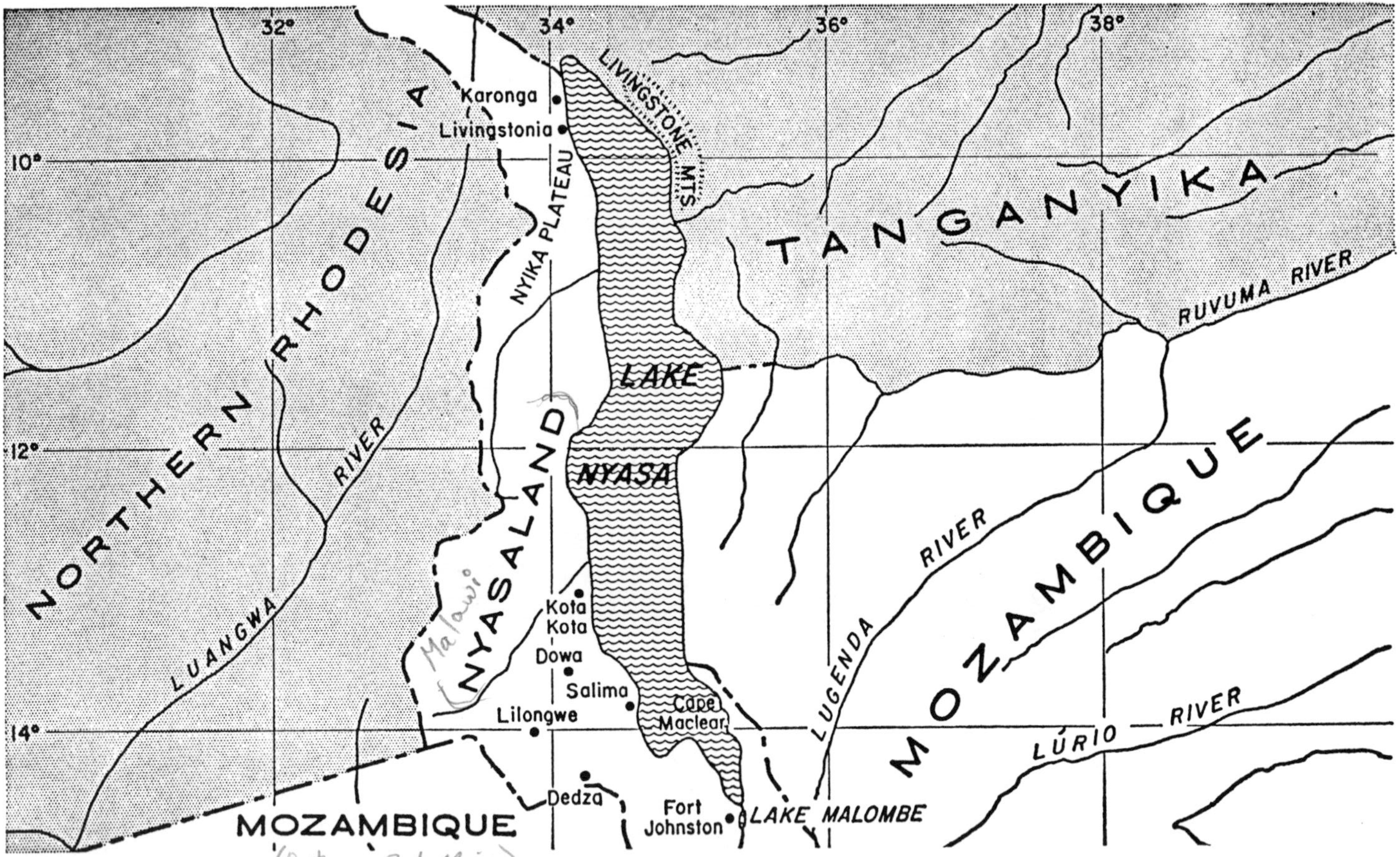

32°
34°
36°
38°
10°
12°
14°
NORTHERN RHODESIA
TANGANYIKA
NYASALAND
MOZAMBIQUE
MOZAMBIQUE
LAKE NYASA
LIVINGSTONE MTS.
NYIKA PLATEAU
Karonga
Livingstonia
Kota Kota
Dowa
Salima
Lilongwe
Dedza
Cape Maclear
Fort Johnston
LAKE MALOMBE
LUANGWA RIVER
RUVUMA RIVER
LUGENDA RIVER
LÚRIO RIVER

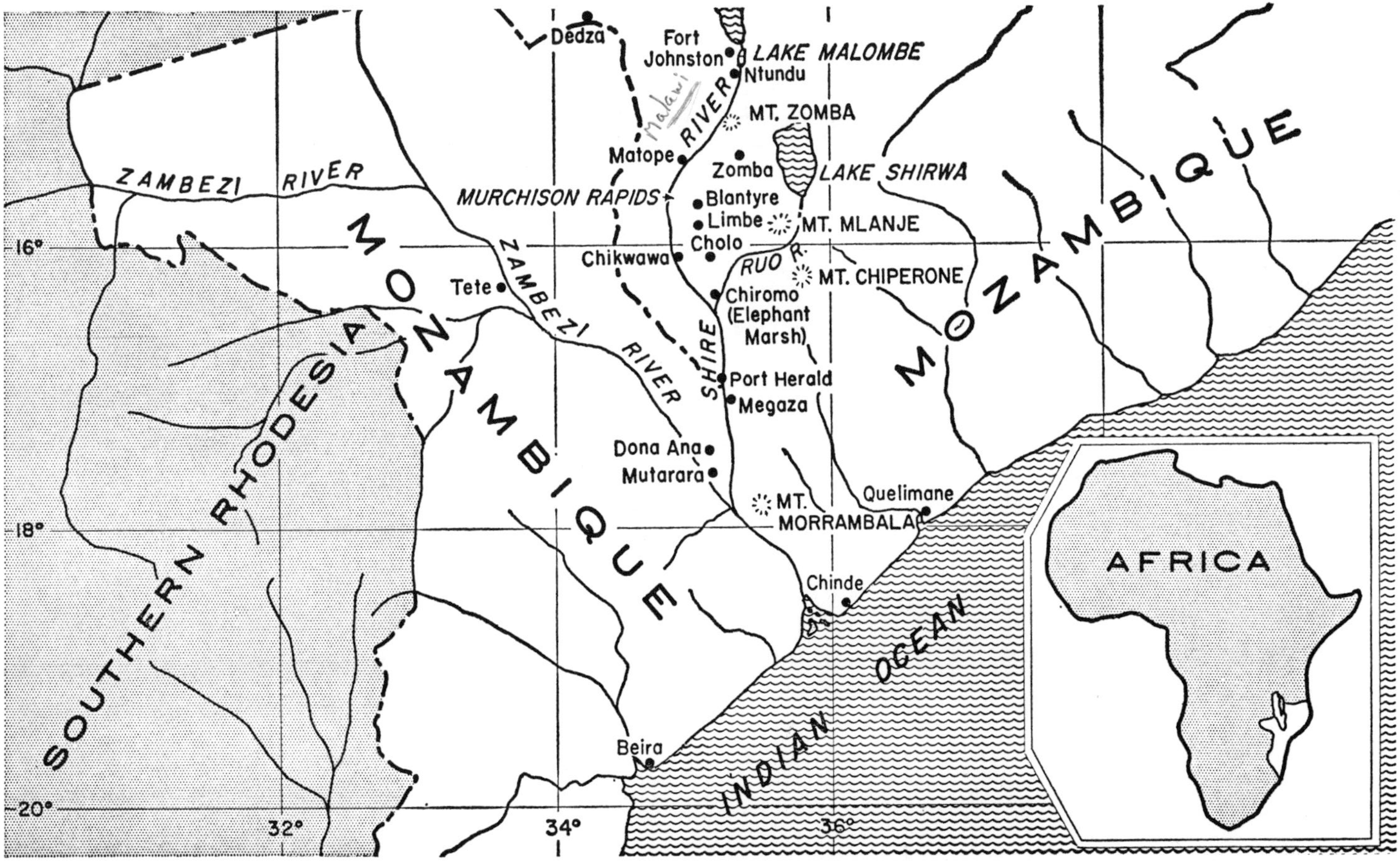

ULENDO

# Sixteen-Mile Safari

IT WAS late afternoon when I came upon the lions. A thin rain had sifted past and blue gaps spread and closed among the plateau clouds. The air drifting over the veld was lowland air, clean from coastal rain, soft from its run through Somalia. The dust was tight down and the grass was gold like old wheat. For a long time I stayed there looking across the dip at the sure sign of lions, at ease now that the day was bound to be a lion day before it ended.

All that afternoon it had been the same—one quick misting of rain after another, and passing jags of blue sky, and all the time the slow wind driving slow waves over the grass and humming in the clumps of twisted thorn trees. It was good country—about the best there is—and animals were in it everywhere you looked, so stanch and free it made me feel perverse to be whining about the lack of lions.

Once we saw a hyena on a ridge, and the African boy with me touched my shoulder because it looked like a lion. Later, a wart hog slanting off in a stiff trot through hog-high grass seemed lionlike for a moment to my over-ready eyes. Another time we came across rawhide leavings of buck, and a vulture plucking among hooves and sinews. A lion had been there clearly, but long before.

At six o'clock we stopped on the side of a low hill and searched the sweep of the land. I got out my field glasses and looked hard at all the far parts of the plain we had not been to. Always there were animals to see but never lions. My driver was worried, and kept saying that lions walk in the late afternoon, trying that way to keep his spirits up, and mine. It was a thing I had read many times, but the light had the look of evening and I had a strong sense of ebbing hope. I began to weigh the thought of spending the last light hunting for eland, which they told us could be found in a valley not so far away.

But we kept on across the crest of the hill. The land beyond it sank in a long slope and then rose to some low trees along a gully. And there, a few yards out in the grass from the rim of the trees was the place where the lions were lying.

It is now that a quick look at the chamber of the Jeffery .404 might be expected, the sliding off of the safety catch, and a sidelong glance at my companion's face for any sign of panic. But there was none of that. The boy was a taxi driver, and long ago Nairobi cabbies lost their fear of lions. The safari car was a Morris Minor and I had boarded it six miles away in a city of sixty-five thousand people. And, as for the Jeffery .404—any showing of

.404's, or of .22's for that matter, would have quickly brought out the Kenya Police.

I hope this turn to my story will not prove irritating. It is really a lot better tale the way it is. You *shoot* a lion and it means your nervous system is normal, and you are pretty well fixed financially. But sit quietly and contemplate a lion from the slight depths of a Morris Minor, and you are seeing a sign that your race has heart after all and is not quite ready to let the past slip away from its far descendants on an asphalt planet.

Even so, I have to admit that the scene across the swale that afternoon in itself held little to make the hackles rise. There was no brown solidity of lion against the grass. There was no lion flesh in view at all. This first stage in my first meeting with lions was only the sight of a ring of cars, eleven little European cars in a tight circle on the wild plain, and one old wooden schoolbus.

That is the usual way you find lions in Nairobi National Park. The lions sleep in the daytime. They lie up in the two-foot grass, and, sleeping, they are something less than two feet high. It is only by chance that someone catches sight of a flurry of rolling or of a head raised in a yawn, and drives over and stops his car by the place. He then becomes a mark for all the lion-hungry safarists on the plain. So the Athi lions spend a lot of time sleeping in a ring of cars; and their willingness to do this makes them probably the most important lions in the world. Their calm patience with people out in the wilderness just beyond the edge of a busy city, their unexpected, unexplained acceptance of the smell and racket of people and cars may finally save the age of mammals now dwindling so dismally away on the plains of Africa.

The Nairobi lions are not under fence. They are wild

lions, free to come and go in the 44 square miles of the Park and in the 200 square miles of the reserve lands that adjoin it. They live there with most of the other high plains animals, killing what they want to eat, a part of the world's most accessible remnant of the waning Pleistocene. It is hard to tell how really natural the Nairobi Park is, what with all the shooting that used to go on there, with the Masai and their cattle coming and going in its near and distant past, and now, with the roads and trails cut and tourists quartering the veld throughout the daylight hours. But it surely *looks* natural; the animals do what they please and the only sign of humanity you see in a day's wandering is people looking at them.

And the animals are everywhere. It is not like looking for sheep in Rocky Mountain National Park. All that afternoon I spent looking for lions, wherever the plain spread flat to the horizon there were beasts in view—a stem-legged ostrich at the least, or a splash of burning zebra stripes; or scores or hundreds of kongoni and wildebeest, the edges of the herds set with elegant gazelles, and with half a dozen other kinds of antelopes sprinkled about singly or in little bands. A bataleur eagle was there, up among the rolling clouds; and close over the plain the cry and swooping of hawks told of a different scale of life, diverse as the antelopes themselves, down among the grass stems. Baboons trooped at the roadside; jackals, francolins, and plover ran ahead in the wheel tracks. In three separate acacia clumps, giraffes were browsing at the top shoots; their sides a pattern of fantastic chainwork among the feathery leaves. And always there was the fine, fair country to see, with the warm wind rippling the veld, smoothing the snowgrass on the hilltops, and stirring a thin song in the pipes of the whistling-thorn.

So, already it had been a trip to remember, this sixteen-mile safari of mine. I had seen a good deal more than a man in a Morris Minor had any right to expect. But no game-seeking safari has full flavor without a lion, and the way my lions were saved till last and were led up to by the long search, which made me more anxious as the light got lower, all built me up keen for the lion feel. I started goading the driver into going both faster to get there quicker, and slower to make less noise.

When the trail we were on started cutting away from the gully, we struck out through the grass to the ring of cars and circled half way around it till we found an opening. We joined the ring between a Volkswagen full of Goanese and a car loaded with an English family. In a taxi beyond them were two men and women who had the look of Americans; and in an old English Ford near the Goanese were five soldiers from a garrison left over from the Mau Mau trouble. At the far rim, drawn up broadside to the ring was the bus I spoke of, a prewar Chevrolet with a body of lapped weather-stripping, and cottagey square windows. Behind them was a swarm of little Indian girls. Painted on the side of the bus were the words "Holiday Bus," and some more I couldn't read. The driver was a thin Hindu. The girls were thin, too, and had vast eyes that showed all the way across the circle.

The cars were all parked at a slant so that the occupants could see into the center of the ring. There were about forty-five people in them, and the first thing I noticed was the quiet patience of their waiting. They fussed with their cameras some, or took another light-reading with their meters. Mostly though, they sat still, talking in voices kept low partly because it was a British colony we were in, but mainly out of respect for the lions. Once in a while there was a squeal or titter from the bus. Each time, the driver looked back reproachfully and the virgins remembered that this was a lion-watch and their eyes got doelike at the thought. In some of the cars there were African Park Rangers, slim, Nilotic looking men in khaki shorts. Their earlobes stretched out into thin rings and then knotted back into lobes again. You pick them up at the main gate if you want to; they know where to find the different kinds of game, and they keep you from getting lost. If anybody should break any Park rule—get out of a car, for instance, or light a fire—the rangers will set him right. But in the circle that day it was not the rangers' presence that set the tone of quiet. It was clearly the thought of the wild lions in the grass only forty feet away.

After waiting a while I leaned out and asked the Englishman in the next car how many lions there were, and he said five. He had seen none of them clearly, but an hour before, someone had noticed the five of them standing briefly by the gully, and, hastening to mark the spot, had found the gap in the grass where they now lay, a dim confusion of brown belly-silhouettes through the grass stems. From the top of your car you could have seen all five lions lying there asleep; but the crowd was, as I said, orderly and nobody tried to get on top of a car.

I thanked the man for the information and he said: "Right you are. Nuisance if they stay down till closing time."

That thought seemed to be occurring to others in the circle. Now and then someone cleared his throat with unnecessary vigor, or started his car and crept forward a few inches, or moved back and forth as if he were after a better parking angle, roaring his engine with uncalled-for power. This last struck others as a good ruse, because night was falling. In no time at all half of the cars had come alive and were revving their engines in protest over the sleeping of the lions. I looked at the rangers to see how they took this mild rioting against the spirit of park law, but they seemed undisturbed, and the lions did too.

Nobody has been able to figure out why lions are so indifferent to the presence of cars. Their detachment is so complete that some think the lion sees a car, not as a container of people but as some separate form of life—bad smelling, amorphous, and because neither harmful nor edible, completely without interest.

Down in Kruger Park, where there are always lots of cars, and where the lion-car relationship has had decades in which to work itself out, the lions show a clear tendency to join up with lines of lion-viewing cars. They walk along the road among or beside them for as long as the cars keep a lion pace. Not by the slightest sign do they show they know there are people in the cars, or indeed that cars are there at all.

The rangers say the lions are stalking impala when they do that. They say they are hiding in the gas trail of the cars. By walking in the reek of people and burnt gasoline, they keep their own smell from warning the prey.

This sounds anthropocentric to be sure, but I'm not altogether sure it is. I went to Kruger Park myself and fell in with lions near a place called Skukuza. For nearly half an hour I traveled in a mixed train of lions and cars, and all that time the lions showed only enough awareness of the cars to avoid contact with them. Even more carefully they ignored the bands of impala we kept passing on either side of the road; and in all that distance no antelope, some of which were only thirty yards away, did more than lift its head over nine lions passing by.

But after a while we entered a curve in the road that partly shut in a band of twelve impala, and all at once the lioness slouching along a tail-length ahead of the car I was in, wheeled and burst out of the scent-screen, if that was really what it was. And before I even saw that it was the start of a charge, a slim doe in the herd two hundred yards away knew it well, and knew it was she who was in the lioness's mind. Three other lionesses broke out at different places and at a fast, easy lope headed toward the doe, which had started dashing back and forth among the bushes, skimming their tops in zigzag loops of terror, fighting her fate out all alone among her scattering fellows. The little doe was the chosen one and all the animals knew it, and all the people in the cars. When the leading lion closed the space to fifty yards, the impala seemed to sense that there was no life left in what she was doing and cut back in a sharp arc toward the road, then came flying in toward the solid line of cars. The lions veered to intercept her, but the spark of the doe's instinct had come too quick for them. They ran together just back of where she soared away with neck straight out, ears flat back, and legs drawn tight against her body, barely flicking at the earth to take power for each new trajectory. Straight into the roadway she came, on a heading sure to collide with a car three cars behind me, burning pure fear in her muscle cells. I leaned way out to look back, and in one moment I saw people with arms flung in front of their faces, the doe like a thrown spear over the hood of a car, and the lions skidding to right and left at the end of the blocked charge.

That was eighteen hundred miles away from the lions sleeping on the Athi Plain. But wherever lions are not shot they seem to accept cars as a part of the natural landscape; and what might have proved to be a big headache in park management—lions crowding into cars or pulling people out of them—turned out to be no problem at all. The problem is making the lions stand up and be seen.

It was over half an hour, out there on the plain by Nairobi, before I saw anything more of the lions than their hidden heaving sides. Close enough for the flies walking on them to show, the lions for all I saw could have been wart hogs, or ant hills, or anything else that was brown and still. When at last I did see a good clear piece of lion, it was one paw stuck up suddenly above the grass and held there on a pedestal of stretched leg while pad toes slowly spread apart, flexed, and pushed out sickle claws like a fast-blooming flower. The crowd half laughed and half gasped at the imagined feel of the stretch and vast spread of the foot.

From then on you could see that the lions were nearing the end of their sleep. There were coughs and wakeful groans. An edge of the clear place would shiver where a lion rolled into new grass. Or a tufted tail would whip up into the clear, or all four feet would show where a lion had stirred and sunk into its last moments of supine rest.

Each new sign of life in the clearing built up the suspense in the circle of cars a little higher. A tone of excitement crept into the drone of the talk. Babies were shifted about, light meters were read again, and shutter settings changed. My driver said: "This lion is getting up quickly," and I thought how the same thing was being said all around the circle in French and Swahili, Afrikaans and Hindustani, and in whatever they talk in Goa. Over in the "Holiday Bus" the feel of climax had come to the Indian girls and they stopped their skylarking and all their eyes showed wide in rows at the windows.

Then, as if with all due attention gained, the male lion rolled, wheezed, and raised his head and shoulders above the grass. He held there steady over the waving grass tips, so vast and red-maned and lionlike that the people, all together as if practiced in it—like the crowd when the grandest final firework bursts saved-up bloom across the sky—went aaaaaaaah, all in one voice together.

For maybe a minute the big lion lay that way, looking off stern and tan-eyed while the people admired him and exposed their film. One way, and then another, he searched the distances—not the ring of cars around him, but the far places showing between the cars. When there was no more there to hold him, he suddenly sank back out of sight.

The people groaned, but without rancor; because all would, come what might, go home in honor with a lion seen. Cases of cameras snapped shut, engines started, and there was lighthearted calling from one car to another. Then, with the dark coming in fast, a last burst of luck let us see the pride of lions.

For quite a while the Britannia, the big turbo-prop airliner on the London-to-South-Africa run, had been whooshing and whistling over at the airport, warming up for the flight to Johannesburg. It was three or four miles away, beyond some low hills, and the noise was not obtrusive. The animals had worn out their interest in noise at the airport years before, and even when the big airplane moved out to the end of a runway and went into its pre-takeoff roaring the lions showed no concern.

But then the Britannia came charging down on her take-off and it seemed to head straight at us. Something about the scream and thunder or sudden flare of an acre of silver in the air struck a lion as odd. He rolled in a start, and must have rolled on a colleague. There was a quick scramble in the clearing and after that five lions stood there in a cloud of their frightened flies, tan-buff in the tawny grass, all statue-still except for their cable tails, all sternly looking through the circle of cars toward different distant places.

The cars all cut their engines and the talking stopped. The lioness stood for a minute, then started walking slowly toward a break in the ring, bending back grass with the strokes of her tail, looking off all the time at the ends of the plain, with no flick of a glance at the flanking cars. Through the six-yard space she moved, and one by one the other lions followed—three grown cubs, one close behind the other, then a break, and then the old man lion, padding off head down the way the others went. The red of his mane still showed when the grass had taken in all other signs of lions.

ए़ए़ए़ए़ए़ए़ए़

Portuguese East

THE FIRST I saw of Portuguese East was corn. Maize, we were calling it by then, at least when we talked with the British boys who put us up. But whatever name you gave it, it was only Indian corn. It was tall and dark green. Its mist-wet leaves were glistening in the sun and its new tassels were beginning to bob in the first breaths of the morning breeze. It stood there across the little river and crowded to the edge of the bluff as fine as corn in Kansas. There was, in fact, nothing to show that it was not in Kansas or that the wind moving it was the southeast trade wind just in from the Indian Ocean. The corn was good; but it seemed all wrong to me, looking for the first of Portuguese East and seeing corn.

When I was seven years old and my range seemed too familiar, I began to feel the excitement of distant places.

There was nothing extraordinary about that, of course. The queer part in my case was how I latched on to certain place names just for the sound, and how they stuck with me as cues for mindless stimulation right up into college and beyond. One of these tingling symbols of mine was the two words, *Portuguese East*. Not Portuguese East Africa. That was geography, without connotation, with none of the careless magic of the shortened form. A little later on I heard *Mozambique*, and its sound distilled an aura, too. I know it was just the sound—the exotic zee-sound, maybe—because for years I had no idea where the place was located. When Portuguese East and Mozambique turned out to be the same, I ought to have been embarrassed, but I only felt happy that two of my symbols had got together that way and reinforced each other.

So you can see why the corn was an anticlimax, over there on the other side of the river. I have nothing against *Zea mays* as a plant. In some places corn is fine, in Mexico or Georgia, in tamales, tortillas, bourbon, or spoonbread. Corn is the great gift of the New World to the Old; and back home it is good to watch it grow, wave in the wind, or turn gold under frost and snap before the happy sickle of a pointer's tail. But seeing it first in Portuguese East was wrong. I don't know just what wonder I expected, but it certainly wasn't corn.

I realize I am making too much of the corn. My reaction was a little simple-minded, really. But it was portentous, too. Although I didn't know it at the time, seeing the corn in Portuguese East was the first of my seeing the smallness of the world, of my knowing the limited, exhaustible nature of the natural earth. Until then Africa had been for me all wildness and romantic savagery, and for some private reason of my own, Portuguese East was its essence. So when I came upon the corn in the legendary land, it seemed all at once that the world would never be quite the same again; and sure enough, in a number of saddening ways it never has been.

That was the special meaning of the maize across the River Ruo; and the first proving out of the portent came only a little later, on Captain Ariano's fantastic elephant hunt. It was there, where nothing at all was shot, that I felt the first dulling of my zest for the pastime of shooting things. Just how this came about is by no means clear to me, but I am going to set the circumstances down anyway.

I came upon Portuguese East at Chiromo, a tired little town in southern Nyasaland, in the angle where the Ruo River meets the River Shire. The railroad crosses the Shire there on the way up to the highlands from the Portuguese port of Beira by the Indian Ocean. There was no highway bridge at Chiromo. The railroad cost so much to build that they let the highway stop at the river to keep down competition from trucks and buses. Before the railroad came, the best way to get to the highlands and Lake Nyasa was up the Zambezi and Shire rivers. At Chiromo there was a choice to make: whether to keep to the Shire for the eighty miles more to the foot of Murchison Rapids, or to take the overland trail that made the long climb up the 4,000-foot scarp to the highlands. Chiromo thus was an important way-station for the early missionary expeditions to Nyasaland. Bishop Mackenzie of the Universities Mission died there of blackwater fever, after a dugout he was traveling in capsized and his quinine was lost overboard. He was buried on a little island in the river. The island later washed away.

Chiromo is a hot dusty village with some big trees, a few Indian stores along a wide street, and the nostalgic air of a photograph of the 1880's. Later, when we spent a week there, we joined the few Europeans of the town in the only social life the community offers. On Sunday afternoons they waited at the station for the weekly train from Beira, and when it stopped, rushed aboard and sat for half an hour in the tavern car drinking cold Portuguese beer from the coast.

But that was later on. The night we arrived, Chiromo was for me only a place across the narrow Ruo from a specially exotic land. For more than a month we had never been far away from Mozambique, lying out there in the sun between Nyasaland and the sea. But at Chiromo you can skip a stone across the Ruo River, and the other side of the Ruo is Portuguese East.

We got to Chiromo after dark. We rolled into the resthouse yard, the Land Rover loaded with bed rolls and collecting gear and our major-domo Wilson, who was the whole African element of this *ulendo*. There were three English engineers staying in the house. They showed us where to sleep and offered us still, airwarm beer, saying that Americans never liked it. This time they were wrong. They knew we were also queer about animals, and showed us a ten-inch chameleon with a sad face and swiveled eyes, bought from a boy against our coming. Then I asked if it was true that PEA was just across the river and they said quite true, but did not look impressed. I went straight to the door and looked out. I saw only shadows and stars and one small light, too low for a star. I had only these to go to bed with.

Before I went to sleep some drumming started up, away back beyond the other shore some place. I asked the engineers what the celebration was about. "Some poor blokes getting circumcised," was all they said.

Two or three times during the night I woke and heard the steady bumping of the drums, and along with it sporadic bursts of din like distant strings of jangling cans. But in spite of this, and of my being across from Mozambique, I finally slept till sunup. Then it was a cup of tea steaming through the mosquito bar that woke me, and Wilson saying, "Your tea, bwana"—which made me feel effete, as that rite always did.

It was only for a moment that I felt anything but that a land once far away was just across the river. I raised the netting and went out on the veranda in my drawers, as if it were Christmas morning, to see what I had waited for. And that was when Portuguese East turned out to be only a *milpa*, a solid stand of corn, tall and noncommittal and distressingly like the things I knew.

I eventually got used to maize in the African landscape. I never was able to stomach bicycles on game trails, but I came finally not to cavil at the corn. I don't know when the Portuguese first brought maize into the Shire country —some time in the early sixteen hundreds, it is thought— but it is now wholly absorbed into the culture of the cornfarming tribes. No way remains to tell that it was some ancient kind of Americans who started corn, and not the Bantus. But as I said, that first sight of maize across the Ruo was a blow to my dream of Portuguese East, and the dream has never recovered.

I went back into the house and had breakfast. Then Lewis and I left with George and the driver in the Land Rover to catch snails at Elephant Marsh and to count mosquitoes in the huts of long-suffering Africans.

Our routine mosquito censuses were accepted with peculiar equanimity by the Nyasa people, even in the backward villages of the Lower River. We went to a village and looked up the chief, then walked around with him and selected the huts in which we wanted to sample mosquitoes. The chief then explained to the people in the chosen houses what we were going to do. The housewife moved out or covered anything that insecticide might hurt—pots of corn or beer, dried fish, setting hens, litters of puppies —and we spread sheets over the floors, filled the place with aerosol spray, and waited a few minutes for the mosquitoes to die.

A crowd usually gathered around to watch the ceremony, with awe or cheerful excitement, depending upon whether they had seen mosquito spray before. After the spray had time to work a while, cockroaches, crickets, spiders, and other unfortunate arthropods began deserting the house in numbers through all of its chinks. This drew in chickens, ducks, and guinea hens like a watermelon cutting, and they ringed the hut in exhilarated ranks to chase and dispute over the fleeing insects. This phase of the work was much admired by all the villagers. The climax came, though, when the door was opened and Lewis and I played our flashlights over the bug-strewn sheets. A wave of wonder then always spread through the craning crowd. They stretched their necks to see all the dead little creatures lying so still on the cloth, and the grand word *udzudzu,* which to any ear could only mean *mosquito,* was buzzed about by every adult and child.

"*Udzudzu, ambiri,*" they all said. "Shee-shee . . ."

Back at Limbe there had been some talk of restlessness among the Lower River people, but we never had any falling out with them over our intrusions. At one town, people started running around restlessly as the Land Rover approached, and when we stopped, they eyed us with apprehension from partly hidden places. We sent the driver to find out what the trouble was. He came back saying that the word had spread that we had "come for war and not for peace." That was the only uneasy reception we had anywhere in Nyasaland, and there was nothing to it, really. It only reminded us of a weird time Mitchell of the Game Department had the month before a little further down the river.

Mitchell had a red jeep and some hounds that he used in taking game censuses in heavy country. He had the habit of feeding his dogs baboon meat. For himself he took on his *ulendos* a brand of tinned beef called *Boy*, which had a colorful label with a picture of a happy African on it.

One day when Mitchell was out looking for nyala in one of the only places where any of these rare and beautiful antelope remain, he was ambushed by Africans. Without warning they jumped out of the bush, threw their spears at the jeep, and ran away. A lot of spears were left stuck through the softer parts of the car and its contents, but none at all through Mitchell. Although the damage was slight, the attitude of the people wounded Mitchell and he went to some lengths to learn what their problem might have been. It turned out that the people figured Mitchell wanted to eat them. To begin with, they look askance upon jeeps in general. They call them *chaframba* cars, and think they are used to chase down Africans in rough country so they can be cut open and their livers removed and carried away for medicine. The red color of Mitchell's jeep further undermined their confidence. There was the skinned carcass of a baboon hanging from it, too. They took this for the body of a young child. The crowning outrage was that Mitchell himself had the bad habit of eating meat from cans with a picture of an African on the label.

As we approached one of the villages near Chiromo and shut off the engine I heard the sound of a marimba. The music was a little wan, but quite clearly it was coming from wooden keys. For a moment, it seemed out of place, like the corn across the river. But then I remembered that marimbas are an African invention, and while George and the driver went to attend to protocol, Lewis and I followed up the sound. We found it was being made by three little boys under a tree. They were beating furiously on five hardwood sticks, spiked loosely across two fat sections of banana stem with splinters of ebony. The sticks had been shaved down to the proper tones with a chopping knife. It was a crude marimba to be sure, with no calabashes hung under the keys to build the resounding notes the marimba of Central Africa is known for. It was a far cry from the Grand Marimba of Mexico and Guatemala. But the mellow, quavering ring of the wood was there; and the boys made up for any lack in the instrument by their own precocious virtuosity. Without collision among the six green-wood sticks with which they struck the keys, they herded an unbelievably complex rhythm along with the weird little tune they played. The boys were maybe eight years old. They played with complete detachment, not once looking at the keys, at us, or at each other. They gazed aimlessly about as if someone else were playing— as if to distract all possible attention from what their hands were doing.

There were people all around under the big tree, but except for some women pounding corn, nobody seemed to pay the music any mind. The women were listening to it though, or feeling it, and I soon began to see that they were using the marimba music to give rhythm to their work. It was not in any obvious Caucasian way, but they were taking from the compound beat of the music whatever signals the African mind needs to hold to the subtle rhythms it conceives. There were four women pounding. Without the slightest seeming effort each was shading the force and rhythm of the fall of her stick in a different way. By listening closely you could tell that the four separately working women and the three little boys were all of one mind in their cryptic rhythms. As far as the other people standing around were concerned, and those who came and went past the tree, the children were just playing at making music. But it was not the sort of thing one expects of eight-year-old white Americans passing the time away.

A thing I forgot to ask was whether the boys might have been made to play as a sort of household chore. Maybe they were there to fill the place with a framework of rhythm and build verve into the work of the women, as in Georgia they used to send out a work-song leader with colored gangs on the railroads.

Anyway, I was glad to see them sitting under the tree beating on their sticks of stovewood. The marimba is one of my predilections, and I used to take part in spirited disputes with Central Americans over where it came from. The Guatemalans say they gave it to the world. To try to convince them otherwise is as unavailing, and I can see now, as pointless and idle as to tell a Sena woman pounding maize that it is not an African plant at all.

One reason Guatemalans believe their ancestors thought up the marimba is simply that they make it better, and play it better, than anybody else. Another reason is that the Maya did in fact have a comparable instrument, composed of graded gourds strung from a rack or tied about the waist of the player, and played with sticks. There is a mountain in Guatemala with the wonderful name *Chinal Jul*, which means "marimba of the ravines." Guatemalans cite this old-seeming name to prove that the marimba is indigenous to their land. But it was surely the old string of the tuned gourds the mountain was named for, and this no doubt was mainly just a percussion instrument. Comparable rows of objects are struck hopefully by people in many parts of the world. They may be fairly exciting to listen to, but they are not marimbas. The essence of the marimba is the set of keys of ringing hardwood, each with a matched resonance box beneath it. Such an instrument is endemic to Central Africa. David Livingstone listened to marimba music during his explorations of the 1860's. His book, *The Zambezi*, has two woodcuts showing marimbas in use, and in structure there is little to distinguish them from the Central American marimba of today. There is no real evidence that the early Guatemalan Indians, or any other Indians, knew anything at all about the marimba in this form.

It is curious that even the origin of the name itself, the pleasantly African-sounding, onomatopoetic *marimba*, is disputed. One dictionary I have says the word is Portuguese; another says Bantu. There has been a lot of give and take between these two languages during the last four hundred years, but in most cases it is pretty clear which furnished a given word, and which adopted it. The dictionary that says *marimba* is Portuguese is one of those big surplus Websters that my wife got at the grocery store. I think it was no bargain.

But I should not make so much of the dispute over where marimbas came from. With all their grand flair for music, the Africans never dreamed of such an instrument as the Guatemaltecos have made of the marimba in the short centuries it has been in their land.

I doubt that it will ever be proved, but I venture to trace the route of the marimba from the Zambezi, say, to a wrecked slave ship in the Golfo Dulce on the Caribbean shore of Guatemala. It did not come in the substance of racked-up sticks and gourds, but only as a thought in the numbed mind of a black man who in quiet times could hear the gold notes float through sweet African air that he would not breathe any more. I judge that the first thing any shipwrecked Africans would do after finding a bite to eat would be to start beating on resounding objects and feeling out old harmonies and times together, comforting themselves with music. The marimba was inevitable on the Central American coast. With every ship that by design or by disaster brought black men in and built up the coastal stocks now known as Caribs and Miskitos—with every party of those people, the marimba came hidden in memories, and bringing it back was one small antidote against their cruel nostalgia.

The marimba getting to America was no wonder, and once in Guatemala it was in a land of fine marimba woods, as good as or better than those of the African homeland. From down on the coast it was, in those days, a long way up to the highlands from which the marimba later spread into the heart of the world. But it was the route everything from Spain had to travel to reach the Captain Generalcy. To me it is good to think of this most magic music coming into the New World through the stupendous jungle canyons of Río Dulce, the most magic river that I know, and then on across Lake Izabal to the old port where the mule trains left to cross Mico Mountain and climb to *tierra fria*.

The first marimba in the highlands must have gone, not to Guatemala City, because there was no city there in the days I am thinking of, but to the plain under the volcanoes Agua and Fuego; out to incomparable Antigua, at that time second only to Mexico and Lima in people and grandeur. And once there, all talk of where marimbas came from became quibbling. The Guatemalans took the African idea, the tuned wood keys and sound boxes, and, through the years since Antigua fell, wasted, and revived as the stunning sight its sleeping ruins are, they built up a versatile instrument on which anything can be played, and which when played well can turn the heart of anyone whose heart is not a stone.

Nowadays the marimba has spread all around and

mixed in with the xylophone and vibraphone. I know nothing about these hybridized forms. But in Guatemala marimbas are still handmade by a vanishing group of craftsmen. The Stradivarius among them is a man named Reyes, who is said to have built thirty Grand Marimbas, and any number of smaller ones.

In Central America marimba keys are made of guachilpilin, red granadillo, hormigo, and a few other of the slow-grown hardwoods of the dry-season forest. The pieces are cut to appropriate lengths and then tuned by shaving wood out on the underside with an adze. Middle C is taken from a tuning fork or another instrument—Señor Reyes takes it from an old bottle he has—and the rest of the keys are trimmed to tune by ear. The keys are laid out on cords stretched on a frame, and the tuned sounding boxes are arranged under the keyboard, one beneath each key. Each resonance box has a hole in its lower wall. A turret of wax of stingless wild bees is built up around the hole, and a thin film of the mesentery of a shoat is pressed over the wax around the opening. This is the vibrator that gives the throbbing, searching after-beat to marimba notes. The keys are struck by thin sticks with balls of rubber at the end. The size and resilience of the rubber balls are varied according to the sizes of the keys they are designed to strike; the bigger, softer ones are used for the lower sections of the keyboard and the harder, smaller ones for the higher notes. The Grand Marimba has 137 keys and is played by seven men, some of whom may use three sticks in each hand.

In both Africa and the American isthmus, marimba music is best when it is heard at a distance at night. To come under the spell of the American marimba requires no training of the ear. You only have to walk out to the edge of Antigua on an evening when the Grand Marimba is set up in the plaza. In about the third hour, say, the time comes to be there, when the night and the rum and the dark-eyed girls have made the *marimbistas* no longer clerks and shoemakers but one many-armed god of the Cakchiqueles, and they send the music out through the *huele de noche* trees in sobs or in paeans as they please. It rolls through the narrow streets and about the lone arches and roofless walls that were convents and cathedrals when the first marimba came into the land. Stand out there in the dark for a while, with the smell of *carbon* smoke and citrus flowers in the same soft wind the music travels, and listen to it whispering and swelling, then losing itelf around the plain. Hear it once like that, in the dark at the edge of town, with Volcán Agua blotting a blue cone out of the field of stars. You will never again be free of the sound of marimbas.

After three days of collecting and counting mosquitoes near Chiromo, the time came for us to move back up the Shire. By then my vision of Portuguese East had dimmed down to corn, ragged drumming, and the little white customs station with a patch of neat lawn and a flagpole.

But the night before we left, when a cock Wilson was stewing stayed tough and the engineers were away and Lewis was writing up the mosquito census, I went for a walk in the dark. I went down the road toward the Shire shore, listening to the evening sounds of the countryside and wondering idly if anybody was crossing on the ferry. The car ferry was a steel barge that ran back and forth across the river. It slid along a cable stretched from shore to shore. The motive power was a five-man crew of Nyanja boys, who sat on the deck and pulled together on the cable. Their work songs were the best group singing I had heard from the Nyasa people. It was not as good African singing as you used to hear on the docks in Savannah; but the boys beat out polyrhythmic time with their heels on the hollow deck and the songs were strange and wild and obviously not from any mission hymnal.

The barge lay at the Chiromo shore and there was nobody waiting to cross. The crew were sitting in front of a thatched shelter, and were eating cornmeal mush with their fingers out of an iron pot. I thought how to say something appropriate in Chinyanja and managed, "No cars." The men nodded and repeated what I had said, because I was a bwana, and because it was true anyway. I felt proud and decided to leave before I should get involved in saying something else.

Going back to the rest-house, I followed a trail beside the Ruo. It took me past two paddle-wheel steamboats moored one behind the other against the bank. They were still afloat but, from the looks of them, surely at their last moorings. Rising there white and dingy in the early dark, they were as outlandish as the corn was, with an air of Natchez and Huckleberry Finn, and with nothing about their architecture to justify their dying in an East African River.

The downstream boat was called *Empress*. Sounds and smells of un-Anglican cooking were coming out of her. As I passed, a voice in the dark asked in some sort of English if I was one of the Americans staying at the rest-house. I said I was, pretty sure it must be Captain Ariano talking. A man in only a pair of trousers appeared out of the dark beyond the rail. He was a big swarthy man, about to bulge into Latin middle age, but for the time still hard. He had a weathered face that was at once tough and affable. He looked like a Mexican movie bandit; or, except for the odd blue-green shading that a lot of Portuguese seem to have around the eyes, he could have been the bodyguard of a Caribbean American dictator.

I knew it must be Captain Ariano. I began thinking of the things I had heard about him, and wondered which might be best to get a conversation under way. At Fort Johnson they had told me that he was a master tigerfish angler. They told me about his ranch, too, and his lion kiosk in the back country across the river. They said that because he was Portuguese he could get at the Mozambique buffalo in the seaward plains, and had shot hundreds of them to sell for biltong, the ubiquitous dried wild meat of southern Africa.

I thought of a lot of other things, and then I said: "Tell me, Captain, is it true that you shoot leopards with a twenty-two?"

With a motion of one shoulder he admitted and disparaged the fact. But it was a good choice I had made, and he invited me to have a glass of wine and to see his rifle—not the twenty-two, but the gun he hunted with. I went aboard and right away we seemed to get along together pretty well. He spoke comprehensible English, but I could see it was a strain for him. When I tried Spanish it put our relation in the clear at once. He showed me the rifle. It was a popular American make and model, and as good a gun as you need for deer. I asked if it wasn't too light for Africa and he said not if you know game and know how to wait and shoot. While it sounded foolish to carry a gun so light in Africa, still, he was a biltong hunter who had killed sixteen buffalo on one two-day hunt. I said how about elephants—did he ever shoot elephants with the little rifle?

He turned the gun over and pointed to a patch of thin parallel lines cut into the stock, back toward the toe. They looked like crude and misplaced checking. The Captain rubbed a finger across the patch.

"Elephants," he said.

My reaction was cut short by Wilson's voice. He was complaining along the shore, probing the dark with his curious English, in a mild pet because I was not back at the house where supper was finally ready. I called to him that I wouldn't be a moment and he turned and went back up the path, still talking about supper but now only to himself. Then I asked the Captain to tell me what it was like across the river.

Our conversation was queer to listen to. We didn't speak anywhere near the same language. I shaded my Central American with the shushings and nasals I figured would instill confidence in a Portuguese ear. The Captain shaded his Portuguese in a way that seemed appropriate to him, and figured he was talking Spanish. Neither of us really knew what the differences between the two Iberian tongues were. The Captain kept sloshing out red wine, though, and we soon worked our way to a fairly firm linguistic middle ground. It was not long before he said that if I could come back sometime he would take me over into Mozambique to see the wild country. I said I would get back all right.

"Would you like to hunt the elephants?" the Captain asked. I said that was out of my line and I mainly wanted to walk around in Mozambique, but that, sure, hunting elephants would be all right if I could get around and see the land.

"Are there really elephants over there?" I asked. The Captain got up, grabbed my arm, and walked me down the deck to a closed door. He pulled it open and struck a match. A terrible stink flooded out past us, and for a moment this was all I could think of. Then I made out a high pile of black, useless-looking stuff rising from the floor of the stateroom and more of the same stacked in bins along one wall. I had no idea what it was.

"Elephant," the Captain said. "Biltong."
"But who eats it?"
"It is worth money on the coast, to feed boys." The Captain dragged a strip of the poor shredded, dried-out elephant off the pile, cut a sliver with his knife, and held it out to me. "Prove it," he said.

"You mean eat it?" The Captain said yes, and I told him I would wait till we got out in the air again. "And thank you," I thought to say.

Then he pulled me a little farther down the corridor and opened a smaller door. By matchlight I made out a row of elephant tusks leaning against the wall. They were not very big but they were a sure sign of elephants and they brought back the thought of Mozambique over there dim and blue across the Ruo beyond the corn. The Captain shut the door and we went back on deck. I saw with relief that the project of my eating the elephant had slipped his mind, so I flipped the meat behind me into the river and said, "Well look, my Captain, are you serious about that *ulendo* one of these weekends?"

He told me to send him a telegram as soon as I would have a couple of days free. If I sent it three days in advance, he thought the boys could locate the elephants. He said I ought to come on a Friday night and sleep on the *Empress,* because it takes a long day for an elephant hunt, as few as they are beginning to be, and as wild. I thanked him and, refusing one more glass of wine, jumped ashore and hurried up the path toward the rest-house and Wilson's indignation. In the morning we went back to the highlands and did more work on the Middle River.

On the Friday night that I got back to Chiromo the Captain was away across the river. He was checking over the hunting truck he kept at the customs house and waiting for the latest news of the elephants. But my telegram had reached him, and his cook was on the boat to show me a cot in a stateroom in the texas. She told me somebody would wake me at three in the morning; and because hurrying a car down the scarp from Blantyre is weary work I let the lap and whisper of the river on the old hull take my thoughts off morning, and quickly went to sleep.

Then the next thing I knew, I was fighting to ignore a pounding at the door, until I awoke and heard a voice outside saying it was three. I said I would get up, and pulled my clothes on without a light. It was black dark in the cabin. When I opened the door it was luminous dark outside and a boy was standing in the river mist with a lantern to take me to breakfast. In the galley it was warm and light. The cook gave me some tea, a boiled fish from the river, and some crusty Portuguese bread from Beira. When I had finished breakfast the boy, who said his name was Diego, led the way aft to where a dugout with another boy in it was tied to a blade of the big stern paddle. The boy in the boat looked wet and cold in the lamplit fog. I crawled down into the bow, wary of the gray water close around, and Diego dropped in behind me and cut us loose. They both took up paddles and swung us around into a course that would reach the far side about 300 yards upstream. After three or four strokes, the *Empress* was lost in the fog astern and we floated blind in an opaque shell of lantern light. The river was coming down from the cold cloud forests of Mlanje Mountain, but she had warmed up along the way. Streams of mist fed off her into the cool country air and rolled away in banks. The voyage across the river seemed no voyage at all, only a state of being in between. The boys did their reckoning from the feel of the current, and blind as we were we soon saw a light flare up on a post ahead. We bumped against a landing, and I jumped ashore in Portuguese East.

I wanted to test the feel of being in the land, but there was no time for it. There was a yell from somewhere and Diego answered it. Then I heard the chatter of an engine starting, and Diego told me the Captain was in the truck ready to go. I got my gun out of the boat and walked toward the noise; I found the Captain sitting in his bush wagon beside a big young Latin fellow behind the wheel.

"He was a boxer in Lisbon," the Captain said. I shook the young man's hand. Casual introductions seem to bother Spanish and Portuguese people.

"Who is he?" I said politely, motioning toward the boxer.

"He is called Jenaro," the Captain said. "A son of mine."

Jenaro nodded cheerfully. This not only confirmed the Captain's statements but meant he understood the way we talked. I got in the car beside the Captain, holding my rifle straight up between my knees. It seemed to be a Chevrolet we were in. Anyway, some of it did. Other sections had been replaced as they were ruined or as the Captain changed his notions of what a hunting car should be. The doors of the original pickup body had been cut off half way up and the roof of the cab had been rebuilt out of fluted galvanized iron. On the rear was a seat held up by a four-foot tripod, which was high enough to let the occupant look over the cab ahead. In front of this there was a pistol-grip spotlight swiveled to a tall standard. The Captain said the light was for night hunting when the savannas were dry and you could drive across them. I could see that it was a good way to pile up biltong all right. Across the river on the British side fire-hunting was illegal and a light like that would have got you into trouble, but the Portuguese are more lenient in such matters.

Diego jumped onto the bed of the truck and said everything was ready, and we bucked away. For a while I leaned out to admire the fire-hunting seat some more, but the Captain said I was going to fall out of the car—or *off* of it, he said—and I could see that he was right. We had one headlight at the start, but as we left the clearing behind the customs house this began to go off and on in a distracting way. After a bit Jenaro shut it off for good and made Diego get up in the high seat behind and play the hunting light ahead to illuminate our way. Any talking we did had to be pretty loud because there was no muffler. There was no real road either. There were only two ruts in sunbaked mud straddling a primordial footpath. It was like driving in concrete troughs. Luckily the fit was perfect. It had to be, because this same car had made the ruts in the last of the wet season, and no other vehicle had come along to tear them up. Once the ruts had taken in the wheels, there was little or no steering to be done. Jenaro put all his energy into keeping the accelerator on the floor.

The engine seemed well preserved, or maybe it had extra carburetors and things. Anyway, it was a strong engine and we went tearing along in the dark, geared into the swerving troughs, chasing the fleeing spot of light like greyhounds after an electric rabbit on a racetrack. We swooped into the middle of an unexpected little town of mud and straw, clattered and veered about till we found the ruts again, and then streaked out into the night, running the spot so fast Diego was barely able to keep it out in front of us.

I was getting curious to know why we were in such a hurry. I was about to ask, in fact, but the thought was beaten out of me by the car flying off the road and ripping through the scrub until stopped by heavy growth.

"The elephants," Jenaro said, backing away from the grip of the brush.

"You mean we hit one?"

"They ruined the road here. They stood around on it in

the last rain. It was a long time ago, but the road is still bad."

We seemed to be back in the road again, but there was no light, and the Captain noticed that Diego had been raked out of the seat by the limb of a tree. We waited till he worked loose and climbed back into place; then Jenaro started the car again, opened up the engine, and relaxed.

"Why are we going so fast?" I asked.

"It is already time for the lions," the Captain said.

"Lions? You mean elephants?"

"Lions first, then elephants."

There was so much noise I knew I would never work out how we had come to add lions to our aim. I settled back with the apprehension of the moment. We turned away from the river and into a stand of timber where the tree trunks crowded close to the wheels of the car. We shook loose from the woods and ran along its edge for a while, following the wall of forest because the ruts had lost themselves on the hard clay of a plain. It was out there with no ruts to guide us that the spotlight suddenly lifted off the road and left us careening blind through the three o'clock black, with the trees of the woods two paces to the left and nothing at all to the right.

Jenaro jerked us away from the timber and cursed Diego. The Captain said, "Waterbuck," and began to laugh in a tolerant way and to pound my leg. He said Diego always lost his head when he caught eyes in the edge of the spotlight.

"He can't help it," the Captain said. "With that light you can see a waterbuck a kilometer away."

When Jenaro banged on the ceiling, the light had already sneaked guiltily back and was holding fairly steady in the track ahead. For a while we raced along smoothly and then overran a pair of dim ruts that left the main track and made off to the right. Jenaro jolted to a stop, backed, and took this track across bare ground so smooth that you needed a road only to keep you away from the scattered bush-clumps and termite hills. After a while we dived into the end of a tunnel through tall grass. We came out again in a broken country, sank into the familiar ruts once more, and for maybe about fifteen minutes drove straight ahead. Suddenly we swerved and jerked up short with the engine already dead. Before the light went off, I could make out a rise of wattle and thatch, and a thin black man with a sack over one shoulder. He was holding a slim spear with a laurel leaf blade, and was blinking in the glare.

"Who is that?" I said.

"The *mayordomo*," the Captain said. "The overseer. This is the ranch."

He got out and told Diego to bring a box that was in the back of the truck, then went over and started talking to the *mayordomo*, who in spite of his rustic look seemed to know Portuguese fairly well. The Captain asked him about lions and the man said they had not come all night but that this was the hour at which they had come the night before. The Captain looked at his watch and saw that it was 4:15. He said that if they were coming they would have to come soon. Then he asked if there was any new word about the elephants. The *mayordomo* said they had been down along the river and were headed back toward high ground. A tracker from the biltong crew was looking along the edge of the woods for the place they had gone in. The tracker would wait where he found the trail going into the woods, and would send word about it to the biltong camp. The Captain told his son to drive over to the camp and see what they knew there. Jenaro got in the truck, started it, and roared away.

I asked the Captain if lions would come with a noise like that going on. He said if they were coming they would come, but that it was getting late and we ought to be in the kiosk. He turned and walked away in the dark and I followed him across a stretch of hard, dung-strewn ground to where a smell of cattle hovered, and a rank of crooked poles loomed before us and faded to right and left in the arc of a circular stockade. It was a high palisade of close-set snags, the silvery, crooked bones of weathered ebony, with the upper parts untrimmed and the spiky branches forking like sunbleached antlers. The poles were all interwoven with barbed wire, and along the top of the fence a wire ran loosely in the forks and was hung, here and there, with clusters of old tinware. I looked between the poles and in the dark made out the cattle lying quiet and wide-eyed waiting out the last of the night. Their horns were upswept African horns that spread away in a field of spires and looked gothic and clean behind the arthritic claws of the palisade.

We walked on a hundred paces or so beyond the corral and the Captain said, "The kiosk." I peered toward a new structure coming out of the dark. It was a little open pavilion with a thatch roof held up by six poles and dropping all around to eye level at the eaves. Inside, there were two chairs facing a table. A short staff rose from the table, and this held up a pistol spotlight like the one on the truck, with wires leading down to a storage battery on the ground.

The Captain said we would stay a while in the kiosk. After he took our guns and set them across pegs behind the chair, he told me to sit down, then sank back into one of the chairs and sighed. I was surprised how comfortable the chair was. The Captain said it was a pilot's seat from a wrecked airplane. Diego came out of the dark with the box from the truck, put it on the table, and sat down with his back against one of the poles that held up the roof.

"I thought a kiosk was a place where you buy newspapers," I said.

"Not this one," the Captain said. "This one is different. This one is the kiosk of the lions." He started taking things to eat out of the box.

"You better tell me what to do if any lions come," I said. "I never hunted lions before."

"I'll tell you," the Captain said. "For the time just tranquilize yourself, and eat."

He felt around in the basket and took out half a ham and a round of hard white cheese, some Beira bread and a sack of oranges and mangoes. He whistled softly and Diego got up. The Captain asked him about the canteen. Diego reached down beside my chair and picked it up. It was a two-gallon bottle of green glass with a hide cover shrunken on it and a shoulder strap. The Captain told me there was wine in the canteen, the red *tinto* so revered in Mozambique. It was diluted with water, half-and-half. It combined the virtues of both, the Captain said, and was what he always took on a hunt. He filled a cup for me and one for himself. Then he cut some cheese, ham, and bread, and we began to eat breakfast. I had eaten breakfast only a short while earlier, but the ride in the bush buggy made me lose all count of physiological time.

I told the Captain I was still surprised to be out there lion hunting like that. He said it was bad lion country, and no good trying to ranch there without corralling your stock at night. He had killed six lions and two leopards, he said, shooting from the same chair he was sitting on. Before he put up the kiosk and the alarm wire around the stockade, a lion could jump in and make off with a yearling while the *mayordomo* went on sleeping.

He said they still got in—you couldn't keep a man in the kiosk all the time—and I said I thought lions would have more sense than to keep coming back where they were shot. The Captain said that sometimes the place got a bad name among the lions for a while. There would be no sign of them for three or four months; but they always came back, maybe different lions, from somewhere. On both the last two nights they had come, just before daylight, and that was why we were there in the last dark of the third night waiting.

When I had calmed the spurious hunger the truck ride had stirred, I lay back in the chair and listened while the Captain went on talking about how hard it was to ranch in Africa. Then he got onto the subject of fishing for tiger fish, which was to him the best subject in the world. Finally, having talked himself out even about that, he closed his eyes and lay there chewing bread and cheese and waiting. After maybe half an hour like that, we heard a sudden racket in the paddock—a shuffling and quick clatter of tin. In almost the same voice the Captain and Diego said, "Nothing—it is nothing," because it was only two yearlings restless to be outside, pushing each other about.

After a while there was some gray to see in the sky, and Diego saw it and said day was coming. But the day took a while longer getting there and I passed the time remembering this waning stage in the hopes of other hunts—of deer hunts with the dogs almost out of the block of scrub where the standers were, and still cold-trailing; of duck blinds with only the night coming in with the cold north wind; of long trips to the sound in a rowboat after the sea run of big channel bass, and the tide already at middle flood and only catfish and little stingarees sucking at the bait. I used to fight off believing the chances were really running out at times like those, but this time I felt no fight in me. I felt only a dim wonder over how I came to be out there in the predawn dark of Mozambique with the cattle corralled behind the lion fence and the Captain eating to kill time before the lions might come. Whether the lions really came seemed not to be the measure of the moment. I could hardly see how this could be, and I wondered, at first uneasily, whether I might be losing my hunter's spirit.

The strange part was, I remember after a while sort of *hoping* so. Very secretly, for the first time, I remember articulating the thought that it might be best for me to try to get rid of my hunting urge. It was an odd decision to make, almost like deciding to submit to castration; but the thought was a valid one and it has ever since been picking up momentum in my mind. The hunting urge is no longer a passion it pays to cultivate, with the future we face in these times. Unless you are very rich, and can keep a big piece of the earth fenced off for your own private, antique joys. Or unless you have the extraordinary sort of mentality that savors the falling of birds let loose for you from cages.

I heard of a woman once who said to Theodore Roosevelt, "Tell me, Mr. President, when will you ever get over your childish inclination to kill things?" Those were not the exact words, but the question was about like that, and in a way it was a good question. We are all going to have to get over killing things pretty soon, for one reason or another. But the problem is not as simple as the question makes it sound. Behind that well-fed woman there were too many millennia with less-well-fed women putting the question another way—saying, "Look, Gug, when are you going out and kill something?" Killing things is in one way childish. In another way though, it has till lately been not childish at all, but the most mature and necessary craft and craving a man could have, next to that for procreation. And when all the need to kill for survival was gone, the old bloodstirring urges stayed with us, as intact as our useless wisdom teeth. Like wisdom teeth they have been far slower to yield to changing times than the need to use them was. For a while men put the old juices to work for the fun of the chase, as a manly recreation. As long as men were fewer than ducks and deer, things went along all right that way.

But now I think fathers are creating misery for their sons when they build in them the false hope that there can be hunting in the man-ridden world to come. The cult of the pioneer is done. The axe and the gun are dead symbols, like the crossbow and the anvil. We are Cro-Magnon no longer; we are no longer Minute Men or Forty-niners. Whatever needs, joys, and rights our grandchildren may have, these will not include felling trees or felling bodies.

I saw a boy not long ago who seemed to embody the dilemma of the hunter in these times. I was waiting for my lunch in the dining room of an East African hotel. A party in the last stages of preparation for a safari came in, and the boy was one of the group. There were two big men in khakis, with shortsleeved tunics over shortsleeved shirts and bullet loops around the tunics. The boy was about thirteen, well grown and very like the men. Two women, clearly the wives of the men, walked in front of the hunters to the table the headwaiter showed them.

The men and the boy all looked like Ernest Hemingway, with maybe a little more of a Texas look. Or maybe it was John Wayne they looked like. The women didn't look like Hemingway at all. They were women who were obviously going to spend a few weeks at the hotel waiting.

They were little, sweet, well-tended women, like secure mice; and as they passed I heard them speak of Neiman-Marcus in voices that seemed correct for Central Texas. They all sat down, and the women kept talking and the men began to speak in rumbling voices about things they ought to buy and people they had to see around the town. The room was full, and the waiters in red fezzes and white robes were slipping about among the tables. I could hear the shuffling sound of their bare feet above the talk of the safari party and the subdued voices of the English people. After a while the boy grew tired of waiting for the waiter and got up, went over to the buffet, and started piling a plate with cold cuts.

He was a manly looking boy, big for his age and healthy, a little heavy perhaps but not soft at all. There was a sort of aura of prepubic virility about him, partly built in, partly no doubt the result of a plan of his to be exactly like his father. The boy was a small big-game hunter beyond any doubt. He was probably going to be a good one. Maybe he already was good. There was an air of poise about the boy that made me feel this was not his first safari. My first thought, looking at him, was that he was a lucky boy. Not many boys have fathers who can give them an African safari for being good and manly.

I listened to the men talking seriously about the great game they were setting out to play, and I felt a little envious because no son of mine would probably ever go out on safari that way. But after thinking a while I was not so sure the boy was lucky. For his youth and a while afterward, he would have a solid thing to hold to— unless the Africans who are taking over their land should suddenly cut it off. But from the religious way the men were grooming him, they seemed to believe they were handing down some heritable asset for generations to come, like a good business or a wine cellar. What would be left of it when the boy would be his father's age? And how about the boys of the boy, I thought. What meaning would remain for them in the cult of the hunter?

That early dawn in Mozambique I felt only the start of such radical sentiments, only a curious unfamiliar lack of concern over the running out of the lion time. After the gray had come into the sky we waited twenty minutes longer, till the stockade poles were easy to see. Then we heard the sound of the truck away out on the plain. It raged up to the house and stopped, and the lion hunt was over.

The Captain stood up and stretched. Jenaro got out of the truck, came over, and cut himself some ham and bread.

"The tracker found where they went in the woods," he said. "They could be in the edge—or we might have a long walk."

He and the Captain started speaking in fast Portuguese and I snatched out of it that the elephants were in a long strip of forest surrounded by marshes and open thorn savanna. If they were traveling, to follow them could take us fifteen miles through the long dimension of the woods—or on the other hand, if they turned and crossed the narrow strip of forest, they might cut back into the open country in an hour. At least it was known where they had gone into the woods, and the tracker was there waiting to start the hunt.

We got into the car with our guns, the canteen, and a knapsack of victuals. Diego and the *mayordomo* climbed up behind, and we rushed away northeastward across the plain. We drove for half an hour or more and came to a clump of low forest like an island in the grass. We ran along its border for a while; then Diego, who was on the roof watching, rapped the tin and leaned down till his face was framed upside down in the window. He pointed ahead and we saw the tracker at the edge of the woods, leaning on an old Enfield rifle. When we stopped, the tracker came up and started talking quietly about the elephants.

He said they had gone in some time before midnight, but not long before. I don't know how he knew. I looked closely at the shattered rim of the woods where the elephants had entered. The work was so fresh you watched for falling twigs or the starting ooze of sap or the slow straightening of bent-down branches. But any spoor laid at night looks fresh at dawn, and the tracker kept saying the elephants could be either near or far. There was no wind to warn them; but there was also no chance of our going quietly through the crisp, clawing scrub.

Just before they had entered the forest the elephants had walked back and forth along the edge. The tracks of the biggest ones were the size of dinner plates and were sunk an inch deep in the firm, grassbound earth. The Captain looked carefully at the ground and spoke with the tracker. He said there were six or seven elephants in the woods. He told Diego to wait there with the car for an hour to see if we did any nearby shooting, and we moved off into the forest behind the tracker.

Inside the woods there was scarcely any need for a tracker. Where the elephants had stopped to browse, their destruction was spread about, but mostly they had kept moving in a close band, and the broken limbs and tilted saplings made a streak of ruin that nobody could miss. In the thickest places, where a man alone could hardly have pushed his way, they left almost an open road for us to travel.

It was rough cluttered country, a confusion of bits of

open wet plain, parkland savanna, and monsoon forest. Trees huddled here in tight coppices, or opened there into orchards where the let-in light let the grass grow in thorn-bordered lawns or head-high brakes. It was unreliable country to walk in. It led you into clean shade for a little, then stopped you short with a barricade of thornbush. Open vistas drew you off unsuspectingly, then narrowed down to nothing, and clawed you back when you saw your error and tried to correct your course. Nobody in his right mind would have hunted on foot in that place without the elephant sign to follow.

It was close to eight o'clock when the cool of the semiarid night had gone, and eight-thirty when it got too hot for a jacket and seemed time to stop for a drink. We did no stopping to rest at all. The fourth hour passed and there was no change in the look of the trail. Whenever I might have started to feel tired, there was the haunted look of the country to lift me up. It was not possible to believe that such country could be as lifeless as it seemed. I kept looking for a patch of tan lion against the grass or for secret mosaics of giraffe, but none was ever there. Scraps of all the African landscapes rose up before me, but except for the trees, there was never a living form. We would come suddenly out at the edge of a little plain of short grass and bare adobe, with an old euphorbia rising like organ cactus beside a low place where water stood, but no rhino would blow, no impala float away, and no elephants could ever be seen among the fever trees at the far edge where our elephants could have stopped their marching.

It was about then that I began to understand a thing I had heard many times and had myself repeated. It was that African wilderness is waning. We had been in Nyasaland for nearly a month and had seen little game. But this was more or less expected. Much of Nyasaland is heavily populated, and even out in what seems bush one is rarely far from a bicycle trail. But here in this unpeopled, wild-looking country, we had walked quietly through a varied terrain for a whole morning, and had seen only landscape empty of wild things. There was the trail of the six marching elephants to follow, and that kept heart in the day. But there was also a vision fading away from me forever, a conception of Portuguese East as a childish symbol, of Africa as a teeming primordial land where the past can be kept forever.

It was nearly eleven o'clock when we stopped for lunch. It was more cheese, mangoes, and tinto. The sun was coming straight down through the open places in the cramped woods. There was no breeze to move the heat away, and it piled up in banks that almost stifled our breathing. There was no call to linger when lunch was over, so we found the elephant way again and started following it, a little more slowly now, into the fifth hour, and after that into the sixth. Jenaro took off his shirt and started berating the elephants, using turns of phrase that seemed more Cuban than Portuguese. But the Captain kept saying that with elephants you never could tell till the last when they would stop and let you see them. Possibly he was just keeping our spirits up and I wondered what he really thought; but then I saw the tracker out there ahead with his old rifle and the *mayordomo* behind him. They had walked through too many days like this to be willing to kid anybody. I was used to walking in the woods myself and I knew it was time I was getting tired. But short of desperate exhaustion, feeling tired is mostly a matter of feeling bored, which is no way to feel on your first day in Portuguese East. And besides, nothing felt quite real, after all the wine for water and talking Spanish with Portuguese men, with the spearman out there shining without his sack shawl and the elephants somewhere off in front laying a trail for us to follow.

We had been walking the elephant road nine hours. It was three in the afternoon. The heat was a thing to push through and the Mauser was finding my bones wherever I tried to hold it up. I began to catch my thoughts straying from the country and the elephants, and wondered how we might ever get home again.

"The animals are in a hurry," I said.

"I told you they sometimes never stop—only walk, walk, pulling down stuff but walking all the time."

"What will we do when night comes?"

"We will have to stop walking. Only that." The Captain looked at his watch.

"And from there?"

"Go home," the Captain said. Then he looked at me closely and said: "Were you thinking we would walk back the elephant's way?"

"I wasn't sure," I said. "What other way is there?"

The Captain hit me on the back, laughed, and said I figured I was on a grand ulendo this time for sure; then he stopped laughing and told me the car would find us and take us back.

"How will Diego know where to look for us?" I said.

"We will come out on the trail of the elephants. This woods has an end."

"Suppose the elephants stay in it and don't come out at all?"

"Then there will be shooting and Diego will hear it and keep flanking to head the herd. If he misses it, he will pick up the tracks and wait for us there."

I asked him where he thought the elephants were. It

was a sort of a simple-minded question, and the tracker looked back, politely, because we were talking too much. So he still had hope.

"They can be anywhere," the Captain said.

That last half hour I began to see that the elephants were not going to stop for us; and for the second time that day a missed chance seemed not to matter very much. Tired as I was finally getting to be—sweated down to lees of red wine and unused juices of prolonged crisis—I began to see a good clear vision of myself face to face with elephants, putting up the Mauser to shoot where the Captain told me to. I saw that it made no sense to me. Suppose I did get the gun up and did hold it true and, after a lifetime of dropping peanuts into the snouts of elephants, loosed the little slugs to streak over and splatter spiteful trails into the dignity of an elephant's head. The end of that would be a heap of bad smelling biltong to go to the coast, or a sudden need to run like hell. Either way I could find little heart for it left in me. I didn't say anything about this; I suppose that if the elephants had stopped I would have joined in the shooting. But when the ninth hour ended and we looked down the elephant road and saw the woods fall away into a plain, I was only glad we would soon stop walking.

We came out where an arm of knee-high grass jutted into the woods from a wet savanna and held the trees apart for a mile or more. It was hot out there in the slanted sunlight, but at least the air was moving. Shallow waves rolled across the grass, and it felt good to be out of the woods. The Captain and Jenaro swore some at the elephants, but I think they were glad to be out of the woods too, breathing the live air in the open again. We walked into the grass a way and looked up and down for the car. We saw it a short way off in the edge of the woods. Diego was standing by it holding a shotgun and peering on down the border where guinea hens were chattering.

We started toward the car. The tracker and the *mayordomo* were ahead and from the way they waved their arms you could tell they were still trying to figure out what the elephants were doing. Suddenly they both stopped short and jumped back and one of them let out a yell. The *mayordomo* ran to a rotting stump, kicked the hard middle out of it, and, raising this above his head, heaved it out into the grass, where it hit with a cracking sound. Instantly the head of a snake showed over the grass tips, and then slowly climbed higher still, the neck spreading wide as the head rose. Facing the men squarely, ten feet away, the snake held there swaying with the grass, the shifting curves of the body rope-thin and nacreous gray in the sunshine. You could see no menace and no fear, but only a standing yard of curving query, all out in the open, and the tongue slowly waving. Even back where we stood I could see the questioning tongue and the glint of the eyes, and could tell that the snake was a cobra.

It was a big enthusiastic cobra with a hood. He stood up there at the edge of the forest at the end of our hunt, not knowing he came in place of elephants. I knew Indian cobras from zoos, and had unwound their melancholy corpses from museum jars of alcohol. But beyond that, cobras had been for me mostly color for far-off places; and here now was one of my own to see, swaying slightly in the slowing wind of the afternoon in Mozambique, while two black boys gibbered and scrabbled for solid things to throw.

Suddenly Jenaro's gun came up, and quickly the Captain batted it down.

"What is the matter with you?" Jenaro said to his father.

The Captain said: "You will scare the guineas," and Jenaro snorted and the boys looked back quickly for a joke because the guineas had quit talking and Diego was half way down the edge of the woods on his way to join us.

The snake sank into the grass a little, but then it gathered itself and rose again, higher than before, and stayed there swaying across the beveling shadows of the grass stems. Then a chunk of rotten wood that the tracker threw looped past its head and all at once there were only grass tips where the cobra had been.

Sparing wild things is not my idea of an Iberian virtue. I certainly never thought I would see a Portuguese biltong hunter spare a poisonous snake. There was something special about the look of the cobra, all right, there in the sun at the edge of the woods; but I never thought the Captain would see it. As a matter of fact I ought to have killed the snake myself. I should have borrowed the guinea gun from Diego, backed off to let the shot spread apart, and collected the snake for Chuck Bogert. It seemed to be an Egyptian Cobra, the kind King Tut made famous, and a species that ranges widely in Africa; but it might have been something else. I was charged with unused hormones of the hunt, though, and with the undimmed feel of Mozambique, and had no sense of fitness. The only specimen I seemed to want, and the only trophy, was the cobra standing there gray and puzzled, higher than the yellow grass, with a mile of plain beyond, then blue woods, and over that the rest of Portuguese East and Mlanje rising hazily from Nyasaland.

We went to the car and got in. The tracker and the *mayordomo* made no move to come but only stood watching us. I asked why they were standing there like that, and the Captain said: "They will stay with the elephants." Jenaro started the engine and we moved away. I waved back at them, the tracker with his old Enfield and the *mayordomo* with his spear. I looked closely for any sign of concern over the night and the prospect of more walking after tireless elephants, but I could see none.

Back at the landing on the Ruo the wind was down, the sun was sinking into Elephant Marsh, and the sky had all caught fire. The dugout had gone over to Chiromo on a trip for the customs station. Down at the river a heavy wooden barge had been hauled half way out for repairs, and beside it a Sena smith was making cleats of iron. He was a real old heathen smith, a sad little gnome of a man with tight peppercorn hair, a heavy sledge and a chunk of iron for an anvil. His forge was a strap-iron basket of charcoal and his bellows was a two-lobed bag of liver-and-white goatskin that his four-year-old son had on like a life jacket. To make the bellows blow, the little boy worked his arms up and down like an unfeathered heron working at how to fly, pumping with vast energy but all the time with a far-off look as if he really were doing nothing at all. The smith's wife was higher up on the bank fussing with some pots over a little fire. The thin smoke rose barely visible from the hardwood sticks and then spread in a head-high stratum that drifted edgeways with the quiet air. There was a hangdog look about the family that was even more than the racial sadness of Shire Valley Bantus. I recalled reading somewhere that in many parts of East Africa smiths are traditionally looked upon with contempt, and wondered whether that was what ailed this family. This got me wondering how a useful craft could ever come to be despised. In West Africa a smith is a happy man, better adjusted than

H. W. Longfellow himself would likely have stipulated, and in some places he is even looked on with mystic awe as one whose art is at once occult and beneficent. The man doing the same sort of thing among the southeastern Bantus is often a pariah. The Sena smith by the river had the look of a beggar, and I asked the Captain about it. He said he didn't know what was wrong with the man— that smiths were like that.

The customs officer came down to sit with us on the bank. He started talking about Laurenço Marques and Lisbon. The Portuguese was too fast for me, and after a while I got up and walked down the path beside the Ruo toward the Shire where I could hear the sound of an outboard motor. I came out on the Shire bank and saw a dugout crossing the mouth of the Ruo. A black boy was running the outboard motor and in the bow there was a tall man with no hat and very little hair. The top of his head was shining red-brown. He was facing the stern and trolling for tiger fish with a long rod of split bamboo. I looked over to the Nyasaland bluff and saw an old Humber parked there. I recognized it as a car owned by a Scot named Horace; and then I saw that it was Horace fishing. I had met him briefly at Fort Johnston. He had retired some years before and now ranged up and down the river and the lake hunting and fishing. He was said to be the only man in the valley who presumed to dispute about tiger fish with Captain Ariano.

The dugout moved slowly up through the eddies that the Ruo was spinning into the Shire water. Horace held the rod with one hand and with the other gesticulated to reinforce the flood of Chiyao he was yelling at the boy in the stern. The boy was so near the motor that he heard nothing, but he saw Horace was talking so he grinned and looked agreeable.

When the boat moved alongside where I stood, I said hello; and Horace, knowing only that I was a chap standing on the Mozambique bank said, "*Bom dia*," and then looked back down the slant of his line and started yelling Chiyao at the boy some more. The canoe worked on up the Mozambique side of the river to a little cove where hippos often groaned at night. Then it turned out into the stream and started to circle back.

I stood there tired as I ever had been. It came to me that I ought to get some tackle and a boat one day and see what a tiger fish was like. I was about to head back up the path when I heard the motor stop. I looked up the river and saw that Horace had his tiger fish. Away back of the boat where the spoon had been running, there was the swirl of a quick thrashing in the water. The boy was ducking to keep clear of slack line and grabbing for a paddle to turn Horace stem on to face the fish. As the boat swung around, Horace reeled hard at the overrun line, but it stayed slack for what must have been half its length, and though Horace was far away, I could see his hope was fading. Then, almost too fast to see, the top of the rod sliced down to the water, and Horace had solid hold of a tiger fish. The hook stung the fish, and it chopped up half out of the top of the river and slung water and foam, then streaked off down the shore toward where I was standing. It jumped not thirty feet from where I was, and hung in the air like an angry stuffed fish mounted for a moment on a wall. Then it dropped back, churned foam and ran downstream again, and the line sang in the water. For a moment Horace held back, gauging his tackle and spirit against the run of the tiger fish. Then he just braked down and let it go, as it was bound to go in spite of anything he could do.

The tiger fish was leaving Horace. He stood there with a

rapt, helpless look, with his drag on so tight the bamboo took the same slant as the line clear back to the butt, while the Yao boy jabbered in the stern. He stood there in the dugout holding on to the rod, with the last of the line slipping away and nothing left to do. There was a deep V sweeping along over where the fish was raging away. When this got to the edge of the Ruo water, it sucked under suddenly in a heavy swirl, and I knew without looking that Horace would be standing with the rod straight, the line loose, and his hope all gone.

The tiger fish belongs to a genus called *Hydrocyon*. It has a slim, compressed body, a longish snout, and terrific teeth set wide apart in the jaw. Its sides are yellowish silver brushed lengthwise with shadowy dark bands. The fins are tipped with red or orange. The tiger fish is rated among the most rambunctious fighters of all freshwater game fish. It quickly chops flies to bits, and anyway a fly is wasted on a tiger fish because it takes any kind of bait, and unless the fly is put on with a wire leader, the fish will take it away from you. The best bait is a spoon. The best places to find the fish are deep, quiet holes or slow eddies in rivers, like those where the Ruo meets the Shire. The excitement with a tiger fish does not end when, and if, it is boated. After that there is the hazardous work of unhooking the fish, with it clearly aware of your part in its predicament, irked about it, and determined to make you pay with your life's blood. The only fish I know that seems so self-possessed and bound to exact vengeance is a moray eel, which looks as if it were about half snake anyway. A tiger fish is a typical fish, and in any fish such well-ordered indignation out of water seems a little eerie.

When I saw Horace playing the big tiger fish—or vice versa—I had no idea what family of fishes *Hydrocyon* belonged to. But its actions on the line brought to mind

Brycon, a Central American fresh-water fish called locally *blanco* or sometimes *sávalo.* I used to fish for *blanco* in Honduras and Nicaragua. Although it is a fish not often spoken of in the literature of fishing, it seemed to me to combine in its athletic body the speed of the bonefish and the aerial skill of the tarpon.

Watching Horace and his fish made me think that the tiger fish and the *blanco* were a lot alike. After I went back to Blantyre I read about the tiger fish and found that it and the *blanco* do in fact belong to the same group, that of the curiously distributed characines, which like the cichlids are found only in Africa and the American tropics. This is the family of the piranha too. It is fortunate that the tiger fish doesn't share the ambition of piranhas as regards the size of prey, because tiger fish are said to weigh thirty pounds sometimes. The Africans say a crocodile is afraid to attack a tiger fish.

Horace and the Captain both said categorically that the tiger fish is the finest sporting fish in the fresh waters of the world. The world is big, though, and the tarpon gets into fresh water. The silver of a tarpon hanging high against blue sky between green walls of a jungle river is not matched anywhere it seems to me. But the point is, for dynamic verve in both jumping and running, the characines are surely among the spectacular game fish of the world.

As I stood and watched Horace out there thinking about his lost fish, I felt sorry for him. I was not sure he would see his loss as I saw the loss of the lions and elephants in Portuguese East. And I wished the boy would for God sake stop his unseemly whooping and beating himself on the legs. I looked to see if Horace might notice a gesture of sympathy from me, if I should make one. But he just stood there in the drifting boat, seeing nothing, needing nothing at all; so I walked away.

The next morning I was leaving early, but since there was a little time before breakfast, I went down to the *Empress* to say good-bye to the Captain again. The mist was rising off the river and there was some thin blue showing in the sky and the start of the day wind was moving the corn on the other side. When I got near the *Empress*, I heard the Captain talking and saw him at the far rail waving at some Africans who were out in the Ruo in a dugout. He was talking Chinyanja. I didn't know what he was saying and don't think the men in the boat did either. They just looked at him, standing at the rail in his shorts, and said nothing at all, but only paddled upstream, looking from one bank to the other as if they were searching for something. The Captain swore at them in Portuguese, and then turned away from the rail grumbling. He saw me standing on the bank and bellowed: "The elephant hunter! You said you were going home."

"After breakfast," I said. "Who are the fellows in the canoe?"

The Captain said they were Mozambique Negroes from somewhere up the river. They were backwoods folks and very ignorant. They came by Chiromo every year on a fishing trip. They usually made a strike or two with their net in the Ruo and then moved on.

"They are very ignorant," he said.

Diego came out of the galley and said: "They eat snakes," and went back in again.

We watched the men heading up the middle of the river, still looking hard at the banks. Suddenly the one at the bow paddle started jawing back at the others and waving an arm toward the Nyasa side up above the town, and after a bit the canoe turned and slanted across the way he pointed. I told the Captain I was going up there to see what they were going to do. I said I had come down to thank him again for the elephant hunt and to ask if maybe we could try the tiger fish next time.

"Sure," he said. "Wait a minute." He disappeared into the cabin and came out shaking what seemed to be a long-handled black paint brush. He drew back and threw the thing over the rail and it looped up end-over-end and fell to the bank, almost at my feet. It was the tail of an elephant. It was still bloody where it had been cut off half way out to the end. I picked it up and looked at it, unable to focus on how it might have come to be there.

"The boys found them," the Captain said. "An hour after we left. Just inside the woods on the far side of the grass, remember? The tracker killed one and went for the biltong crew, then walked out to tell me. He got here at daylight."

"The tracker is a man," I said.

"You take the tail to your children."

"That is about right," I said.

"You can have a foot, too, if you want it. You skin them out and they make elegant wastebaskets."

I thanked him but said that, even skinned out, the foot would be too heavy to carry home in the airplane. I told him I would be back down if I could get away. Then I said good-bye, and trotted up the shore toward a mud bar where the fishermen were coming in. As I passed the rest-house the cook warned me that breakfast was almost ready and I said I would only be a minute.

When I reached the bluff abreast of the bar, the men had already started their strike. One was standing on the shore anchoring an end of the net. It was stripping off a mound in the middle of the canoe, which was working out into the river again. There was a man at the piled net paying it out, and the two other men were paddling. There was a strange stiff look about the way the man in the stern paddled. When the boat turned back toward shore, I looked at his face and saw that his eyes were gone. The current made laying the net in a circle a tricky maneuver, but the blind man paddled steadily all the way around, and nobody seemed to be giving him any directions. When the dugout cut straight in to complete a drifting circle with the net, the man in the middle picked up a paddle too and they all worked hard to take in a patch of dimpling eddies that played about the slow inside of the bend.

As they came near I slid down the bluff, jumped the slough inside the bar, and saluted the anchor man. He was standing shin deep in the water, holding his lines. He did not look at me at all. I tried my kind of Portuguese on him, then English, and finally, all the Chinyanja fish names I had learned, pointing at the net and saying each word with an interrogative lift. It all brought nothing. The man would not even look my way. I went over and fingered the two-inch mesh of the net. I had fingered a lot of nets along the Shire and up at the lake. This one was made of some sort of plant fiber and I tried every nuance of sound and sign I could think of to find out what plant it was. I even stripped bark off a drifted stick and held it questioningly beside the net, but the man only looked aloof. He was really a fink, as my daughter says, and I finally said to hell with him.

The men in the canoe jumped out and started pulling the upstream lines ashore. They too seemed unwilling to admit that I was there, and I saw I might as well quiet down completely. When about twenty arm-lengths of net had come in, there was a fish stuck in the mesh, and one of the men took it out and threw it into the boat. The blind man groped about in the water in the bottom, caught the fish, and put it in a basket. After that, fish came fairly often. There were various kinds of cichlids, catfish, tiger fish, and other species out of the Zambezi fauna like nothing I had seen before. Some were gilled in the meshes of the net and some skidded back and forth in the fold along the ground line.

The men took out the fish and threw them one by one into the canoe. There were quite a lot of catfish in the haul, two kinds of them. Both had murderous barbed spines in their fins, and I watched with apprehension to see what the blind man would do with these. When his hand finally touched catfish skin, and the poisoned javelins locked straight out stiff with menace, I could hardly keep from yelling. But the merest touch told the man what it was he had. He gentled his motions and felt for the head, slipped his hand over it and squeezed tight, leaving the fins sticking out between his fingers. Then he lifted the impotent fish from the bilge and, rolling his lips back out of the way, took a fin in his teeth and bit the spine right out of it and spit the broken shaft into the water with a great show of distaste. For quite a while I stood and watched him. As he gnashed away at one poor catfish after another my own lips curled back in spite of me. Then I heard the cook down the river tolling me to breakfast and left the fishermen with their harvest.

After I finished eating, I stowed the last of my gear in a bag, picked a chameleon off the screen, and put him in a basket. A boy from Tenghadzi ran up and asked if he could ride as far as the camp there and I said sure. The cook, who carried my bag to the car, gave me a bottle of tea because the trip up the scarp would last through morning teatime. I handed him some shillings and a note for the engineers when they came, then got in the car and started the engine. We bumped out into the grove of blue gums beside the rest-house. The tires cracked sticks as we wound among the trees. I leaned out for a last look at Portuguese East, and saw it in snatches down the long runs of shade. As far either way as the crowding trunks would let me look, there was only the smoking silver of the river and the corn standing in prim ranks. We jolted onto the highway and the Indian stores rose beside the road. Then even the corn was gone.

Nyasa

WE WERE down below unpacking our bags when the voices on deck took a different tone. The other passengers were all up at the bow in the wind and sun, and for a time their talk had been an unformed drone over the rhythm of the engines and the small noises the ship made rolling in the troughs of the tradewind waves. But then the words grew louder, and a woman called out something urgent that ended, ". . . cyclone," and the voice of a man said, "Couldn't be. Weather much too fine."

I remember clearly that the overheard phrases for a moment meant little, because the weather was, as the man said, fine. And that suddenly the thought of kungu spouts came to my mind. I dropped what I held and ran out of the stateroom, up the companionway and into the blazing light on deck. And there it was, the awesome thing to see, the sight that alone would set apart our short voyage on the lake and place us on the list of the blessed among *Ilala* passengers. Out to windward, rising black and crooked in midlake against the thin blue sky of the Portuguese side were the legendary kungu spouts, the midge clouds of Lake Nyasa.

These hosts of tiny flies make one of the grand spectacles of African natural history. There is much to tell about them, and I shall tell some of it a little later. First, however, there are things to be told about the lake in which they pass their infancy.

We had gone aboard the *Ilala* two hours before at Kota Kota, after spending the night in the rest-house on the hill behind the town. It was a good rest-house and a welcome one. We had arrived there after a long drive up Nyasaland from Blantyre to Dedza, out through the Angoni country to Lilongwe, and then on through *Brachystegia* forest, with no game in fifty miles except one band of forest pigs. When we came to the lake shore at Kota Kota, the sleepy old Arab slave port, the rest-house on the hill looked good. We ensconced ourselves in it, then looked up the Medical Officer to get help for our ailments —Lewis for a cold, I for some new set of small African creatures in my insides. Afterward we walked down the hill to look at Kota Kota and the lake.

Kota Kota is the biggest native city in East Africa. As we walked down through its shady recesses, we saw the different Arab look of the people and thought back to times not long ago when the Arabs were there as slavers. We looked up the famous Kota Kota ivory carvers, but they seemed jaded by too much attention from gift-shop agents. We saw the Universities Mission compound, and the tree where David Livingstone received the local chief in 1863. We talked with the people at the Rice Co-operative Society, which mills and exports the rice grown by African farmers of the region and furnishes the main bulk of the cargo that is lightered out to ships in the shallow Kota Kota roadstead. We went out on the waterfront and watched the traffic of dugouts from villages up and down the shore. We looked out over the mid-section of the long lake toward Mozambique and saw no land at all in that direction.

Nyasa is one of the Great Lakes of Africa. To the geologist, to the zoologist, and to any amateur of landscapes it is one of the great lakes of the whole world. It is 2,300 feet deep, 350 miles long, and from 20 to 50 miles wide. The surface is more than 1,500 feet above sea level, and the bottom 700 feet below it. The River Shire—pronounced not *shyre*, but *sheeray*—leaves the lake at its southern end and runs 310 miles to join the Zambezi in Mozambique.

"Nyasa" means "lake" in Chinyanja, the Bantu dialect most prevalent in the region. It is the same word that elsewhere turns up as *nyanja*, or *nyanza*. So to bilingual folk of the area, to say "Lake Nyasa" is the same as saying "Lake Lake," which has a humorous redundance.

The queer dimensions of Nyasa suggest that it was made by glacial action, but this is clearly impossible, because the Ice Age never reached down into Nyasaland. To see how the lake got its curious shape, it helps to look hard at the shorelines along both sides. Their conformation calls to mind the old controversial theory of continental-drift, the idea that the continents floated into their present disposition on molten magma underneath. Proponents of the drift theory pointed to the complementary contours of the coastlines of West Africa and Brazil as evidence that the two lands had broken and drifted apart. That notion is a moot one. On the eastern and western sides of Lake Nyasa there is a similar and even more suggestive reverse agreement in the juts and jags of the opposing shores. In this case there can be little doubt that the two edges of the land were really once in contact. The lake is a crack in the earth. It is one of a long series of confluent cracks that begins away down in the eastern Transvaal and runs all the way up the body of Africa and to the Red Sea, the Dead Sea, and the Jordan Valley in Asia Minor. This vast fault is known as the African Rift. Other big lakes lie in the Rift and so does the Nile River.

Nyasa is an ancient lake. It has varied markedly in level, but there has been water in the Nyasa trough continuously far longer than most lakes have existed. The water still rises and falls in a way that confounds the builders of installations along the shore, although recent engineering at the outlet has steadied it down in this respect. Besides its sporadic changes in level the lake pulses with peculiar internal tides of the kind known as seiches.

Traffic on the lake is harassed by petulant squalls called *mueras* that come in unannounced and rave down the trough of the lake with great violence. In 1947 the *Vipya*, a new ship on her third run up the lake, was caught in a *muera* in the specially stormy midsection of the lake where the winds sluice down between the Livingstone Mountains on the eastern shore and the Nyika Plateau on the Nyasaland side. The *Vipya* capsized several miles offshore, and one hundred and fifty people were drowned.

Lake Nyasa was discovered, or located, by David Livingstone. The Portuguese had found it long before, but as far as any opening up to the outside world was concerned, it was Livingstone who discovered it. He came in overland from Tete on the Zambezi, after finding the *Ma Robert*, the sleazy steamboat sent out from England for his explorations, too unreliable for the trip up the Shire River. The whole huge spread of interior Africa was dark in those days, and Nyasaland was in the darkest part. Livingstone was looking for information with which to strengthen his campaign for British action against the slave trade. He groped through a nebulous web of thin, fantastic clues and legends before he came at last to the shores of Lake Nyasa, on September 15, 1859.

The first steamboat on the lake was called *Ilala*. It was sent out by the General Assembly of the Free Church of Scotland, with Bishop Laws and the party that founded the Livingstonia Mission. Ilala is the name of the place where Livingstone died and where his heart was buried. The first *Ilala* was built in 1875 by Yarrow and Headly of London. She was a stern-wheel steam launch forty-eight feet long, with a narrow funnel, two masts, and a three-foot draft.

The logical route into Nyasaland was by way of the Indian Ocean and the Zambezi and Shire Rivers. This required a portage around Murchison Rapids in the Shire, which blocks the approach to Lake Nyasa with a series of cataracts that fall 1,300 feet in 54 miles. The original *Ilala* was designed with these rapids in mind. Her hull was made of steel plates joined not by rivets but by bolts. Each plate weighed fifty pounds, which was an average carrier's load. Another bit of foresighted planning was sending out with the party a naval lieutenant named Edward Young, who had been with Livingstone on his Zambezi expedition, and later had gone out to Nyasaland again when Livingstone was erroneously reported dead during his second visit to Lake Nyasa. Three years after Livingstone returned to England from the Zambezi explorations, he went back to East Africa. He landed on the Indian Ocean coast at Mikindani and made his way overland to the south end of Nyasa. There most of his African helpers deserted and took word back to the coast that Livingstone had been murdered. When the news reached England, Edward Young was sent to investigate. He carried out the tough errand with characteristic courage and good sense, laboriously tracing out the routes of Livingstone's wanderings and finally accumulating proof that the missionary was still alive. Putting Young in charge of the Livingstonia Expedition was an even shrewder move than bolting a hull together out of fifty-pound head loads.

The first *Ilala* was taken to Cape Town, where she and the expedition party trans-shipped for the Zambezi on a German schooner. At the mouth of the river the keel was laid, the hull assembled, and on August 10, 1875, the trip into the interior began. The *Ilala* drew too much water for river travel and she ran aground repeatedly in the 200 miles from the Kongone mouth of the Zambezi up to the rapids in the Shire. Time and again she had to be emptied of all cargo and hauled over bars and banks. When Murchison Rapids was reached she was once more taken apart, and a thousand carriers put her pieces and cargo on their heads and carried them to the head of the fast water. The boat was reassembled there without the loss of a single bolt, Young's account says with pride, and she steamed on up the Upper Shire and entered Lake Nyasa on October 12, 1875.

One of the important things Young did while cruising with Bishop Laws on Lake Nyasa in the first *Ilala* was to meet with an Arab slave dhow off Kota Kota and steam around it in circles to show the awesome speed of the Mission steamboat, and to suggest, without saying it, that no dhow could hope to escape if a steamboat should seriously pursue it. The Arab fled for shore. His ignominy was taken as a straw in the wind by the slavers and they soon afterward moved their headquarters to the northern end of the lake.

East Africa and its Indian Ocean coast were very far away from the United States in slave times. A lot of American slaves came from there nevertheless, and most of these were recruited among the villages of the Nyasa region. During the earlier days of their slave traffic, the Arabs and their local Bantu henchmen, the Yaos, marched caravans of shackled people the 500 miles or more around the southern end of the lake to the ports of the Indian Ocean. Later, when the British came into the Shire Highlands and flushed the Yaos from their homeland southeast of the Lake, Kota Kota became the main center for mobilization of the slaves. They were stacked like cord wood in the dhows, ten thousand in a year, the Arabs boasted, and sent across to the Portuguese port of Losefa on the eastern side of the lake. From there they were walked to the coast and either shipped to Zanzibar to be distributed to Old World markets, or were picked up by the American slavers who for decades played cop and robber with the British gunboats that patrolled the coast.

The suffering of the Negroes aboard the dhows was grisly, although not to be compared with that of the far bigger cargoes of misery in the American slaveships during the transatlantic crossings. The Arab dhows were light sailing craft, open or partly decked and fitted with supports for bamboo platforms that were built in tiers, one above the other, with a space about equal to the thickness of a human body in between. After walking the 500 miles down to the coast, a hundred or a thousand in a caravan, each with his neck in the crotch of the dreadful *goree*, or slave stick, and usually with a heavy load of ivory on their heads, the slaves were loaded aboard the Zanzibar dhows in bulk. They were laid out horizontally; the bottom was covered first. Grown people were put in and children were laid on top of them to fill the spaces; then the boards of the first platform were put in place an inch or so above the bottom layer of people and another tier was stowed, and so on until the load was built up gunwale-high. Because Zanzibar was only a two- or three-days' sail away, little food or water was given the slaves and on some voyages none at all. Sometimes the winds were fitful or the dhows ran into contrary storms that prolonged the crossing. There was great loss of cargo then. The Arabs complained that, although the bottom layers of people always died first, these could never be removed until the upper tiers had died and could be thrown overboard. According to estimates made by Livingstone and others, five slaves died in transit from the Nyasa region for every one who reached Zanzibar alive. In one dhow examined by a British officer after a stormy ten-day crossing, there were fewer than a dozen survivors in a cargo of three hundred.

For many of the Nyasa villages, life at home was no less gruesome than the journeying to market. When a town was raided, half the people might be carried away and most of the rest would die slowly of famine, because of disruption of their delicately balanced agriculture. The lake shore and Shire Valley were at one time one of the most densely populated regions of Africa, and when Livingstone found Lake Nyasa it had become the center of the East African slave trade. The British Consul at Zanzibar estimated that 19,000 slaves a year passed through the customs house there, and many more went out uncounted from Portuguese ports. But no figures could measure the misery involved in the harvesting of such a crop. The nightmare in the land is made plain in Livingstone's

Expedition to the Zambezi, the book in which he tells of his discovery of Lake Nyasa. I have picked out a few passages that give the feel of the times:

page 413

We never realized the atrocious nature of the traffic until we saw it at the fountain head . . . Besides those actually captured thousands are killed and die of their wounds and famine, driven from their villages by the slave raid proper. Thousands perish in internecine war waged for slaves with their own clansmen and neighbors [that is, it was not always just the Yaos capturing slaves for Arab and Portuguese dealers, but as the chaos spread, Nyanjas sold Nyanjas, and sometimes were even able to catch detached Yaos and sell them to the openminded Arabs]. . . . The many skeletons we have seen among the rocks and woods, by the little pools, and along the paths of the wilderness, attest the awful sacrifice of human life . . . A small armed steamer on Lake Nyassa could easily, by exercising a control, and furnishing goods in exchange for ivory and other products, break the neck of this infamous traffic in that quarter; for nearly all must cross the Lake or the Upper Shire.

page 140

The trade . . . crosses Nyassa and the Shire, on its way to the Arab port Kelwa, and the Portuguese ports of Iboe and Mozambique. At present slaves, ivory, malachite and copper ornaments are the only articles of commerce . . . nearly all the slaves shipped from the above mentioned ports come from the Nyassa district . . . it is only by the ivory being carried by the slaves that the latter do not eat up all the profit of a trip.

pages 474-475

The Shire having risen, we steamed off . . . It was not long before we came upon the ravages of the notorious Mariano [a Portuguese half-caste slaver]. The survivors . . . were in a state of starvation, having lost their food by one of his marauding parties. The women were in the fields collecting insects, roots, wild fruits, and whatever could be eaten in order to drag on their lives, if possible, till the next crop should be ripe. . . . Dead bodies floated past us daily, and in the mornings the paddle had to be cleared of corpses, caught by the floats during the night. For scores of miles the entire population was swept away by this scourge. . . . It made the heart ache to see . . . the river-banks once so populous, all silent; the villages burned down, and an oppressive stillness reigning where formerly crowds of eager sellers [appeared]. . . . The sight and smell of dead bodies was everywhere. Many skeletons lay beside the path, where in their weakness they had fallen. . . . Ghastly living forms of boys and girls, with dull dead eyes, were crouching beside some of the huts.

I think it must be the slave raids so recent in their background that make the rural Nyanjas of today seem so repressed, so unlike Ghanians, say, in temperament. It has been less than seventy-five years since the slaving stopped around the lake, and its marks are still there like unseen chains on the necks of the Nyasas. The quiet in most Nyasaland crowds is eerie; the contrast with the cheerful hullabaloo of any comparable West African group is puzzling. In Nyasaland you walk through a sea of women seated in a market or at a ferry stop or maize station, and the stillness is so deep and un-African it makes the faces around you seem like a hallucination. The quiet is not the morose, anti-white silence that spread through crowds of Kenya people in the days just before the Mau-Mau trouble. It is rather a listless melancholy, a lack of any of the usual Negro gaiety. In West Africa or Martinique or Bimini, any gathering not drawn together by some grave accident is an occasion for loud good-natured talk and jibing. The incongruous absence of this struck me at once in Nyasaland, and I took special notice of crowds that had no idea a white man was anywhere about. Compared with Negroes at other places the Nyasas are a quiet, melancholy people, and I can only think it is the mark of slave times on them still.

The final struggles to rid Lake Nyasa of the slave trade took place in the middle 1890's. The fighting was all at the north end of the lake. The first *Ilala* had a part in it, and the Germans from Tanganyika—then German East Africa—helped the Nyasalanders drive out Chief Mlozi, the last of the Arab slavers. The fights with Mlozi brought the old *Ilala* into friendly contact with a German gunboat called *Hermann von Wissman*, which later was involved in the first naval battle of World War I.

I think it is not widely known that the first naval engagement of 1914 took place on Lake Nyasa. It was certainly not known to me, until I happened to read an account of the event in the *Nyasaland Journal* written by a man who took part in the encounter. The battle took place on August 6, 1914, only two days after war was declared. The ships involved were the *von Wissman* and the British *Guendolen*, which was the most imposing ship that ever sailed Lake Nyasa. She was a 135-foot, 350-ton twinscrew steamship, built by Rennie and Company of Greenock, Scotland, in 1897, and assembled on the Shire River at Matope above Murchison Rapids. When Nyasaland got word of the outbreak of war, the *Guendolen* was sent on a surprise foray up to Sphinxhaven, home port of the *von Wissman* on the German shore of the lake. The *von Wissman* was a 91-foot gunboat named after the German explorer, Major von Wissman, who led an expedition in 1891 against the Arab slave traders. The *Guendolen* mounted two six-pounder Hotchkiss guns forward, port and starboard, and one three-pounder aft. The *von Wissman* had a single one-pounder, mounted high in the bow. Though she had the heavier armament, the *Guendolen* moved cautiously up the German shore, mindful of the superior sweep of the German's gun. To the relief of everybody on the *Guendolen*, the *von Wissman* was found helplessly ashore in the Sphinxhaven dry dock. The action that followed is described in the *Nyasaland Journal* by Dr. Meredith Sanderson, the surgeon on the *Guendolen:*

As we cleared the point and swung towards the bay, the swell caught us broadside on and the *Guen*, wide in the beam but shallow of draught, began to roll, not really heavily but enough to embarrass an amateur gunlayer. Then simultaneously a voice from above rapped out the order "Open fire, 2000 yards," and the *Wissman* slid into view, a sitting duck, still on the slipway. Jock belted away making a lot of noise between duds, but partly owing to some over-estimation of the range and partly, no doubt, to the rolling of the *Guen*, all the first shots that were not misfires soared away over the hills behind the target, probably scaring the daylights out of peaceful villagers far inland.

The ammunition was Victorian in date and about one in four was dud, so that when Jock found that none exploded during the period of waiting before opening the breech, as decreed by the Lords of the Admiralty, he soon dispensed with that formality altogether, though he barked at his crew if they delayed in dumping a misfire overboard. Then without warning, just as Beaumont had strolled over to offer advice, Jock scored a hit on the slip, a shower of splinters went up and everyone cheered.

That was the only score—a bye, so to speak—for immediately afterwards a small white dinghy put off from the shore, in which was a European clad in a singlet and a pair of shorts pulling furiously straight for the *Guen*. Rhoades ordered, "Cease fire," and a blessed silence fell. It was his drinking pal, the skipper of the *Wissman* with whom every meeting was a party. The accomodation ladder was lowered and Rhoades descended from the bridge to receive him at the gangway.

The dinghy came alongside and its infuriated occupant, having flung his oars into the boat, leaped to his feet and shaking both fists above his head, exclaimed, "Gott for damn, Rrroades, vos you dronk?"

The news that Der Tag had arrived had not yet reached him.

The notice of this struggle in the London *Times* bore the headline, "Naval Victory on Lake Nyasa."

The scenery along much of the Lake Nyasa shore is spectacular, but the landscape does not hold many of the big animals that one associates with African wilderness. Along the shores of some of the lakes to the north, game still can be seen from boats. There was a time when people shot elephants from the decks of Nyasa steamboats. Nowadays on the lake, and on the river too, you cruise for hours past country that looks wild, and the scenery is as grand as it ever was, but no shape of even an antelope shows gray buff against the gray buff hills. The kungu midges of Nyasa are exciting, and the fishes there are a fantastic lot. I am going to tell about them a little later. But the kungu are not seen on every cruise. They don't look much like wildlife anyway. The fishes stay mostly down under the keel and add little to the landscape. But there is one bit of savage Africa left in the lake and that is the islet of Boadzulu.

Boadzulu is a rocky little island near the southern end of the lake, about twenty miles north of Fort Johnston and five miles off the western shore. The vegetation there is sparse and scrubby, and from a distance its rocks gleam white in the sun, because a myriad cormorants nest on the island and through the ages have whitewashed it with the uric acid of their droppings.

Boadzulu is no island menagerie. Besides the cormorants, its only conspicuous inhabitants are a colony of monitor lizards. But the monitors are unaccountably abundant, and some of them are bigger than those found anywhere west of the Lesser Sunda Islands, where their kinsman, the Komodo dragon lives. Why monitors thrive so well on Boadzulu is not known. They are said to eat both the eggs and the young of the cormorants, but this resource must be too seasonal for year-round subsistence. The cormorants probably contribute to the diet of the lizards in other ways. Wherever water birds congregate, a lot of untidy regurgitation goes on. This is not because the stomachs of the birds are easily upset; it is just their way of bringing fish home to the nest. Anyway, cormorants everywhere throw up a lot, and the ground under their nesting trees is usually strewn with fish that they sloppily drop. On a little island off the Florida coast known as Snake Key, I once counted eleven species of fish, both salt and fresh-water kinds, lying on the ground in a forest in which cormorants and other water birds were nesting and roosting. It is probably not mere coincidence that this island, although wholly without fresh water, has an abundant population of cottonmouth moccasins. Four miles out there in the Gulf, surrounded by salt water, and in what seems to be wholly inappropriate habitat, cottonmouth moccasins are more numerous than in any other place known. One reason for this is, almost surely, that for several months of each year, fish are spilled by the birds in the trees above, and fledglings fall out of the nests.

Whether the Nyasa monitors are fed by regurgitated

fish that fall from cormorant nests is not known. But there is a suggestive similarity between Boadzulu Island and its many monitors and Snake Key and its unnaturally abundant cottonmouths. Neither island looks like a proper habitat for its reptile occupant. In both places that reptile is present in unprecedented numbers and is living intimately with water birds. In the case of the cottonmouths, it is known that they really do eat both the dropped fish and the occasional egg or displaced young bird that falls to the ground. As far as I can determine, nobody has examined stomachs of the Boadzulu monitors, but they must be doing the same. There is evidently nothing else on the island for a big carnivorous animal to eat. Though the Nile monitor is a good swimmer and often jumps into water to get away from an intruder, it is not known to be able to catch fish in the water.

The Boadzulu monitor is *Varanus niloticus*. It occurs from the Sahara to the Cape of Good Hope. There are about twenty-four kinds of monitors in the world, all in the Old World tropics. In size they range from an Australian species only eight inches long to the Komodo dragon, the biggest of living lizards, which reaches lengths of up to ten feet. Monitors are of special interest because they are probably involved in the ancestry of the snakes. It is not thought that snakes came from monitors as such, but the question of the origin of snakes is a very dim and troublesome one, and the snakelike character of monitors seems a straw in the wind, at least. A monitor has an extraordinarily long neck and a narrow head, and from the shoulder forward is clearly snake-like. The impression is enhanced by the sinuous movements of the neck as the creature forages. The tongue is long, forked, and, like that of a snake, is used as a sensory organ. It picks up smell-particles out of the air or from the ground, and passes them to a structure in the roof of the mouth called Jacobson's Organ, where they are duly smelled—or tasted if one prefers. Some other lizards do this, but it is one of the specially characteristic features of the snakes. Another way that monitors resemble snakes is in their ability to swallow whole pieces of food of great size. Still another is in their unbreakable tails. Most lizards have tails that part easily at special zones of weakness. The breaking is an adaptation that no doubt saves the lives of many lizards, when the body crawls away and leaves the tail with an attacker. In some the tail can even be snapped off at will when the bearer is touched or even merely menaced by a predator. The tail of a snake or a monitor is not built that way. It stays on the animal unless it is bitten off.

The Nile monitor is one of the few good-sized land vertebrates still conspicuous throughout much of the continent of Africa. It is found in all sorts of country. Low bluffs and natural levees along rivers are the best place to see monitors. Along the Shire River, even where all other vertebrate life has been shot, trapped, or crowded out, the big gray-black monitors still slip into the water ahead of your boat, or drop with a crash from a low tree limb, just as iguanas drop from trees into Central American rivers.

Monitors are evidently in no immediate danger of population depletion. But there is no real reason to wait for the near-extinction of a species to give it protection. If Boadzulu remains unruined—if hide hunters have not gone out recently and shot all the monitors there—the island ought to be made a preserve or a monument. At least it should be given whatever protection is needed to insure to the monitors and cormorants a future in which they will be looked at but not in any way molested. To do this would cost nobody anything, or at most would cost only the fees for the necessary surveillance; and this could be done from shore with field glasses. So there is no reason why the wild little island should be lost, and good reason why it should not. It is compact and useless, in the usual sense of the word, and it looks like a grand small scrap of the prehuman earth.

Nyasaland has already established a surprising precedent in the matter of declaring reptile preserves. It once had what I judge was the only snake preserve in the whole world. This was a python preserve on the high, dry island of Chidiamperi in Lake Shirwa, a few miles south of the southern end of Lake Nyasa and about twenty miles west of Zomba, the capital. Lewis and I went there to collect snails in the marshes around Lake Shirwa. The python preserve was pointed out to us, a rocky island out in the lonely lake. To learn what had motivated the government in such an extraordinary bit of wildlife preservation, I wrote Mr. B. L. Mitchell of the Nyasaland Game Department, and he sent me the following extract from the Report of the Game and Forest Reserve Commission.

CHIDIAMPERI (Python) ISLAND. (Zomba District) Area 1 sq. mile.

This island, in the western waters of Lake Shirwa, was found to be inhabited by a considerable number of pythons, in December 1929. At that time the island could be reached by canoe, and, partly with a view to preventing any undue slaughter that might have taken place following on a demand for python skins, partly with a view that at some time the island might serve as an attraction for tourists, the suggestion was made that it should be proclaimed a Game Reserve.

Gazetted: Proclamation 5 of 1930. (11 March 1930)

No further notice appears to have been taken of the reserve by anyone until 1934 when the Advisory Committee on

Nyasa

Hides and Skins to the Imperial Institute asked for information about this reptilian reserve—possibly with an eye to commercial exploitation. Thereupon the District Commissioner and the Assistant Chief Secretary made a very uncomfortable journey on foot to the island—the lake having more or less dried up by then—and reported no snakes at all, except one (python) seen by a native who accompanied them. Their report also stated that native information was that the python had mostly left the island in the dry year of 1933 and the remainder had been eaten by wild pig.

It is now reported (August 1945) by Chief Mwambo that python again inhabit the island; the number of Europeans who have ever set foot on it, however, must be very limited.

At the end of the extract there was a penned note that said, "Chidiamperi has been abolished on the recommendation of the Commission."

So the world's first python preserve is gone. But it showed there were once people who were willing to save their snakes, and who might now think of saving Boadzulu. It is time to start ransacking the earth for the little landscapes that need saving. If the outlook for wilderness preservation is in any way brightening, it is with respect to the more spectacular spreads of earth, the big wild lands in which the public can play; to which people from cities can go and build new woodland cities of tents and trailers. People in growing uneasy masses are longing for something somewhere out of town. In parts of the world, they have shown that they will pay high fees for what they want from wilderness.

But besides these places in which the public can fish, hike, or in some other way lose itself, there are the Boadzulus to think of saving, and they are a different kind of treasure. They are delicate bits of balanced landscape that can be kept only if nobody ever sets foot upon them.

The tiny community of living beings on Boadzulu could go on into the distant future only if always it were savored from a circling boat.

That kind of preservation makes for austere public relations. But public relations, like everything, are related to time, and to the public you have in mind. Besides the aimlessly multiplying public of today, there are our more civilized descendants to think of. There are people of *Ilalas* of a long time from now, who will line the rails and raise binoculars to Boadzulu. Depending upon what we do today, the monitors will still slink there and wave their tongues and search among the whitened rocks under twisted trees where lean-faced cormorants flap and bicker like some lost colony of Archyopteryx; and the passengers of another age will have this small relic of the world we found to see. Or, they will lower their glasses from bare stones and wonder again what kind of men we were.

Kungu

I HAD READ most of these things I have told about Lake Nyasa before we went aboard the new *Ilala*. I had read of the kungu too. The very first published account of the kungu clouds—unless some old lost Portuguese chronicle tells of them—was this bit in David Livingstone's *Zambezi:*

clouds, as of smoke rising from miles of burning grass, were observed bending in a southeasterly direction, and we thought that the unseen land on the opposite side was closing in, and that we were near the end of the lake. But next morning we sailed through one of the clouds on our own side, and discovered that it was neither smoke nor haze, but countless millions of minute midges called "kungo" (A cloud or fog). They filled the air to an immense height, and swarmed upon the water, too light to sink in it. Eyes and mouth had to be kept closed while passing through this living cloud: they struck upon the face like fine drifting snow. Thousands lay in the boat when she emerged from the cloud of midges.

Since Livingstone's time nearly every traveler who has written of the lake has told of the kungu as a thing that filled him with awe and wonder, or simply with amazement, depending upon whether he saw it in the shape of casual cloud or in that of a water spout. So I had read of the midge clouds, but even briefed this way, the sudden sight of the sky-tall funnels trailing crooked stems across the lake was a jolt to me. Water spouts stir me unnaturally anyway. It began I think with a harrowing woodcut in some old book we had—one of the Doré style of demoralizing scenes that must have left a trauma in the minds of many who looked at them when young. Certainly, they did in mine; and then later the idea of water spouts was sharpened for me when some fellow seascouts and I got into a whole pride of them off the Georgia coast. We had simple-mindedly sailed out in an open lugger one July day to look for the Gulf Stream that was said to be out there some place. We were long out of sight of land, and the sea had changed to the indigo of deep water, when all at once the weather thickend too fast to run from, the water got black with white teeth, and one tongue after another licked down from the straight lower edge of black clouds, touched the sea, and here and there licked it back up in spinning tapers to the cloud again. Pretty soon six frightened boys in an old whaleboat were flying to Warsaw with a double-reefed foresail, in front of eleven separate funnels, exactly like the fly tower the *Ilala* was leaving to the northward.

That was in my background when I peered out of the companionway to see what the stir was among the people on deck. I could see why one woman had shrieked, and why her companion's reassurance so lacked in comfort. What they were looking at was so very like a tornado that for a moment I forgot that some travelers had found kungu clouds in the image of tornados and water spouts. Nobody seeing the crook-stemmed hyperbola out there in the east, rising from its spread-out contact with water a thousand feet deep in a stalk a thousand feet tall that narrowed, then spread, then joined a great cloud sailing over the lake—nobody I know could have seen that object and felt sure it was not a tornado. But as I went on deck the captain leaned out from the pilot house and said, "Kungu. Fly spout. Only midges, you know. Ought to see more presently."

And so we did. As we moved southward down the middle of the lake, we began to make out a zigzag line of fly spouts, anchored on the one we had seen first and making off down the lake just over toward the Portuguese side of center. Eventually, there were thirty-seven kungu clouds in view at once. We figured that they extended about thirty miles. Out there over water hundreds of feet deep, over bottom in places lower than sea level, thirty-seven separate seething eruptions of life swirled over the lake in fogs and eddies, mounted in towers and columns and joined the sweeping clouds. For two hours steering south we kept this line off the port beam—just toward the Portuguese side of midlake, the captain said, while we cruised a few miles on the Nyasaland side. As time passed, the swarms spread and joined, and the dense blue-black smoke thinned to a gray mist, except here and there where twisting air gathered it into a dark vortex like the one first sighted. Then for a while there were no clouds to be seen. We cruised on toward the south-southeast at 14 knots, and at 10:40 we picked up the northern end of another line of kungu, nine clouds in all, strung out for

10 or 11 miles, moving with a 12-knot wind toward Nyasaland from somewhere to the east of midlake. By 11:30 this belt was thinning and at noon we had to look hard back northward to make out the two last swarms, both black-stemmed toadstools tying the clouds and lake together like the first we had seen.

You can name me the wonders of Africa, and tell of Ruwenzori or Serengeti, of the great falls of the Zambezi, or of Cape Town harbor—or of any of the other great things there are to see there. But I know of nothing in Africa that more wholly astounds the mind than the kungu clouds of the Great Lakes. There is nothing anywhere that so overpoweringly seems to show the mindless drive of life as these vast up-pourings of protoplasm show it. They come up out of an almost bottomless lake—from the bottom of that lake—through piled fathoms of blue water and enter the alien air as billions of transformed insects. They somehow get done their mystic reproduction in the narrow space between being mature and in a man's sense ready for life and being swept off by the streaming trade wind to go where the clouds go, with no more sway over their fate than the dust or moisture in the clouds themselves.

The kungu fly is *Corethra*, or as they call it now *Chaoborus*, a midge in the mosquito family. It is old-fashioned to call it Corethra, but so long as you don't italicize the name, and thereby seem to give it technical status, it ought to be all right. Anyway, it's a lot prettier name than Chaoborus, and I'm going to go ahead and use it. Corethra is an ethereal, two-winged insect placed by most entomologists in the same family with the mosquitoes. Among usual mosquitoes, only the female bites. Neither sex of Corethra bites. Like real mosquitoes, Corethra passes its larval life in the water, but while mosquitoes

Kungu

develop in ditches, marshes, or tree holes, the larval midges live in big lakes, passing through three or four separate metamorphoses before finally emerging for a brief life in the air. Corethra occurs throughout most of the world. The young stages of Corethra are called phantom larvae, because, except for the eyes and a few inner works, they are invisibly transparent. They figure largely in studies of the open waters of lakes. Their presence or absence is one of the criteria used in classifying the lakes of the world. Because of the peculiar life history of Corethra, to call a lake a Corethra-lake tells a limnologist a great deal about what kind of body of water it is.

I have a right to speak of Corethra with some authority. Not a specialist's authority, but that of one who has known Corethra for many years, and who at its hands has come under strong stress on two occasions. One was the time we saw the kungu spouts over Lake Nyasa. The other was a time three decades earlier.

The very first Corethra I ever saw was two jet black eyes and four silvery sacs, all hanging still together in a jar of clear water. Professor J. Speed Rogers held the jar. He held it up to the light, got a look of controlled rapture in his face, and said, "There he is. Now you find him."

It was Speed's way of proselytizing. I had come to the University preternaturally inclined toward reptiles. Speed wanted a student he could put to work in limnology, to learn something about Florida lakes. Showing me Corethra like that, making me look hard through the clear water, seeing at first nothing and then the floating eyes and silver sacs, was his plan of seduction. I took the jar and twisted it about. All at once the light slanted in just right and revealed the whole watery phantom shape of the strange little animal floating there motionless like a short string of ice beads with eyes and, fore-and-aft, a pair of silver sacs. Dr. Rogers handed me a lens and I fumbled the vial about until I could focus all along the air-clear body. It was a cylindrical chain of jointed segments. There was a swollen head with a pair of flexible antennae, and it was connected to the second joint by a thin necklike stalk. The last segment had a comb of swimming hairs and at the very end a wisp of gills. I moved the lens away and held the jar two feet in front of my eyes once more, and again the body of the Corethra went clear as water and only the eyes and lumps of silver were hanging there together.

Such was the phantom larva, the child of the midge Corethra, the only insect in the abyssal zone of the earth's deeper lakes. The air sacs I saw were hydrostatic organs, used to hold the creature at the depths proper for the stages of its life. The antennae are not just feelers, but prehensile tentacles for grasping the small planktonic animals that young Corethras eat. Dr. Rogers had picked the Corethra he showed me out of a pan of mud that had been brought up from the bottom of a Florida sinkhole. The Corethras in that sinkhole made it, in Speed's eyes, a hallowed place, and the way he told about it held even my snakeman's ear. When he said we could go out and catch some more Corethras I was glad to have the chance.

To press the advantage Speed hustled me out to the edge of town to Townsend Sink. We took a canoe off the top of his car and loaded it with gear: screen-bottom buckets, enamel pans, an Ekman dredge, and a Kemmerer-Foerst water bottle. Then we got in and pushed off onto the gray gleam of the pond.

The water was losing curls of mist into the chill of the March morning. I remember a big sow rooting at the edge of the sink. I even remember how we seemed to be hanging there as we floated in the little canoe on the top of the burnished dark disk of water with the ring of sweetgum trees around it. Speed looked very big, I recall, in his half of the little boat. His breath steamed like the pond, his middle was covered by a complicated bandoleer vest he had designed to hold vials of alcohol, forceps of two kinds, a suction bottle for catching bugs, and a few different sizes of killing jars. He took up the Eckmann dredge—a square brass box with jaws like a trap and a trigger to spring the jaws when a brass runner slid down the line. He held the dredge in one hand and the brass runner and rope in the other. He puffed air over his shoved-out lower lip, and looked about to get bearings to find the deep place where he knew Corethras were sure to be.

"Let's try it here," he said.

I slowed the boat with a paddle, and Speed dropped the dredge. When it had settled, he let the runner go and there was not a sound down under us to tell that the brass weight had tripped the catch and that the strong jaws had gnashed up a load of the mud from the bottom. Then he started the ticklish job of pulling in a brass box of mud over the dipping gunwale of a three-yard canoe. But Dr. Rogers was an old hand at this. He knew how to shift back to the off side with each pull of the rope and keep us, on the whole, fairly steady. Before he got the dredge up, though, he remembered that we ought to take a water sample too, a liter of water to take back and test for oxygen; and he told me to drop the bottle over. The water sampler was a brass cylinder which, like the dredge, would slap shut at the right depth when a runner slid down the rope. It was not very heavy, but it was heavy enough; and Speed felt the big dip that meant I had dropped it on the wrong side—over the same gunwale where he was still pulling in the dredge—and yelled, "The other side," as if to stop the falling bottle. Being a student, in awe of Speed, and overanxious to save face, I got a wrong reflex and jerked the rope, so that suddenly there were two ropes pulling down on the port side of the silly coracle. The canoe spun smoothly over, and all at once I was down with the Corethras at the dark, cold bottom of the pond, and Speed was down there too, although there was not enough light for me to see him. I clawed back up to the surface, and Speed came up a little later, spouting and blowing and looking reproachful with the part of his face that stuck up above the water.

We got to the bank all right and bailed out the canoe. The bucket and pans were gone for good, but we fished up the dredge and the bottle. We carried the mud back to the lab and there were plenty of Corethras in it. I went on with the lake work Speed wanted done, and I went on, too, with a strong feeling of knowing the phantom midge.

With all the kinds of aquatic insects there are in the world, it seems queer that only the phantom larva has joined the drifting fauna of small beasts and vegetables known as plankton. Not much is known about the life of the Nyasa kungu, but elsewhere some things have been learned about Corethra. A little while after the female emerges from the water she lays her eggs on the surface, a hundred or so, spirally arranged in a buoyant disc of jelly. The eggs sink to the bottom, and have the odd ability of developing in the oxygenless environment of the mud. They hatch after 48 hours. The larval life has four separate stages, each ended by a change of skin. In its first two stages Corethra drifts with the plankton, as a needle-thin, ice-clear sliver that gorges its ghostly body with its fellow plankton, caught with its prehensile feelers. The third and fourth stages are spent skulking in the mud of the bottom by day, and back up among the plankton at night.

In some Corethra lakes the phantom larvae are the most important item in the economy of the life chains there. Their total mass may outweigh that of all other inhabitants of the lake combined. Down in the mud they are relatively safe from fish. In fact their special niche in life is the exploitation of the safety of profundal zones so devoid of oxygen that most fish can't follow them down.

The little sink where I met Corethra once yielded 23,000 larvae per square meter. The record seems to be a count of 33,800 per square meter made by the famous limnologist Juday in Lake Mendota, Wisconsin. If you multiply this figure by the body weight of live larvae, it gives close to a quarter of a pound of larvae for each square yard of lake bottom. As an average, Juday gave 1,070 pounds per acre. Considering the off-beat nature of the bottom environment—the lack of light and oxygen there—this seems an imposing yield of meat. It is more than you can expect for beef from an acre of cultivated pasture.

There is one kind of fish, the weird-looking elephant-snout fish, in the East African lakes that ventures a short way into the suffocating depths to patrol the bottom and suck up aquatic insect larvae. But by a lucky timing of its daily movements, Corethra keeps mostly out of the clutches of even the elephant fish. In Lake Victoria it was found that the elephant fish feeds by night, while Corethra leaves the mud to join the plankton at sunset. As a result, even in places where Corethra is more abundant than any other bottom insect, stomachs of elephant-snout fish were found to contain no Corethras at all.

Juday found that Corethra enters the bottom mud by the end of the first half-hour after sunrise, and leaves it again at a time corresponding to sunset in the outside world. Once out, he found, they come up fast, in one case rising about 75 feet in an hour, apparently timing their movements by the waxing and waning of light. The great emergences of the clouds of adult flies are not scheduled by the sun but by the phase of the moon. In Lake Victoria there is a peak in the swarming during the two or three days after a new moon. The activities of many marine animals are timed by the moon, mainly because of the importance of tidal movements in the sea; but this is one of the few known cases of a lunar rhythm in the life of a fresh-water animal.

So much for the biology of the kungu clouds. The thing that makes them so imposing a phenomenon is the overpowering, unexplained vastness of the swarms. I have driven through fogs of May flies that swept over the roads like a blizzard. In Florida I have seen the blind-mosquitoes stream up out of lakes in hosts, blind motorists behind smeared windshields, and scare off who knows how many mosquito-shy tourists who don't stop to see that blind-mosquitoes never bite. But nothing in my background prepared me for the sight of the kungu clouds rising black against the sky of Mozambique, smoking up out of the lake not in one swarm but in one after another in jagged file for thirty teeming miles. There was a grand, elemental quality in the sight. Like the northern lights or a hurricane, it was a thing to be seen with awe.

It was also a thing that cried out not to be left unexplained. I have many times stopped to watch a little mist of gnats dancing in simple-minded fellowship, staunch in their group spirit, holding the form of their wan little band before wind or rising air. I have often wondered about the causes of such swarms and the ends they serve. Wherever you find great gatherings of animals, you have a right to look for some gain they get from the crowding. Only man gathers to his clear detriment.

Fish swarm—school, we call it—to gain a mystical sort of protective anonymity, thought to confound a predator unable to concentrate its hunger on any one of such a host. Or, being condemned to the sere rites of external fertilization as a way of reproduction, male and female fish come once a year together for a mass release of sperm and eggs. There are mouselike lemmings in Scandinavia and springbuck in Bushmanland that mass and march away in growing suicidal hosts till they die or drown in the sea. In their great scale, the flights of the migratory locust suggest the kungu clouds. But all these sporadic mass goings-out from the homeland, though they are not thoroughly understood, surely bring some gain to the race involved. At the very least the migrants go away as an adaptation to relieve famine at home and insure survival for the few that stay there, a way of keeping a race alive by sacrificing most of its individual lives. In the kungu clouds it is hard to see any advantage. The exodus occurs just as the aquatic pupa becomes a breeding adult, an aerial creature that could not possibly have stayed in the home of its youth, and can never go home again.

To the eye the spouts are simply billions of flies rising from the lake in fields, swirling into the air traps, and joining the marching clouds. As infants the phantom midges are water-plankton. As mature insects they join the plankton of the air, the creatures that ride the drifts of air and are wafted on the winds. Although one sees little of the air-plankton from the ground, it is always up there moving by in the currents of the atmosphere, a myriad light seeds, spores, and resting stages of vegetables and lower animals, aphids, hairy caterpillars, and ballooning spiders of many kinds. If you tow a net behind an airplane, it will catch a great variety of living things.

Some of the Nyasa kungu surely join this host; but I

doubt that it is for the reasons that send spiders ballooning away. The other regular travelers in the winds are able to reproduce and pioneer in the new lands they come down in. They sprout or germinate when they fall in proper places, they arrive gravid and lay fertile eggs, or they seek out a waif of the other sex and set up the race again. As far as I know, all the small beings that habitually drift with the high air do so as a fundamental adaptation for dispersal. They are all qualified not just to ride the wind but to colonize, if they should ever reach a place appropriate for their kind. The world-wide ranges of the most confirmed members of the aerial plankton prove the validity of their unpromising escapade.

But why do the kungu gnats dance off in their vast hegira? From the little I can find to read about their reproductive behavior, it seems most probable that they mate and lay their eggs before they swarm away. Their power to colonize would thus be lost after the brief mating and dropping of fertilized eggs on the surface of the water. From that moment they are a sterile sidebranch of their stock, a pointless eddy of the main stream of their kind. Moreover, if you look at a map of Africa downwind of Lake Nyasa, you wonder whether the agelong flooding out of flies could possibly do anything more than seed the baked veld with the corpses of the emigrants. There is nothing on the map to show why the midges of Nyasa go soaring off to limbo in such teeming unanimity.

While I was looking at the fly spouts from the deck of the *Ilala*, my first thought was, why should the creatures do such a seemingly suicidal thing. Lewis is an entomologist—a May fly man—and May flies swarm to mate. So I naturally asked him why, in the biological sense, the kungu came up in such hosts together, and he said what most entomologists would say: to mate. They do it to get the sexes together for breeding, he said. But then I could see him looking slowly up the thousand-foot climb of the fly column to where it became cloud, and I could see some doubt diluting his confidence.

"No, up there," I said. "What are they doing up there?"

There was a woman standing by us, the one whose shriek had spread the spout alarm, and she was thinking too. She said: "Perhaps the eggs fall to the water." This thought seemed unlikely to us all.

No matter what those billions of slowly metamorphosed prime adult animals had in mind, they seemed doomed and cut off from their germ line forever. What need or end could ever have built into their strain a design for a dance so desperate? What makes them stack their breaths of bodies into towers of life and sweep to death on the far-off steppes? Why should the phantom larvae leave the peace of their instars in the dim abyss of the lake and climb to the sky, only to die on distant rocks? It seemed to me a fair question. It is not an easy one to answer.

It took me quite a while to see that there are really two questions to be answered: Why do the midges—why do *any* midges—swarm? And, why do the kungu swarms join the clouds? The first question seemed simple and straightforward—just a matter of looking up papers on the behavior of mosquitoes and their kin, or of asking the entomologists who study these matters. But start asking why midges swarm and you find that it takes you at once into a quietly seething turmoil of controversy. Fly students, it seems, are not by any means agreed on the function of swarming. My own poking about in the literature on the swarming of flies only got me confused with respect to both the reasons for swarms and the mechanisms that hold the bands together.

At least a part of the integrating force is, they say, the singing of the flies, the irksome keen buzzing they make in flying. It was once believed that the males sang the females into the swarm. Later studies show it may be just the reverse—if two sexes are there at all. In some swarms there aren't any females to speak of, and in others no males. In still other cases, more than one species of fly may make up the swarm. And as to what goes on inside the swarm, one observer says that blind-mosquitoes hover against the wind for a second or two in a weaving figure-8, dart off for a few inches, then stop and repeat the movement, and so on and on. Another man found that the individual mosquito in a swarm makes a circle 10 to 20 inches across, and reverses the direction of his circle each time its circumference intersects a line in the direction the wind is blowing. In strong winds, he says, the circle is drawn out into an ellipse. With still stronger wind, it becomes a reversing straight-line course. As to what force holds the insects all together and draws in more to dance —some say it is the sweet sing-song they make, some say it is sight. The whole subject seems to be, like the schooling of fish, a thing not well understood, and scientists are only now beginning to study it with purpose and energy.

As to the possible utility of the swarming habit, most entomologists appear to accept the old idea that the swarms of mosquitoes and midges are breeding groups—that swarming and mating go together as they do with frogs or herring. But in the case of the Nyasa kungu flies, this seems to make no sense at all. If swarming is mating, then the habit is a catastrophic vice of the Corethras of Nyasa. I poked peevishly about for quite a while without finding a better answer, however, until finally I thought to write Maurice Provost, director of the Entomological Research Center of the Florida State Board of Health at Vero Beach. The mosquito menace in Florida being what it is, Provost is naturally interested in the phenomenon of swarming, and his organization has given it a great deal of attention. My letter to him brought this surprising response:

Dr. Nielson, of our staff, who has made a lifelong study of swarming, explained the fallacy of the "mating swarm" idea in this fashion: It is as though one were to notice some cases of epigamic human behavior going on in city parks and conclude therefrom that parks were the mating areas for *Homo sapiens*, and furthermore that this was the main if not the only function of parks!

. . . We believe that insect migration and swarming are consummatory rather than appetitive behavior, to use the current ethological idiom. As such they serve no special survival purpose.

That relieves the pressure one way, but in another way it leaves a mess. It leaves you having to look at the prodigious display of a kungu cloud and say they are simply up there having fun. It is not that I am afraid of the fun part. There is nothing offensive to me, for instance, in saying that puppies play for fun. The idea of flies swarming for fun, just aimlessly following inborn urges for the joy of functioning, seems fine—until you see a kungu cloud. The trouble comes when you realize that the play of puppies is useful fun, activity that strengthens dogs, and that could conceivably figure in the evolution of the race. This makes you look for some shred of utility in the kungu cloud. You look at the mass of those billions of flies up there cavorting about in the sky, and the thought wells up that fun or not, such a prodigious pageant has got to have bearing on evolution, on the final survival, extinction, or remodeling of the race. But just you try to tell what the bearing is.

I have finally managed to shed my prejudices and open my mind to one fact that was really obvious all the time. This was that, whatever the initial reasons for the Nyasa kungu swarms, they soon stop being a biological phenomenon and become a part of the weather. Like some buzzards I shall tell of in a later chapter, the flies have entered and have become a part of twisting columns of rising air. The trade wind comes in over the hot Mozambique country and the air warms, lightens, and rises; and here and there goes up in spiraling eddies. These thermals feed into swelling clouds, and when they move out into the lake they keep their spin for a while and pick up the flies. What the flies are doing before they get into the vortices I have not, as I said, been able to learn. But once they are sucked into the twisting air, they hold to the mushroom shape of the eddies and turn them opaque and fearful-looking for as long as they hold together.

So the kungu not only looks like something wrong with the weather but is actually mixed in as a sort of special meteorological manifestation too. It looks like mist and settles on ships as mist does. It looks like deep fog, and boats get lost in it. Four men in a boat once got lost in kungu fog and choked to death. It both looks like cloud and merges with cloud till the cloud is midges as well as moisture. It can take the form of the tornado in the slow vortex of an ordinary thermal, or it can mix in with real tornadoes. And on Lake Nyasa this queer complication of weather occurs on a lake that is already infamous for its murderously capricious *mueras*. To see the mixup this can cause, consider this stirring passage from the log of an early expedition.

Kungu

It is impossible to describe the awful combination of whirlwinds, thunderclouds and lightning that seemed to throw the lake into the wildest fury, and it will be many a day before my companions and I forget that tempest. Gusts of wind came like hurricanes from every quarter. To set sail [i.e., to set a sail] would only have heightened the imminent danger we were in of being swamped altogether, and seldom has any vessel been more tried than the *Ilala* was on this occasion. The water appeared to undergo some fearful agitation. At one period we counted no less than twelve water-spouts around us and we had literally to steam in and out amongst them. Of a sudden there was a dead calm. At once clouds of "Khungu" mist hung over the Lake, then came the most appalling thunder and lightning, with rain such as can only be felt in these latitudes, and after these more water spouts, any of which would have smashed our deck in and sucked us down like a stone if we had been so unfortunate as to be struck by it.

That was no timid, land-bred witness talking but the redoubtable Edward Young himself. The time was 1876, and the ship was the *Ilala*, the first steamboat on the lake. Young was no emotional traveler made oversensitive to small disasters by nostalgia and diarrhea. He was as tough as they came, and sensible, and yet in his journal, *Nyassa—A Journal of Adventures*, he talked that way of the weather of the lake.

So on Lake Nyasa it is not really easy to know what is flies and what is weather. The ship we were on was the second *Ilala*, and from the rock-steady comfort of her deck we saw spouts too, and that day there was no *muera* at all but only the gold and blue splendor of East Africa in August after rain the day before. The only clouds were shining cumulus, coming in from the Indian Ocean. There was no menace in the weather they came with, and the spouts on the lake that day were surely only myriads of midges. I have no doubt that what Young saw were real water spouts, but you may be sure they were blacker, more menacing water spouts, because of the kungu in them.

It is really not possible to keep swarming insects and weather apart. In a little swarm of gnats the size of an orange, swinging and bobbing over a cypress knee, one can be sure the shape of the swarm is being made and held by the overt behavior of its members. The bond that integrates the band is some small joy and drive in the mind of each of the dancing flies. But how could anything flies do mold the colossal kungu columns? How could any acts of the members determine the boundaries of any structure so immense? Quite clearly they do not.

The confusing part of this is that the real sociological swarms and the weather-built masses of flies should look so much alike. I remember a swarm of blind-mosquitoes I saw once in Florida that embodied this ambiguity. Driving past a broad pasture at the edge of our town one day, I noticed a dusky shape in the air dipping down to the grass from the trees at the edge of a lake. I slowed, looked closer, and saw a gray turnip shape twirling. The top of the bulb was spinning slowly over the pasture, and the tapered tip was trailing just above the grass. The object was about fifteen feet across at the top. It had the shape of other insect swarms I had seen. It had the shape of a whirlwind too, and the spinning run of a whirlwind; and it was moving across a field in which I had noticed whirlwinds in dry times when there was dust to pick up and give them body. All the way down the field it held its shape, moving along at the rate of a man's walk, bobbing and swinging over the grass, and breaking up at last against houses at the edge of town.

When I reached home the telephone rang. A friend of mine who lives on the lake the flies had come out of was on the line. He said he just saw the damnedest thing—and, following a perverse urge one gets sometimes, I cut him off by telling him what it was he saw. I told him he saw a whirlwind of blind-mosquitoes. It irked him some to have the words put into his mouth that way. But he got over it. He went on to say he had seen the swarm condense over the water, and move over the trees and out across the pasture, where I had chanced to be driving by and to see it too. We talked about the matter and then let it drop, as one not likely to be explained by further talking. But I was left wondering what it was that held that band of midges together and trundled it down the field. Was it the hopes and hormones of its members, or just the passionless swirl of air?

If Dr. Nielsen is right that swarming is only aimless fun, then I am going to be left forever wondering about the state of mind of the flies in a kungu cloud. Does the joy die, do you reckon, when the gyre takes in the celebrating band? Or does it maybe mount and swell to unknown limits of delight, as the midges soar away in the turning wind, dancing over the joyous pointlessness of the rest of their lives?

The cook of the *Ilala* gave me a different slant on the kungu clouds. He told me about a folk belief held by some of the people who live along the western shore of the lake, where the cliffs rise straight from the water, and the clouds collide with the land. Living there, finding the water deep and the fishing hard, subsisting in steady deprivation of protein, they have concluded the kungu is sent in with the clouds for their particular good. That is what the *Ilala's* cook told me.

That first day of our voyage on the lake the talk on deck was mostly of fly clouds. It was not just among the passengers. The captain joined in it too; and gradually, one by one, the whole crew got in words about the phenomenon that had stirred us up. You could see it was a thing the lake people were proud of, like the breathtaking scenery of the lake itself. But unlike the scenery, it was a part of the trip not shown every set of passengers. So, there was a lot of kungu talk on the ship that whole day. The next morning at breakfast the cook sent in to each table an unordered small omelette set with bits of a black and unlikely looking substance. I got mine first and before the waiter moved on I asked him what the dish was.

"Kungu, bwana," he said. "This fly we hob seen yes-tiday. The cook send especial."

As the kungu was served, a wave of comment went around the room, most of it not happy. Lewis and I tried to set an example of zoological objectivity and to approach ours without passion against eating flies as such. We gave the omelette a fair trial. We were not in the slightest seasick at the time. It was not, I have to say, very good eating. The kungu added nothing needful to the flavor of eggs. It had a taste of dry chocolate and badly kept anchovy paste, and right after breakfast I went to the galley to learn what the cook had in mind, to have flies in the eggs that way. I found that he spoke no English, but our weeks on the river had given Lewis and me some useful scraps of Chinyanja, and by chance there were among them the words to make my errand clear.

"*Kungu alipo?*" I asked, hoping I was asking if there were any kungu flies.

The cook grinned for half a foot, and said, "*Alipo.*" He reached into a high shelf and drew out a black mass that looked like a burnt loaf of bread.

"Kungu," he said, and flooded me with fast Chinyanja

—or it could have been Chiyao—that made me sorry I had misled him with my meager words. But then a steward came up and he was Standard III, from Blantyre. He took over the encounter, and soon got from the cook the folk hypothesis I mentioned, the one that explained the prodigious self-destruction of the kungu flies. They are a gift, the cook said, from some high source, to feed the people of the lake. He laughed indulgently as he told of the superstition, but you could see he had a good deal of secret confidence in it.

When the fly clouds and spouts come to land, along much of the shore it is the high-rising scarp they hit. They drop in a steady rain and pile up at the foot of the cliffs in deep drifts. The people scoop them up in baskets and mold them into rolls and cakes. These are wrapped, as everything is, in banana leaves, dried on the rocks, and then smoked for a long time over a slow fire. So the lee-shore tribesfolk, not being bound by any conventions of behavioral animal ecology, conclude thankfully that the kungu comes ashore to furnish relish for their *ufa*.

Ufa is the porridge the Nyanja people make of finely ground corn. In much of the country it is the staple— the rice, the cassava, the taro of the land. They eat it out of a family pot, each person thrusting in his hand, balling up a wad, and tossing it into his mouth with a quick movement. *Ufa* is full of calories, but by itself it is depressingly bland. All about the Shire Valley and on much of the lake shore, protein is scarce, and the people scratch for any odd scrap of meat to piece out their diet and add zest to the mush. When found and added to the *ufa* pot, any such small proteinaceous embellishment is spoken of not as meat, but as relish. The kungu is a great windfall of relish for the tribes along the western shore of the lake. I don't know how much it raises the level of nutrition, but it plays an important role in building morale.

To a newcomer to the lake it is not, as I said, a very engaging flavor that kungu has. None of the passengers finished their fly omelette—not even Lewis and I. But to the people of the lake, the fly cake is by no means just endured for the sake of a balanced diet. To Nyasa people the cake is a delicacy. The cook had brought kungu aboard to enhance his own fare; and he was the cook, mind, with the pantry and freezer of the ship at his disposal. I have no doubt that if you were to offer a lake man a choice of fly cake and black caviar—and they look much the same—he would take the flies every time.

It is all a matter of what you're used to. Neither of the two objections outsiders raise when fed kungu is really valid. They say ugh, *flies*—but flies are meat, and insect meat looms large in human history. Our forebears no doubt passed much of their time as a hen does, scratching for grubs and insects. It is only pastoral Western man who has come to shrink from the thought. Getting our sustenance from big creatures like cows has bred up horror at the thought of eating little living things. In an article in *The American Scholar* called "Insects in the Diet" Marston Bates set the limits of the taboo as land-dwelling invertebrates—backboneless animals, not of the sea where we take avidly after molluscas and crustaceans, but of the dry land, where worms and insects are the common invertebrates.

But that only defines, and does not explain, the taboo. A good part of the trouble is the small size of the creatures, as I said, and another part is the eating of them whole. I remember the days when mounting concern over victuals for the future first set people to thinking of straining the ocean for the tons of small beings that float there. This plankton is the biggest crop the sea produces. It could be an almost inexhaustible food reserve for man. It doesn't taste good, and it might constipate you; but these flaws can no doubt be worked out.

But for the sake of the planners of the future who make the big step and give up cows and cornfields to farm the seas, let me say never, *never,* permit people to see what it is they are being fed. Some thinkers are pessimistic about plankton as food for our teeming descendants because it tastes odd, others because it is hard to strain out of the water. I say it will be the magnified looks of it that will scare off clientele—its unsettling miscellany, its untrustworthy subvisible size. Prettily packaged, in cakes or oozes, it may find a limited vogue; but some idle person is sure to tease apart a bit of the stuff under a lens one day, and see the chaos of organs and shells and little feet —and then there will be hell to pay.

There is more to the taboo than Bates says—it is not just backbonelessness that people dread. One thing that horrifies is for a creature to have lots of feet—"Oh think of all those legs," you hear them say—and another bad thing is to have no feet at all. Snakes and palolo worms are both good eating; but ask any friend why he would never shop for these for the table and he'll almost surely say, "No legs; oh, God, just think, no legs at all."

I took a piece of kungu cake back to Florida and my wife doctored it up some and served it in harmless small heaps on crackers at a cocktail party. There were few compliments, to be sure, but there were no complaints. Later, when I divulged what the spread was, no one struck me, but they quite clearly thought they had been imposed upon. After all, the consensus was, the rules for *hors d'œuvres* are pretty slack, but *gnats.* . . . And these were people, mind you, who were stuffing themselves with smoked oysters and anchovy paste. And anyway, they said as a last thrust, the gnats taste like they're spoiled.

With the kungu cake I took home some biltong to excite my children, some elephant biltong that I got from Captain Ariano. My wife served some of that at the party too, shaved thin as you can buy it all about South Africa, in cellophane bags like peanuts or potato chips. The guests said this was rotten too.

It is discouraging when guests say the food you serve them is rotten. Such prejudice is a little puzzling when you get to thinking about it.

When I was young, for example, there were things to be feared called ptomaines. I never knew what they were and don't to this day, but I lived in fear of ptomaines, and have lately come to wonder what ever became of them. They were supposed to occur in spoiled victuals, and most insidiously in seafood. Even quite sophisticated gourmets, who would carefully ripen a canvasback duck or a steak, shrank from the thought of tainted fish. Worst possible place for ptomaines, they used to say. And yet in parts of the world, there are other people who care little for a fish till it gets a bit of an advanced taste to it. For instance, one of the most widely eaten fish in the world is the cod; but it is not the firm, white, gentle-flavored natural cod that finds an almost global market. It is the racy bacalao, the dried cod slabs glazed over with exudations from a ripening inside, and with a taste no cod on earth was ever caught with.

In Nyasaland there has for centuries been traffic in fish between the lakeshore tribes and the people inland. Today there is some refrigerated transportation by truck to the highland towns, but much of the fish still goes by bicycle. Boys coast down the scarp, load fish baskets at the lake, then walk their bicycles back up the long slopes and out the narrow trails to the inland villages. By the time they get to the back country their fish is not the same. This regimen has bred into the inland people not just a marked indifference to decay but a real preference for ripened fish. David Livingstone remarked this. Lewis and I saw a most spectacular example of it.

On the eve of one of our first trips from Limbe to the lake we left our Humber Super Snipe—the palatial staff car provided for our field work—in a garage near the office. The engine had dropped out of the Super Snipe on three previous trips. This time we were going down the long rough scarp road to Chiromo, and had borrowed a Land Rover for the trip. As we were about to shut the door of the little tin garage where the Humber stayed, a boy on a bicycle stopped and handed our African driver a fish. It was a once handsome but now dejected-looking *chambo*, a highly edible kind of cichlid, from the lake. The driver took it gratefully, found some newspaper in the trunk of the car, wrapped up the *chambo*, and stowed it in the trunk of the Super Snipe. Then he shut the door of the garage and locked it. We chided him for what seemed a most irresponsible lack of foresight, but he waved our complaints blandly aside, got into the driver's seat, and drove us away. We came back three days later. When we opened the doors, the fish seemed all to have distilled out into the baking air of the little metal building. We stepped back to let the solid reek push past. But the driver went in and opened the trunk of the Humber, took out the parcel, and tenderly cradling it in his hands to hold in the now liquid contents, told us good-bye, and went away to find a cook.

Thomas Barbour once told me of some folk somewhere in southeast Asia who put fish in a bag, hang it in the sun, and as the fish liquefy, collect the drippings to use as a sauce. There is more to this matter of ptomaines than meets the eye. It seems bad to Western men when people do that sort of thing; but I suspect it may be we who are the mystics, the ones burdened with taboo. Anyway, the Nyasa people ripen their fish as we ripen cheese, and always have done so, and are not hurt by it. Perhaps they even get some extra unknown good out of fish prepared that way. But that is a digression. It is not decaying fish that have brought fame to Lake Nyasa. The live fish there are one of the wonders of the world, and a thing I am bound to tell about.

Archie Carr and Wilson.

PHOTO BY LEWIS BERNER⟩

Kikuyu village in Kenya. The able and vigorous Kikuyu will be an important factor in the future of African wildlife.

Hippopotamus yawning. Queen Elizabeth National Park, Uganda.

Vultures on the body of a young elephant killed by poachers. Lake Manyara National Park, Tanganyika.

Elephants in a dense forest. Manyara.

(PHOTO BY LEWIS BERNER)

The Piri Piri on the Zambezi near the Shire's mouth. Mozambique.

Zebras. Ngorongoro Crater, Ngorongoro Conservation Area, Tanganyika. The incomparable crater shown, a 100-square-mile volcanic caldera, is practically a microcosm of the plains' wildlife.

Cheetahs. Masai Amboseli Game Reserve, Kenya.

Elephants winding. Amboseli.

Rhinoceros with cattle egrets. Amboseli.

Giraffe at Ol Tukai. Amboseli.

Elephant in village. Murchison Falls National Park, Uganda. Some elephants quickly learn about the easy pickings around the lodges and the quarters of the park personnel.

Thomson's gazelles. Nairobi Royal National Park, Kenya.

Vultures waiting for the photographer to go away from a carcass. Manyara.

Ankole cattle. Uganda.

Crocodile. Victoria Nile, Murchison Falls National Park, Uganda.

Young lion. Nairobi Royal National Park.

Lioness keeping an eye out. Nairobi Royal National Park.

Wildebeests. Amboseli.

Oribi, one of the smaller African antelopes. Queen Elizabeth National Park.

Hippopotamus irked at photographer. Queen Elizabeth National Park.

Cattle herons on elephants in grass. Queen Elizabeth National Park.

Waterbucks. Queen Elizabeth National Park.

Elephants and egrets. Queen Elizabeth National Park.

Fish eagle. Queen Elizabeth National Park.

Cattle egrets and snowy egrets with cows. Marion County, Florida.

Giraffes at Ol Tukai, Amboseli. Mt. Kilimanjaro in background.

[105]

Chambo

As STIRRING in their way as the kungu clouds, and to the student of evolution even more so, are the cichlid fishes of Lake Nyasa. Of the vertebrate animals of Africa the greatest number of most distinctively African species are not mammals, birds, or reptiles, but fishes. Even in such bizarre company as this the Nyasa fishes stand out. There are more endemic species there—more kinds found there alone—than in any other lake. Ichthyologically Nyasa is the most extraordinary body of fresh water in the world.

There are 200 species of fishes in the Lake. Most of them are found nowhere else. About 180 of them belong to a single family, the Cichlidae. It is the evolutionary escapades of this family that account for most of the eccentricity of the fauna. The particular whimsy of the family in Lake Nyasa is that it breaks up into constellations of similar but slightly different kinds called species-flocks. The cichlids show the same tendency in other East African lakes, but it is more pronounced in Nyasa than anywhere else. One genus there, *Haplochromis*, is composed of 101 slightly different species. This is by far the biggest species-flock known in the world.

Most Americans and Europeans are acquainted with cichlids chiefly in the person of a brash, chunky aquarium fish that looks like a sunfish. The group as a whole has a curiously discontinuous distribution. It occurs in tropical America, in Central Africa, and hardly anywhere in between. On both continents there are distinguished aquarium fishes among the cichlids. One of the Nicaraguan cichlids and one of those in Lake Nyasa must be among the best of all fresh-water food fishes. They are real gastronomic delights. The Nyasa species is the *chambo*, a *Tilapia*, relatives of which are now being widely used for restocking and fish-culture projects all over the tropics. The Nicaraguan delicacy is a *guapote* that lives in Rio Tipitapa, a short and obviously enchanted stream that connects Lake Managua and Lake Nicaragua. When this *guapote* is cooked by one of three little restaurants that specialize in it, the result is a spectacular gastronomic event.

Cichlids have arresting breeding habits. Most kinds do not tend the eggs and young in nests, but hold them in their mouths until the fry get big enough for independent living. This way of reproducing their kind lets cichlids colonize in all kinds of places that have things to eat in them but lack decent ground for nesting. It probably took a great deal of evolution to produce a reliable mouth-brooder among cichlid fishes, because they dearly love to eat fish eggs—their own as well as those of other species. But now, in many of the species, one sex at breeding time is always able to resist the awful urge, and to hold the new generation safe in its mouth until it has grown big enough to cope with the world outside. In such an unorthodox group of fishes it should be no surprise to find a peculiar quirk in the distribution of the mouth-brooding habit. In Central Africa it is mainly the female who tends the young; in West Africa and the American waters it is said to be the male.

Africans around Lake Nyasa know about the mouth-brooding habit, and embellish it a bit in their folklore. They say the young are born from the mouth of the parent. This is an error. Actually, the eggs are first laid in a fanned-out cavity, much like the nest of a sunfish. Then, instead of being fanned and tended there, the eggs are picked up by the female and held in her mouth. When they are able to swim the little fish are spat out periodically to forage. They gather in a small school and pick out tiny particles suspended in the water. When anything scares them, they rush back into their mother's mouth again. With many fish carrying on mouth-brooding in narrow quarters, it is not surprising that the wrong offspring are sometimes taken in. Female fish may even pick up young of a different species. Miss Rosemary Lowe of the British Museum saw a little *chambo* try to force its way into the mouth of a *Barbus,* a kind of cyprinid fish that knows nothing about mouth-brooding at all. If you put mouth-nursed cichlid fry in a tank with a predaceous fish, they will rush hopefully into the willing mouth of the fish-eating fish.

But the most imposing and bewildering feature of this singular family of fishes is the species-flocks it forms in the African lakes, above all the *Haplochromis* flock of Lake Nyasa. This group confronts the zoologist with the anomaly that the greatest number of closely related species of any vertebrate animal in any restricted area in the world should be in a *lake*. Not in the Galapagos Islands, or in a varied geographic area like the Republic of Colombia; but all dumped together, as it were, in one long, narrow basin of water. Anybody with a shred of curiosity about such matters is bound to be stunned by this situation, and to cast about for a way to explain it.

To get ready for the work in Nyasaland I read a lot about bilharziasis, elephantiasis, and the other animal-borne diseases that our job there would be concerned with. I tried to acquire a smattering of Nyasaland herpetology too, because reptiles and amphibians were a special interest of mine. But I went off to Africa wholly unprepared for the phenomenon of the Nyasa fishes. I had heard of them, but the things I had heard were too heady for quick absorption, and I left the subject, to go on with more necessary preparations for the trip.

One day after our first two weeks on the Shire River we went up to a fish house on the southeast shore of the lake above Fort Johnston.There were fish all over the place, and I hopefully started asking what kinds they were. I soon gave it up, however. People appeared to be slinging names around in an irresponsible way. They seemed to be telling me different names for the same kind of fish, or for slightly different phases of a single species. It was the same way whenever we saw canoes come in with fish on the bottom, and when boys on bicycles out in the bush trails gave us names for the fish in the baskets between their handlebars. Then I saw one of the big Nyasa dragnets landed on the lake shore, and for the catch that this brought in, there was a wholly bewildering tautology of terms.

These big Nyasa seines are the cultural *tour de force* of the people of the Lake. You rarely see longer nets in use on any ocean shore. The first chance I had to watch one being used came unexpectedly, when our majordomo, Wilson, took me to his village to buy a ceremonial mask. I had once, in Wilson's presence, admired some wooden masks in the window of a Blantyre craft shop. These had been made by Zulus for the tourist trade, and although they looked pretty good to me, Wilson sneered at them. He said the people in his village made them better.

Our man Wilson—our boy, he called himself—was an extraordinary fellow. He did not have the usual Nyanja look at all. His skin was a reddish brown, for one thing, not the regular gray-black of Nyasa Africans. His face was broad through the middle, with high cheek bones and somewhat oriental eyes and a gnomish look. He always wore a pink silk shirt and muslin pants that he made himself, and went barefoot. They told us he was a Yao, when they sent him to be our boy, to make tea and keep things straight and cook for us if the camp we were in should have no special cook. Wilson acted like a Yao all right. The Yaos are the tribe who used to help the Arabs in their Nyasa slave raids. They have tamed down now, but still they are more self-assured than the usual Nyanja, a little more cocky and outspoken, and often they are fey and fantastic in their thinking. In those ways Wilson was a lot like a Yao. Maybe he was part Yao. He didn't know. His chief qualification for being our caretaker was that he knew some English and knew all about Americans. As a youth he had gone to Southern Rhodesia and worked for an American in Salisbury. He learned English there and came to know about the outside world. Wilson was the scion of an old lake-shore family. He was in fact a sort of prince, and had been in line to become chief of his village. But knowing the world outside had made life at home seem dull. Wilson went back only rarely, for short visits.

One afternoon when we were camped near Wilson's village, he asked if I wanted to go there and get the mask we had spoken of. He said his mother had died two days before, and he had walked to the village that afternoon to help his sisters arrange the funeral. He said a man had a mask for sale, and we could get it if we went up after tea. I was curious to see Wilson's village anyway, so we got in the Land Rover and drove six or seven miles down the lake road and turned into a track that made off toward a straggling cluster of thatched-roofed houses. We were in the midst of the town before I saw that there was no street or aisle to show the way to travel. I stopped, confused, but Wilson told me to keep on going, and started waving his arm to guide me to the proper side of a given hut or dog. We got along all right that way. As we went among the huts and chickens, a train of young boys formed and ran behind us yelling over the jeep being in town, and over the grandeur of Wilson's coming home. We passed a pot-bellied baobab tree. Under it was a mound of mud bricks surrounded by a thin fence of thorn. Beside the mound three women in loin cloths, bedraggled and dusty, were kneading mud in a pot. All three were crying.

"That my sisters," Wilson said.

"What are they doing?" I asked.

"That my mother under bricks," Wilson said. "Sisters make more bricks so animals not get mother."

A little farther on Wilson told me to stop the car. He got out and went to a hut where a dog lay like a dead dog in the dust before the door. The dog woke up and at once came bounding over in a rage to bark at the jeep. A wary-looking man came to the door, and Wilson started talking to him. They stood there quite a while talking and moving their hands in the air. Every now and then they rolled their eyes in my direction. Finally they seemed to reach an agreement, and after ducking back into the house, the man came out with a cloth sack and followed Wilson to the car.

"Going get mask," Wilson said.

The man smiled to show he understood what Wilson said, and that it was true, and, to make up for the lack of any introduction, I asked him how he was. The man only smiled some more. They both got into the car and we followed a footpath that made off through the grass to the edge of a swampy lagoon that was separated from the lake by a narrow grassy ridge. We got out and the man led us to a place on the bank beside a clump of trees that stood in the water. He stopped there, and looked all about in a surreptitious way, then reached into the grass behind us and pulled out a six-foot pole. He walked out knee-deep into the water and started poking about with the pole on the bottom among the swollen bases of the flooded trees. All the time he kept looking back uneasily over his shoulder, making admonishing gestures now and then as if to quiet us, although neither of us had said a word or done anything but stand quietly watching.

"What is the matter with him?" I said to Wilson.

"He finding mask," Wilson said.

"You mean the mask is down there in the water?"

"Stay there all the time," Wilson said. "So any women can never see."

"You mean women can't look at the mask he's selling?"

"Not any women can see."

"What's wrong with women looking at the mask?"

"Bad," Wilson said, raising a stern finger at the thought of women. "Very bad for women see."

"Oh," I said, though I didn't understand.

Just then the man hit something solid with the stick, and turned with a look of triumph in our direction. When once again he had peered carefully up and down the shore and back along the trail, he shoved his arm away down into the lagoon, until his ear was in the water, and felt around on the bottom and quickly got hold of what he was after. He pulled it out and I could see that it was a wooden mask, tied to a small boulder. The man came sloshing out to shore, carefully holding the muddy mass close to his body, cradling it against the disaster of women coming. Wilson and I crowded in to look.

The mask the man had brought up was not a dramatic object, as ceremonial masks go. It was really not the usual frightening face one associates with African masks at all. It was a mild, ineffectual face, actually. There was not much character in it, but there was nothing sinister or vicious either. It had an unready, melancholy, fetal look about it, with the bulbous forehead of an early embryo swelling out over a set of pinched, unfinished-looking features. The eyes were only gimlet holes; the mouth a slit beneath a long Greek-style nose; the cheeks and chin were like halves of crabapples, stuck on at slightly inaccurate places. The face was painted a dim maroon, with black bars over the eyeholes. It looked up through the mud on it with an expression that seemed to combine surprise and a piteous, unbelieving resentment, as if it were recoiling at a first look at the world. A half-grown mussel had somehow got itself wedged into the lipless slit of the mouth, and this stuck out half way as if the face were smoking something. It was not fair to judge the face in that condition, covered with mud, with a piece of rattan passing through one eye to tie it to the anchor stone, and the mussel jutting from the mouth. But the impression one got looking at the mask was not felicitous at all.

The man was pleased though. He untied the rock and started splashing water on the mask to get the mud off, carefully standing between it and the shore, in case of women. When the mask had been untied from the rock, the mud scraped off, and the clam removed from the mouth, it looked a little better, but not a great deal, really. It still was a somewhat depressing thing to see.

But the man was looking relieved and happy over the way he was carrying out his mission. He went over to the bank, got the sack from where he had dropped it, and put the thin, sad wooden face inside. Enfolding the bundle in the sparse cover of his arms, he sidled over to the car and put it inside between the two front seats. Then he turned to Wilson, looking very relieved and triumphant. He said a few things in Chinyanja.

"What is he saying now?" I asked.

"He says take care not any women see the mask," Wilson said.

"Ask him what I owe him," I said.

"Already he tell me this," Wilson said. "He need three-and-six for the mask and sixpence for the sack. Four shilling you pay."

I didn't specially want the sack, but I knew it would worry the man if I carried the mask bare through the village. I paid him, with a small tip to go with the price, and he turned and quickly went away into the grass. When he was out of sight, I tried to get Wilson to tell me a little more about why the man acted as he did, but it was not any use. All I could learn was that the man "was ashamed if any women can see the mask."

As we started to get into the car there was some shouting up the shore. Wilson listened a moment, then asked me if I wanted to see people catching fish. I said I did. Wilson told me to come along then, and struck out down the trail along the bank. We soon came to a blind end of the lagoon and the trail cut around it and out toward a brighter look to the sky, over where the lake was lying. We went through a strip of tall grass with wet ground underfoot and came out suddenly on a short beach at the head of a shallow cove.

The beach made a clean white arc in the green reeds of the lake shore. There were really two arcs there, the shallow one the beach made and the convex sweep of a fish net that curved out from one end of the beach, went half way across to Mozambique, or so it seemed, and then curved back to shore again at the other side of the cove.

The sun was flooding in from low in the west, and a slow, small surf chopped green and white at the ivory slope of the sand. Clumps of people were scattered out along the shore. At either end of the beach, three men were hauling at the ends of the net, plodding in to the edge of the grass, then going back to the water for a new hold and another slow haul inshore. The two teams were only two hundred yards apart along the beach, but it was a quarter of a mile or more out along the noble curve the net floats made, and already big piles of landed net had grown behind the men. It was late afternoon and the sky was deep blue over the deeper blue of the body of the lake. The net floats hung out there in a long ellipse, like a thin necklace of strung beads, with its ends hanging from the ends of the little beach and its farthest curve almost out of sight. Among the reeds that cut off the arc of the beach the wet linemen shone black in the slanted sunlight.

It was a good bit of the earth to see at the time, and I stood for a while at the edge of the grass to soak in the geometry and color. Then Wilson poked at me and pointed into the lake beyond the farthest floats. Away out beyond the last reach of the net a dark break was rearranging the ranks of low waves coming in from across the lake. It was a crocodile out there, cruising just outside the net; and he was a vast big one. Judging him against the spaces between net floats, I figured the bumps of his nose and eyes were farther apart than the nose and eyes of any crocodile I had seen. He was not going anywhere, only moving back and forth along the outside curve of the net.

There was no way to tell how big the crocodile really was, or how old he was, or how many years he had watched the men of the village draw in their nets. Or how long before his day his forebears were there sharing the catch of ancestors of these men for centuries back into the earliest times when Bantu people pushed out Bushmen or whatever other folk may once have fished along the shore. Before the Bushmen came, for all I know, crocodiles of the kind and kin of this one were at that place when handaxe men bashed at fish with shaped stones, or let their females slosh out too unheedingly when they brought the water in.

The sight of the big crocodile out there, so unhurried in his cruising, brought up thoughts like those, of things it would be good to know. Just watching the hauling in of this one net, all you could see for sure was that the fishing of the men was a thing long in the life of this crocodile; that he knew just what was taking place and that the outcome of the acts of the men would surely ease the life of a grand old crocodile who had known a hundred years of hungry days. Keeping a sixteen-foot crocodile fed must be a heavy chore, one that must call upon all the resources of the crocodile involved. It seemed no wonder that this one should so well know the ways of the villagers. You could see in the system of his patient cruising that the net was a part of his life. You could see it, also, in the way the people accepted the crocodile as a necessary part of their fishing. Europeans would have sent for a gun, and the crocodile would long before have changed his way of life; but in this village there were no guns able to do more than make the crocodile wonder why the men didn't get on with the drawing in of the net.

I killed an hour or so thinking about the crocodile, and picking up snails and mussels among the reeds. After a while I could begin to see the belly of the net shrinking and its arc closing in to the curve of the beach. People began to chatter with the sense of the climax of the landing. Women passing with pots or baskets on their heads stopped and put down their loads to watch the end of the haul. The coming in of a long net is a grand thing to see, and it stirred even these Nyanjas to an unwonted lighthearted expectancy, and took them out of their native reticence and made them seem like fishing Krumen for a while. It conjured up the jubilee spirit of a seine coming in on Trinidad.

As the float line flattened toward the shore, the crocodile reached at last the limit of his confidence and came no closer, but only kept cruising slowly back and forth a hundred yards offshore to wait for the windfalls of addled fish that would soon come fleeing from the net. Every now and then someone would point at the crocodile and punch somebody else, and they both would laugh and hit their legs in a spirit that was good to see, but not easy to understand exactly.

At last the final bight of the half-mile net came into

the chopping surf, and fish began to jump the float line and flutter in piled-up confusion in the bagged webbing. The Africans scurried about picking up the fish that dashed ashore, and trying to bat down those that jumped the float line. Then finally the net-bag stranded and slid up onto the sand. Hands reached to pull it high to safety, other hands held the webbing up as a fence between the fish and the lake, and still others began to sort the catch out into baskets.

The haul was not big, considering the length of the net and the manpower it had cost to set the net and bring it in. There were maybe fifty pounds of fish in the haul, and they were mostly small. But the great strike had gone through three different habitats of the rich south end of the lake. It had swept through open water, reedy flats, and the mud-sand bottom of the shallow inshore zone. I was still far from ready to appreciate the bizarre prodigality of Nyasa fishes—even the fraction of it shown by this single sample. But I shared the excitement all the same, and started dashing about among the gatherers of fishes, trying to write down the names of the different kinds, with a phrase or two to keep them apart in my notes. I had no trouble with the carplike kinds, the lake mullet and lake salmon as the English people call them, or with the several sorts of catfish that were there. The elephant fish was there in the catch, and it gave me a flash of false confidence because it is so easy to know. It has a long tubular snout, used for sucking up larvae out of the bottom mud, that gives it a downcast look not like the look of any other fish. It was a comfort to see the elephant fish there so easy to identify, but it was not a healthy thing for me. Because the main body of the catch was a tumbling galaxy of shining cichlids. Among these the diversity that I was able to make out seemed to be nowhere near as great as that of the names I was taking down. I got a little desperate, and Wilson followed me about anxiously and did what he could to help out with his English. But he was not a naturalist at heart, and the fish had few translatable names anyway. After a while I gave up the census in disgust and tore the pages of names from my notebook as worse than useless.

Later on I learned from Dr. Ethelwynn Trewavas at the British Museum that the Africans do not recognize all the kinds of cichlids there are in the lake. But to me, with my casual acquaintance with cichlids in Central America, the names in use around Nyasa seemed rife with synonyms. But the names I heard were partly Chinyanja, and partly Chiyao, and a few were Swahili, English, or Portuguese; and so for a time I set the difficulty down to my own linguistic troubles. Now I know better. The trouble is real. The fishes of the lake are an incredibly finely subdivided spectrum of kinds of life. The plethora of vernacular names corresponds to a real and far greater plethora of species, to an extravagant redundance of fishes that has no counterpart anywhere else in the world.

As I said, I came away from the Nyasaland trip without comprehending the full stature of what I had seen, and this I regret. But some of the richness of the fauna is reflected in the fishing techniques of the Africans, and these I was able to see and savor. I would rather go to a fish market than to a movie, anyway. The landing of a net is fine drama to me; the geometry of a wicker fish trap half under water draws me with all the allure of the animal tent at the circus.

On Lake Nyasa and its tributaries, fishing is the central focus of native ingenuity. The diversity of the fishes has called out all the creative energy of the poor shore people. The net I watched come in at Wilson's village was of a type known as *khoka*, the biggest of various kinds of seines used on the lake. The hauling ropes were twisted of a crawling, vinelike plant. The webbing was made in a series of connected panels. These were only about six feet deep near the ends of the net, but out in the middle section were twelve feet deep, or more. Each panel was made of cords that had been laboriously clawed out of the bodies of truck tires. Some nets we saw were made of plant fiber. All of them used to be. But this was one of the more fashionable kinds made by carding short chunks of truck tire through a small forest of nails sticking up in a board. The threads freed this way are only a few inches long, but these tied end to end in an infinity of square knots were the twine from which the nets of Nyasa were knitted. I was told this before I went to the lake and didn't believe it. But later I saw the carding of the tire rubber, and the knitting of the nets. There is no way of escaping the surety that on Lake Nyasa mile-long nets are made of threads salvaged from tire cord.

Ranging down in size from the giant *khoka*, there are several other kinds of seines, used both to herd in bottom-feeding fish and to surround schools of *usipa*, a little fish like whitebait. In rocky places where there is no room for seining, gill nets are set. Offshore, a sort of fine-meshed purse seine is used. In this the middle part is a great deal deeper than the ends, and the net balloons to surround a school of *usipa* and close around them as it is drawn in over the gunwhales. This net is played out between two canoes, usually at night, and another canoe with a light in the bow moves in between the others and drives shoals of *usipa* into the bag. Another Nyasa net, from a distance, makes you think you are in Mexico watching the butterfly boats of Lake Pátzcuaro. It is not the same net, really, but from a distance it has the same look of a slim insect body with filmy wings spread out. The African butterfly net is just a big square of webbing hung from two poles. When the poles are crossed, the net opens in the fork. To use it the fisherman holds the poles in one hand at the point where they cross, thrusts the net into a school of *usipa,* and sweeps it in toward the boat and over the gunwale.

In the most athletic form of fishing done on the lake, a piece of mosquito net is used. Lengths of netting are sent or brought home for the purpose by travelers from the lake-shore villages. I was not able to learn whether this custom was handed down from a time before mosquito netting came to Nyasaland. It must have had an indigenous counterpart, however, because we came upon one pair of youths using a length of sacking as a net. And anyway, a method so bizarre and unlikely would hardly have been thought up recently.

In using the mosquito nets, two men fish from one canoe. They locate the shoals of *usipa,* which can be seen as dark or ripply patches on the surface, like a cloud-shadow on the water. When a school is sighted, the fishermen paddle up to it in their dugout, and when they pull up alongside they jump overboard into the shoal. They stretch the net as they hit the water, swim under water briefly, and then come up and bunch the net into a bag to hold the catch. The most improbable part of the operation is the two men leaving a canoe in a headlong plunge without ever turning it over. This fishing adds just the right acrobatic zest to a necessary chore, and exactly suits the amphibious nature of the young lakeside Africans.

Besides these nets, various kinds of traps, weirs, and baskets are used in lagoons, reedy shores, and tributaries, and among rocks of the lake; and before they became il-

Chambo

legal, several kinds of vegetable fish poisons were used.

The diversity of the Nyasa fishing art is imposing; but it does not approach the diversity of the fishes themselves. In fact, if one has any sense of responsibility at all about such matters, the Nyasa fishes pose two questions that keep off sound sleep until they are answered. One is whether the fishes all originated in the lake, or came in from somewhere else. The other is how they are all able to live on there, so many kinds so closely akin, doing so very much the same sorts of things.

The questions can be put in those two ways, but really there is one great resounding riddle. It is to know what sort of isolation, what kinds of barriers, built and maintain this unequaled exorbitance of species. Ichthyologists began writing astonished papers about the situation long ago, and there has been a fairly steady flow of printed thought by a few people groping for an answer. But the world as a whole, even the world of zoologists interested in learning how evolution works, is living too peacefully with the enigma of the Lake Nyasa fishes. That unaccountable and unprecedented welter of species in a single body of fresh water is not an easy thought for a biologist to absorb. But once the thought is accepted as reality, it is hard to escape the feeling that the Nyasa fishes are one of the truly bizarre anomalies of natural history.

It is a shame that this marvel is of such a specialized kind. It is not a thing that explodes into the mind of a person not accustomed to pondering problems of speciation, the processes of evolution by which new species arise. To marvel at a hurricane or at the kungu clouds or at Victoria Falls, no special background is needed. But to feel the force of the Nyasa fishes one ought to have fretted at first hand over problems of how evolution and ecology work together in multiplying species in the earth.

I foretell a time when this bewilderment of Nyasa fishes will, like the mammals of Australia or the reptiles and birds of the Galapagos Islands, be one of the classic examples to show how evolution has gone about filling the earth with different kinds of beings. And even though the subject is not one that will keep most people awake at night, it seems to me that anyone who is willing to meditate upon it, and who brings with him a smattering of familiarity with the process of natural selection, will go away full of awe over the cichlids of Lake Nyasa.

One trouble with the fish over there is that they seem to have broken Jordan's Law in a blatant way. You hear little about Jordan's Law nowadays, because it appears to oversimplify complicated matters; but fundamentally it was a good law and if you allow for the different ways people feel about certain words, the law still works. What Jordan's Law said was that the nearest relative of a kind of animal should not be looked for in the animal's own environment, or in some far-off place, but in an adjacent place, living separated from the first animal by some kind of barrier. Obviously your feeling about the words "place," "environment," and "barrier" will determine the amount of good you see in Jordan's Law. But all the law really says is what Darwin himself said, and what every biologist believes today—that to have speciation there has got to be isolation. For a kind of animal to split and become two species, some kind of a barrier has to separate two sections of the population so that little, accidental hereditary changes can accumulate, instead of being passed about in the population as a whole. Without the barrier any small changes that arise are bred right back into the whole group. But if any hindrance to free breeding occurs, the changes accumulate, and after awhile, in the aggregate, they may produce two different strains that are no longer able or willing to breed together. When that happens there are two species, where only one was before.

The separating barrier doesn't have to be a wall of fire—that is, an ocean, a desert, or a mountain range. It can be little hidden features of the environment, or traits of the body or even the mind of the animal itself. It can be anything that cuts down interbreeding. Once two species have become different, they can move back into the same territory and live on separately together, each the closest living relative of the other, each held in its mold by some small difference in structure, habits, or psychology. One of them may breed only in the wintertime, say, and the other only in the summer. Maybe they are still alike in many ways, but the new differences keep them apart as effectively as if they were living on two sides of a wall. If you are willing to say that a barrier can be a state of mind, and that a place can be a way of living—a place in the environment—then Jordan's Law makes about as much sense as Jordan figured it did.

The reason for my going into this elementary discussion of speciation is that the evolution of cichlid fishes in Lake Nyasa seems at first glance to have violated all the rules. The diversity of the Nyasa fauna is of a most peculiar kind. In this one long, deep, narrow lake there are whole suites of fishes the members of which are more closely related to each other than to any other fishes in any other place. And besides that, many of them spend their time doing disconcertingly similar kinds of things; that is, they seem to have almost the same roles in the environment. That is as jarring to the preconceptions of an ecologist as the lack of barriers is to the student of evolution. The two violations may be the same really, but they make two kinds of biologists separately indignant.

The epitome of the Nyasa incongruity is the species-flock of the genus, *Haplochromis*, with its 101 Nyasa species. This genus is a real zoogeographic monstrosity. Most of the special ways of life of the Nyasa fauna, and some of its tendency to duplication of roles, can be seen to lesser degrees in the less explosively evolved, but nonetheless marvelously redundant fishes of other East African Lakes—Lake Victoria, Lake Edward, and Lake Tanganyika. Comparing the fishes of the various lakes reveals some beautiful examples of evolutionary convergence—the separate molding of similar stocks in similar environments. But it does little to explain the origin of the species-flocks, or to tell what mechanisms hold the species in them apart—that keep them from competing to the point of extinction, or prevent their interbreeding and flowing back together again. The explanation for this will not come easily, and will no doubt be complex and composite when it comes.

If the lake were an oceanic island, the answer would seem a little easier. Good-sized islands, remotely located and with complex physiography, often have faunas which, like that of Lake Nyasa, are made up of many species all clearly the nearest living relatives of others on the island. But the two situations are not the same. An island is land, and it may abound in physical barriers. There are endless ways for animals living in a varied dry land topography to become separated and break up into enclaves and colonies. But Lake Nyasa is all water, from top to bottom and from end to end; and water is an even, unsegmented living space. It is hard to imagine a lot of fish living in one body of open water ever finding themselves on two sides of any kind of wall.

When an island fauna, or any fauna, is made up this way—of a set of closely related animals that have fallen into all the varied ways of life the island affords—the fauna is said to have been produced by adaptive radiation. The phrase gives the zoogeographer a warm feeling of having explained a situation. The mammals of Australia, for instance, though a varied lot, are all marsupials—pouched animals. Almost every kind is just a special conversion of the ancient possum-plan, in which the young are born as helpless embryos and kept in a pouch on the mother's belly. A zoologist will tell you this is a grand example of adaptive radiation; and it is; and everybody feels good about it. So, in groping for an explanation of the species-flocks of the East African lakes, some people have hopefully suggested that the lake must just be a peculiarly diversified environment. This is not so, in the case of Lake Nyasa, at least. Even if it were, it would not explain the species-flocks; but it is simply not true. Of the several biologists who have thought and written about the problem posed by the Nyasa fishes, Geoffrey Fryer seems to have put together the most pieces of the puzzle. One of the important contributions Fryer made was to show clearly that Lake Nyasa is not, as big lakes go, an exceptionally varied environment at all, but rather the reverse. Because there is no oxygen dissolved in the water at depths of more than 250 meters, nearly half the area of the lake is unavailable as habitat for animals that need both oxygen for respiration and contact with the bottom, as most of the Nyasa fishes do. So for many of the species in it, Lake Nyasa is not the 11,000 square miles of habitat that its dimensions suggest. Instead it is only a thin ring of living space, a flattened circle of shore waters running 800 miles or more around the suffocating interior of the lake. In the habitable zones, the temperature changes are not strong, and the food supply is neither rich nor diverse. The fauna as a whole is somewhat poor. It is mainly fishes, snails, and clams. The kungu midges make a spectacular show; but for most of their lives they live out in the depths of the lake, where all but some of the plankton-straining fishes are unable to go. So in spite of its great length, depth, and age, the lake offers only a lean spread of opportunities, in the usual sense of the word. It is obviously no varied array of ways of life that accounts for the species-flocks.

In fact, it is probably the poverty in food resources that has engendered one of the most fantastic evolutionary specialties to be found among the fishes in the lake. Three groups of Nyasa cichlids—three different genera—have independently hit upon the habit of eating the scales of other kinds of fishes. Each has evolved a taste for scales, and the cunning to steal them, and a set of teeth specially designed for taking them off. You might set down a single case like that as just a quirk of adaptive radiation in a competitive environment. But how in the world can three cases in one lake be explained?

One of the scale-stealing species is known by the Africans as *capitao*—that is, boss—of the *chambos*. The *capitao* lives closely associated with one of the succulent *chambos* of the genus *Tilapia*. Inside its mouth it has a set of teeth especially adapted for scraping scales from the base of the *chambo's* tail; but outside its form and coloring make it look like a *chambo*. Another of this same genus is also a scale eater, and it lives with some of the fishes of the *Haplochromis* species-flock. It too has the undeniable look of the fishes whose scales it takes.

Besides being an extraordinary way to make a living, the scale-eating of the *capitao* gives a fascinating small twist to the phenomenon of mimicry. Mimicry is the adaptive resemblance of one animal to another. In the most clearcut examples of mimicry one animal, spoken of as the "model," is dangerous, or nauseating, to eat; and another animal, the mimic, though he may be really quite sweet-natured or delicious to eat, has a color pattern or body-form like that of the model, and so, theoretically, avoids attack by enemies that know the look of the model and habitually leave him in peace. This is the simplest form of the widespread adaptation called mimicry. In the case of the scale-eating fishes, the situation is in a way like mimicry, because one fish has for utilitarian reasons come to look like another. But the advantage involved is very different from that in the classic cases. The resemblance in this case is not for protection at all, but to enable the mimic to live more successfully as a parasite—providing the word parasite can be used for an animal that lives with, but not on or in, another animal, and that now-and-then eats little pieces of him but does him no serious harm in the process. I don't care what you call the scale-eating fish. The word parasite makes me think of ticks and tapeworms; and the word predator brings visions of lions and barracudas. The scale-eating fishes are not like any of these, and they don't seem to fit well into other slots that animal sociologists have set up for the kinds of relationships that exist between species in nature either.

Nevertheless the *capitao* is clearly guilty of a deception, a form of concealing resemblance; and it is a particularly underhanded kind, it seems to me. It is not the usual sheep-in-wolf's-clothing kind of mimicry, but a wolf-in-sheep's-clothing kind. By looking like a *chambo*, a *capitao* is able to go and come at will among *chambos*, accepted in good faith as a fellow, with normal motives and appetites. Then all at once, without any warning, a *capitao* will turn on a *chambo* that he has been consorting with amiably and take hold of his caudle peduncle. The caudle peduncle is the narrow place where the tail fin joins the body. The *capitao* has no intention of biting the peduncle off and taking it away, but the *chambo* has no way of knowing this. In a panic he struggles to free his tail, but the *capitao* keeps biting down hard with the lot of rasp-like, flat-topped teeth he has; and when finally the *chambo* does get loose, a few of his scales are always left behind. These are the diet of the *capitao*. That is his way of living. I don't know what you call that way of living, but mimicry is certainly involved. And it is one of the most reprehensible forms of mimicry that I have ever heard of.

In a way, the *capitao-chambo* intercourse suggests an odd kind of fish partnership known as "cleaning symbiosis." In the sea there are at least two dozen known kinds of fishes that make their living by removing and eating parasites from some other kind. Most of the cleaners police the outside of the host, but some of them enter its mouth and rid it of interlopers there. Though suggestive of the scale-stealing habit, this cleaning role is really fundamentally different from what the *capitao* does. The cleaners contribute a useful service, while the *capitao* only pilfers from his victim. He is no better than the mosquito that takes juice out of a man. He is worse. The mosquito comes openly, in his own clothes. He even tells of his coming by the bravado of his buzzing. The *capitao* comes quietly, in the garb of the trusting victim.

Although there seem at first to be important differences between predation, parasitism, and the various kinds of mutualistic exchange as ways of life, the evolutionary shift from the one to the other is probably fairly easy. For instance, cowboys on the Pacific side of Central America drive cattle into rivers and make them stand there deep in the water while hosts of little silvery fishes pick the ticks off their hides. This is obviously a profitable give-and-take arrangement, to both fish and cattle. Cattle are of course not indigenous to the Central American landscape, but in the racial memory of the fish they probably represent some more natural member of a former fauna—deer, bison, or other big mammals the fish may have lived with in past times. Anyway, the cows get rid of their ticks and the fish get fed. But then, just as nature is seeming grand, I shall reveal that we used to go swimming in the rivers where those fish were, and that they would all come running in swarms to pull and tweak at the moles on our backs. Though we slapped at them furiously, they never went off for more than a yard or so, and quickly came back to snap at the moles again. They would keep it up until the moles started bleeding and we left the water in disgust. In this aggravating habit, the courtesy the fish had done the cows was obviously moving over toward the sort of clear disservice the *capitao* does the *chambo*. And then, to see the full circle of this odd adaptative eddy, consider that this tick-plucking, mole-snipping fish is a close relative of the redoubtable piranha of South American rivers, which removes not moles but moderate gobbets of meat out of horrified cows, peccaries, or people.

In another way, what the *capitao* does to the *chambo* is like the relationship known as social parasitism. Ants have guests that live in their anthills, and some of these have come to look like ants. Cowbirds and European cuckoos are notorious for leaving their eggs in the nests of other kinds of birds. A kind of cuckoo usually parasitizes a particular kind of host bird. Some cuckoos have eggs that are similar in markings to those of the involuntary foster parent—more like those, that is, than like the eggs of any other cuckoo. The young of some cuckoos, incidentally, have hollow backs that help them push their fledgling foster brothers out of the nest. The only social parasitism I ever heard of among fresh-water fishes was the two cases discovered by my wife, Marjorie. Marjorie worked on the life history of the largemouth black bass at the University of Florida. In studying bass embryology, she began to notice that eggs from a single nest sometimes hatched into larvae that eventually grew into two different kinds of fishes. Some of the fry were proper little bass. What the others were remained a mystery for several days. Finally they got big enough to identify, and the extra fry turned out to be chub suckers. Before Marjorie had finished her work, she found six nests in which sucker eggs were mixed in with the bass eggs. All were being guarded and fanned by bass parents, and even after the fry had got their swim bladders and had begun schooling over the nest, the male continued to guard his mixed brood of little bass and suckers.

If there is one noticeable thing about young chub suckers it is that they look like young largemouth bass. If you get yourself a bowl of one-inch suckers and one-inch bass and stand off five feet away and watch them, you will have a lot of trouble telling the two apart. The color pattern is the same and there is no conspicuous difference in the form of the body. You have to hold them close to see what they really are. Up close and inside, the two turn out to be as different as a dog and cat. But as larvae or eggs on the bottom of the nest, and as fry all in one school together, they look like the same kind of fish. I don't say this is mimicry, but I do say it is so.

A few years later Marjorie found another case of social parasitism in fish. There was a creek behind our house. Marjorie had still not started having a lot of children, and in her moments away from housewifery, she began to observe the nesting habits of another sunfish, known locally as stump-knocker, that lived in the creek. One night when I came home, Marjorie met me at the door and said, well, she had done it again. She looked as if she had done something wrong, and was dejected about it. I asked what the trouble was and she said, "I've got them again," and I tried to think what she might have again, wondering if it could be some minor disease she might have had before, which I had forgotten. But then she led me in to the dining room table, and there was a binocular microscope on it, with a finger bowl under the objectives. She pointed at the bowl and said, as if she had termites in the walls or worse and might start crying about it, "They're in there too. There's something else in there with the stump-knockers." I looked down through the scope and could only see a lot of fish larvae lying around on their sides as they do. They all looked pretty much the same. It was only a matter of a different oil droplet, as I recall, that Marjorie was in a sweat about; but she had grown sensitive to the signs. And sure enough, sets of eggs from stump-knocker nests began growing into fry of stump-knockers and fry of something else. This time the foster children turned out to be not suckers, but golden shiners. And this time we were both able to watch the social parasites in the creek going about their sly work, the two sexes dashing into the clean-swept nest of the sunfish when his back, as it were, was turned, and reproducing right there in the flash of an eye on the run. It was the fastest job of fertilization I ever saw. A rabbit would seem slothful by comparison.

   This second case of social parasitism was too much for Marjorie's ichthyological career. She got a master's degree, but she never went on for a Ph.D. She published her observations, but those on the bass were read by probably a dozen people in all. None of them were fish people and most of them are probably dead by now. The stump-knocker paper most likely was never read by anybody.

Besides the scale-eating cichlids, at least three other sets of closely related Nyasa fishes all eat the same thing in the same places in the lake. For instance, Geoffrey Fryer found a cluster of 27 species, belonging to 9 different genera, all living together on the rocky sections of the shore and all feeding on algae. Twelve of these are members of a single genus. They all scrape off the thick mat of algae that covers most Nyasa rocks. Another group of species eats only bloodworms and other little animals that live in the bottom mud. Another suite of 16 related kinds all strain animal plankton out of the open water.

It is plain that no ordinary adaptive radiation, no usual process of evolutionary role-filling, has produced this fantastic fauna. Obviously, none of the familiar sorts of barriers to interbreeding are keeping the skeins of fish life apart in Lake Nyasa. How then can the anomaly be explained? What features of the lake, what factors of history, what innate foibles of cichlid germ-plasm, have worked to mold this strangest brotherhood of fishes in all the earth?

One thing that most people who have pondered the species-flocks have mentioned as a probable factor is the great age of the lake—or rather, the combination of its long life and the drastic changes in level it has undergone. Nobody knows how long there has been water in the Nyasa section of the Great Rift. Maybe there has been a lake there since the Miocene, possibly even much longer. What matters most is that during the stressful times of the Pleistocene, when in temperate regions ice ages alternated with warm times, Central Africa was having what are known as pluvial and inter-pluvial cycles, an alternating sequence of rainy periods and droughts. During the dry inter-pluvial times most lakes probably disappeared. But because of its great depth, Nyasa kept its water. Falling levels may have subdivided it into smaller lakes, however, and these may have stayed separate for varying times and then run back together again. This history of repeated fragmentation may account for some of the speciation in the lake. In any case, the overall long life of water in the Nyasa basin surely is deeply involved in the bizarre make-up of the modern fauna.

Even though modern Lake Nyasa is one body of water, and not a particularly varied one, it nevertheless has features that could tend to reduce breeding contacts among its fishes. The ends of the lake are very far apart, for one thing; and the shore zones of the two sides, where most fishes live, are for most kinds of inhabitants effectively separated from each other by the deep water and oxygenless lower depths of the interior of the lake. Moreover, as Fryer points out, the shoreline is not by any means homogeneous. It is a chain of alternating habitats, with rocky shore following sandy shore all around hundreds of miles of margin. Fishes could pass easily back and forth in any adjacent pairs of these habitats. But the enormous linear extent of the shore would almost surely reinforce any parochial tendencies that might arise in more widely separated populations, and would also tend to preserve differences inherited by the fishes from ancestors that lived in the separate dry-age lakes.

That is to say, the alternation of rocky and sandy shoreline, and the fragmentation of the lake basin in the dry inter-pluvial times may have worked together both in building diversity into the Nyasa fishes and in furthering the queer duplication of life roles that they show. If the lake periodically became half a dozen smaller lakes; and if each lasted for a time long enough for its fishes to undergo small hereditary changes in ways and structure; and if the water then came up again and the little lakes all ran together, the big lake would now have six slightly different sets of fishes in it. Each set would include kinds of fishes specializing in all the usual, expected roles. Each of the six specialists would be a little different from its counterpart because it had developed while isolated from them. Perhaps this history accounts for the beginning of the diversity. If the various slightly different faunas of the inter-pluvial lakes were dumped back into a perfectly homogeneous environment, a lot of them would no doubt breed together and become one again, or would compete so violently that most of them would disappear. But in the 800-mile ring of alternating shoreline environments, some sequestering would occur. Any sequestering would be bound to help preserve differences, and might even reinforce them.

Earlier students of the Nyasa species-flocks had the impression that there are few carnivorous fishes in the lake, and suggested that low predation might account for the exuberance of the evolution there. That reasoning is hard to follow. There is really no need to try to follow it, however, because predation is not low in the lake at all. Fryer pointed out that there is actually an extraordinarily long list of fish-catching fishes, both among the cichlids and among the few non-cichlid kinds, and that this feature may itself have something to do with the speciation riddle. Pressure exerted by the carnivores might work in two quite different ways. The inroads of violent predation might favor the evolution of new species by keeping the sizes of populations low and keeping them from eliminating one another by competition, even though they might still be so similar that they would have essentially the same roles in the ecology of the lake. What Fryer is really saying here is that the predators keep the subdividing bloodlines from violating Gause's Principle, the rule that says that no two animals can occupy the same niche. This simply means that they cannot have exactly the same roles in the life of the community. This seems logical, and even self-evident. But it is only true if the roles in question are filled to capacity. So long as they are not, you can keep putting all the animals in them you want to and competition will not eliminate them. So in Nyasa, Fryer says, the heavy predation keeps the niches from filling up and many different bloodlines are able to go on sharing in the exploitation of the same opportunies.

The other way in which the carnivores would abet evolution would be by weeding out the ill-adapted and therefore weaker individuals in each population—by grabbing off any fish that strayed from its habitat or from the narrow path of its growing adaptive specialty. I judge this is a sound idea that nobody would quarrel with.

There is still another way in which the drain imposed by fish-eating predators might possibly further evolution among the cichlids of the shore zone. It might just possibly favor the sort of chance changes in hereditary make-up known as "genetic drift." To go into this would lose me readers right and left, and I don't intend to do it. But the idea is worth thinking about, if one is inclined that way.

An attribute of cichlid fishes that somehow, and to some extent, has been involved in their prodigious branching is their own odd reproductive habits. Nearly all the members of the species-flocks—the groups in which subdivision has been most frantic—guard their young in their mouths. The advantages of mouth-brooding are easy to see. The habit brings some of the same advantages that mammals exploited when they hit upon the grand stratagem of internal fertilization. Instead of releasing thousands of tiny eggs into the hostile world to shotgun the forces against their survival, to hatch into clouds of feeble, mostly doomed larvae as a bass does, most female cichlid fish lay a few big eggs, and then cut down the odds against their survival by holding them and the fry that hatch from them in their mouth. The eggs they lay are bigger because they have more yolk in them. They produce better developed fry, which are more quickly able to fend for themselves.

As to the bearing of this habit of mouth-brooding on the formation of species-flocks, the reasoning is as follows. Most fish that build nests on the bottom of a lake have to make drastic changes in their way of life at breeding time. They leave their places and their special roles in the environment and move to wherever the proper nesting ground may be located. Here they build a nest, court, and spawn, and one sex or the other—or both—stays on to tend the fry till these are able to leave. No matter where a ground-nesting fish may live, or how it makes its living, when breeding time comes around it has got to stop what it is doing and move away to the bedding ground. No matter how specialized a fish may be for living profitably in strange ways during most of the year, at nesting time it must give up its specialty and move away to build a nest and care for a cloud of fry. So, ground nesting can be thought of as a factor that damps down specialization.

Mouth-brooding, on the contrary, can be thought of as furthering it. The mouth-brooder produces young in a well-developed state, ready for successful living. They are not even faced with the need to move to whatever distant place their parents came from for the nesting season. The plan exposes the parent fish to no alien surroundings and requires of them no drastic changes in their habits. The young are born, reared, and released in the same habitat they will occupy as grown-up fish. Mouth-brooding thus takes away some of the penalty of specialization. It is probably no accident that most of the explosive evolution in the East African lakes has happened to mouth-brooding fishes.

Geoffrey Fryer, who must be a very thoughtful fellow, suggested that this habit the cichlids have of guarding their young in their mouths may in another, more specific, way help explain their plasticity. He pointed out that the plankton-straining fishes in the Nyasa fauna, like herring and anchovies in the ocean, all travel in schools. They don't cruise separately around, filtering food out of the water like a whale, but move about their constant business in beautifully drilled and integrated bands. Why fishes travel in schools is not well understood. Nearly all pelagic kinds do it, however; and since plankton-straining is bound to take a fish out into the open water, there is a close bond between schooling and the habit of feeding on the small things suspended in the water.

Fryer's idea is that the mouth-brooding habit would make it easy for the schooling habit to be built into a race by simply retarding the development of the fry. This is a fairly common way for evolution to work. In the case of the Nyasa cichlids it might operate this way. When a mother mouth-brooder spits out her fry, they all stay close together in a tight little crowd, moving about together to pick out of the water the tiny bits they eat. In the case of the baby fish, the main advantage of schooling no doubt is that it keeps them ready for the mother to take back into her mouth if danger arises. With this juvenile tendency to school in its background, a strain of cichlids should find it no great evolutionary trick at all to move into the plankton-straining way of life. Instead of having to be fitted out with new equipment—new habits, outlook, and anatomy—a population could enter the open-water niche by simply switching hormones around a bit, so that the infantile nursery schools could grow to maturity without giving up their childish social and feeding habits. That this is what really happened in Nyasa obviously cannot be proved. But it looks like a logical and expedient way to fill a niche that has been entered an astonishing number of different times by the fishes of the lake.

It seems obvious that no one theory will ever explain all the evolutionary escapades of the Lake Nyasa fishes. The explanation must be a composite one. It must have been a chance combination of factors that caused the riotous branching of this limb of the tree of life. Features of both the lake and of the fishes themselves must have worked together to bring it about. The exuberant subdividing happened because the lake is old; because through its long life it has varied markedly in level, and has been at times a lot of smaller lakes; because most of the fishes are thinly deployed along hundreds of miles of shore, in a sequence of different environments. Heavy predation by carnivores may have goaded strains out into subtle enclaves, and the habit of mouth-brooding may have taken away some of the usual penalties of specialization.

I hope it will not bother anybody if this is not all clear. It is not all clear to anybody, I am sure. But light does come through here and there, it seems to me, in fascinating ways. The light is uneven, but it is a comfort to know that there is time to go on pondering. The Lake Nyasa fishes, like the kungu there, are out of the main rush of ruin that is changing the African earth. The time is not far off when the last lion landscape will be fenced about or scraped away. The last Masai will put on shoes one of these coming decades, and the last crocodile will bake in his drained bog or go off to the zoo. But long into those times, two of the old wonders of Africa will last on in spite of us. The kungu will teem up out of the cold mud and climb to the clouds. And the cichlid fishes will go on living the fine-spun secrets of their lives.

The Snake

THE PROPELLER raced and caught air, lost its grip and spun free for an instant. The motor coughed and quit. The boat settled and took the speed of the stream, then slowly turned beam-on to the current and drifted down in front of the thatch-and-wattle village on the bluff. The snake and I rolled together in the bilge.

It would have been bad enough if I had been alone with the crisis, drifting there in the pretty white boat with the dead motor and the angry python. But I was nowhere near alone. The noise of the motor on the river had brought an idling of little Nyanja boys to the edge of the bluff, and it must have been the urgency in my movements that made them wave up a lot more of their kind. When the motor stopped in mid-stream, it was cause for adult interest. When it began to be made out that I was hauling lengths of snake out of the works of the engine, it was no time at all before the whole village stood there on the Shireside cliff. As I continued to pull out resisting meters of python and stand on them, a murmur ran along the shore. Then the whole snake and I tumbled back out of sight in the bottom of the dinghy, and for a while the people could see only an arm or a leg, or a rising arc of snake. The voices grew to a long hum, and from that to a roar of pure African wonder over the ritual madness of bwanas.

But the sight I made there in front of Ntundu Village was not the worst of my position. The three-mile current of the Shire was sweeping me down to the landing at our camp, where Lewis and George and a number of lighthearted British engineers would be coming down to see my bag and learn what meat there might be for the next day. Telling about it, I capture—I am recaptured by— the same feeling of frenzy with which I scrambled out of the heap of snake, hopped over the seat, and stood trembling in the bow, clawing about my mind for what could be done to save some shred of dignity for the landing. Or even to make a landing at all.

It was not all my fault, really, this mess I was in. It was not as if I had gone off half-cocked in the python venture —had gone off to East Africa wholly mindless of pythons. I met pythons early, in the Bicolored Python Rocksnake that whipped the Elephant's Child in Kipling's *Just So Stories;* and I have cherished the idea of pythons ever since. As a zoologist I even acquired a smattering of python herpetology—I never plunged headlong into the subject exactly, but picked up an odd fact as I went along. I knew that the Royal Python of India was probably the longest snake in the world, with a top length of at least 28 feet; that the African species is the rock python, known technically as *Python sebae,* and found all over the tropical parts of the continent; that it gets to be maybe 18 feet long and, when grown, can eat medium-sized antelope and pigs and calves. I knew that pythons rarely bothered people if they acted decently, although Arthur Loveridge told of a credible case of a python that killed a well-behaved woman in Tanganyika.

So you see I had some grounding in pythons. It wasn't a specialist's grounding, but for my shortcomings I had the ready excuse of the half-versed: I knew where to *find* the answers.

And besides, I had in my head one item of python lore that was real proof of foresight. On the way out to Africa we had waited over a day in New York for our plane to London. One of the things I did that day was go by the Bronx Zoo and ask Jim Oliver how big a python a man could handle alone. I remembered that Raymond Ditmars or somebody said you needed a man for every four feet of snake, plus one for each end. I never put much stock in that. I had caught ten-foot boas. There turned out to be nothing but common sense required in the operation, and hardly room on an eight-foot snake for the three men called for by Ditmars's formula. So I asked Jim what a man could expect to do by himself, and he said it depended on the man, and while I disliked the way he looked at me when he said it, I pressed him till he suggested 14 feet as a conservative figure. This seemed a little big, but Oliver is a sound man—a scientist, a celebrated serpent-husbandman, and now Director of the American Museum of Natural History. I had no cause to doubt his word.

I took the 14-foot figure and clung to it all the way out to Africa. It was there the day I caught the python I was telling about. Otherwise you may be sure I would simply

The Snake

have shot the snake on sight and skinned it. Fourteen feet as an abstract dimension may not sound lethal; but see it in snake, live and self-possessed in the quiet woods, and it is a vaster dimension than you think.

Besides that fundamental datum, my field equipment that day was a borrowed rifle, a ten-inch collecting bag, and an almost reverent feeling of being alone in the unaccustomed role of hunter in the stillness of Africa. I was not after pythons at all. Three days before, I had taken out the rifle and killed a little antelope for the camp. This livened our victualing for a day, and the esteem the contribution brought me from my housemates tempted me to try again.

On the settled Ntundu side of the Shire there was little left to shoot. I took the clinker-built English dinghy with the long-shanked Sea Gull outboard motor and kicked up the river beyond the village to look for the mouth of a creek on the other side. After a couple of runs into dead-end coves, I found a break in the sudd, the densely rafted, floating vegetation, and turned into it. The inlet opened into a little bay that was hidden by tall grass on its shoreward side and flanked by drifted rafts of misty-headed papyrus and a jetty of blue-green water lettuce. There were hippo runs through the wall of cane grass. The still pool of the bay was set with frosted pads and blossoms of a blue lily. A little breeze tossed the heads of the papyrus, and they swirled on their stems like blown smoke against the blue sky across the river.

There was a mound of low treetops on the shore. I headed for it and found an opening, hovered by the trees, hardly broader than a hippo run but clearly the mouth of a creek. There was fast water rushing out of the creek. When I ran the fat hull over the fan of outflow and into the hole, the boat staggered and slipped and I had to put on power to push between the crowding banks. The harsh swell of the racket was a scandal in the peace of the place. The dim light under the trees and the rise of worn ground and spread of parkland behind the head-high levee all put the spell on me and suggested game, and demanded quiet above all else. But for a moment I could only sit and buzz and tilt with the sluicing current till I crept abreast of, and then a little above, the clean-sloped bank where the trees were. Then I turned quickly and dashed in under the swooping limbs and cut the engine. The bow whispered on the clay in the quiet of the shore.

I stepped out and pulled the boat higher on the bank. I tied the painter to a vine, picked up the rifle, and climbed the slope to the terrace. It was a good-looking place. In Nyasaland any country that lets you see in sweeps is good to come on. Most of the land is chaparral on the slopes and tall grass in the bottoms, and though you may hear fauna, your eye can rarely pull free from the clutter and see what made the noise. But here in the triangle between the river and the creek, there was a terrace covered by short grass, except where it was burned bare by drought, and densely wooded only where old termite hills rose like Indian mounds and made heaps of different soil that trees grew on. The Shire side of the plain dropped through a tangle of brush into a grass marsh and anchored sudd-fields, and toward the creek there was real forest in a narrow strip along the flood levee. There was room in the place, and an unhindered feel—your eyes could find ways to see without probing. Even in the creek forest there were long lanes for free seeing among the trees.

I came upon a lot of little traces that led away from the banks of the creek and river, and converged and headed inland along the outer edge of the levee forest. The trail

The Snake

they ran into was a deep old thoroughfare. There were new tracks in it, in the thin dust layer over the hard clay. Among these were hoofmarks of big antelope, and they seemed to validate the setting. I kept to the straw-free center of the trail and walked with all the quiet I could keep. As the trail ran along, side tracks kept coming in, some from the woods along the creek, some from old sloughs or dry oxbows on the plain, which now was filling with a confusion of brush and Raphia palms. It was the most promising game trail I had ever walked on—old as the land and deep-cut with the ages but clearly a current way for creatures of many kinds. There were tiny hoofprints no bigger than your thumb and tracks as big as those of a yearling steer. The dust was nowhere marked by the footprint of a man.

I had followed the trail for perhaps two hundred yards when a guapi, one of the tiniest of antelopes, jumped from behind a bush to the right. Without thinking I threw the gun up and shot. The guapi bounced away untouched and I suddenly felt low and inadequate, not because I had missed but because I had wrecked the quiet and promise of the woods for a mere guapi. Maybe that was my shot, I thought, the one shot the woods would allow in the distance I would walk before dark. I thought this out before I shucked the empty cartridge out of the rifle, and I stood there quiet for a while, somewhat disgusted with myself. Then I started easing the bolt handle to empty and refill the chamber, and all of a sudden a new image began to condense and I froze stiff, with the bolt handle half way up.

The trail ahead ran in a long aisle of brush-free ground for a hundred and fifty yards or more. Down this freeway there was nothing to catch the eye to the end; but at the curve of the trail, a buff solidity blotted the green of the brush. Far and still as it was, it was surely the shape of a great live thing; and then slowly I saw that it was a tall, proud kudu bull standing crosswise in the trail, still as a tree, looking straight at me as I looked at him.

In the weeks before, we had been hunting mostly mosquitoes with tea strainers, forceps, and aerosol bombs. I had seen no other proud big-game animal in the whole Shire Valley, and it seemed to me that this might be the only time it would ever happen. I remembered the crisis of my first white-tail deer, and shook a little, but not too much. Then I thought of the bolt of the rifle, still half unlocked from the guapi shot. Not moving anywhere else, I eased the handle on up till it freed for the slide, and it slid back soundless in its greased grooves till the cartridge was clear of the chamber. I caught the case between two fingers to damp the small clatter of ejection, and then started the bolt back the way it had come from. The new cartridge was engaged, lifted secretly out of the magazine, and nudged along to the chamber and seated there with no breath of a rattle. There remained only the hazard of locking the bolt-handle down, and I pressed it with hesitant force, to keep this last move silent; but the last snap got away from me, and a whisper of a click rent the woods like dynamite.

The kudu could have gone then, but he stayed on, still as a weathered snag suggesting the form of a kudu. I started raising the rifle to my shoulder and got the butt set on the outer end of my collarbone, bent to the sights, and lined up the ball and the pit of the buckhorn and held there, with the field of kudu shoulder broader than my range of trembling. Then, not hurrying and hardly tense any more because I had him, I laid on the slow mounting pressure and waited with all confidence for the bang. But a hair before the firing pin let go, a crash down

The Snake

the lane stopped my pressing finger. There was a blur over the sights—then green showed, where a second before the kudu had hidden the green. I dropped the butt of the gun to the ground and stood looking down the trail at where the game had been.

I was standing there like that with the waning feel of the kudu, sinking back slowly into being only a man walking with a gun, when a certain slight sound grew behind me, and a suspicion with it grew to certainty. An unseen creature in the brush took shape in my mind. It was that way that I came upon the snake.

Most people have probably never noticed the sound a snake makes in its unhurried traveling. People are generally too noisy to hear the subtle noise of snakes; and once confronted by a snake the average man is so upset by the sight that he has no mind for the noise. Even a big indigo snake prowling is not often heard—even a boa on dry leafmold must be listened for, and once you have verified the source of the sound it will have stopped or changed because the snake will be coiled in defense or moving off in precipitous flight.

The noise of a prowling snake is like no other animal sound I know. It is maybe most like the pervading many-footed whisper of army ants advancing. The sound trail of other animals is a broken, usually rhythmic, pattering or pounding, a set of footfalls or of separately snapped twigs or of repeated rustlings, thumps, or crashes. Even a four-inch ground skink, one of the smallest quadrupeds, if heard at all lets you know he has legs by covering the ground in audible starts and stops, and not by flowing over it as a snake flows.

In a way the progress of a snake is itself a series of separate steps. A snake moves by the separate efforts of his many belly-scales, each of which tilts downward, reaches forward, and then claws back to shove its section of the body along. But looking down on a snake you see little of this, and listening you hear none of it, any more than you hear as footfalls the marching noise of army ants. As the snake slips forward, the separate sounds of the inching ventrals stirring a straw here, breaking a leaf blade there, run together in a stream of whispers more like the wind than like any animal walking. I am not talking about the racket of a scared snake looping away in disgust from under your blundering feet, lashing the dry brush in crackling panic. And I don't mean the obviously noiseless moving of a snake on your lawn, or on bare sand. I remember a diamondback rattlesnake in the Ocala Scrub of Florida that wandered right up to the stump where I sat waiting for deer. The first I heard was the strumming of his scales on the scales of the bark a yard beneath my rump. But that was the Scrub, where the sand is silent under a moving snake. The thing to listen for is the slight, hissing whisper of the unhurried snake in dry brush or leaf litter. It is a sound not many people know, but one all their ancestors knew, and one likely to stir ancestral juices when suddenly you know you hear it.

It was such a sound that took the place of the lost kudu on the trail beside the creek. I had heard the sound before, and though the volume of it coming out of the ledge of thorn behind me was outside of my experience, it was no real surprise when I turned and peered for an opening through the tangle and saw the pattern of a python.

I hope I have made it clear that, in a general way, I was not unprepared for pythons. I had Jim Oliver's word that with average sense and agility I ought to subdue a python 14 feet in length. So now, when I had made sure the snake in the brush was a python, I circled for a view that would let me see most of him at once. I tested his

The Snake

length, pacing off his yards with my eye. It was an easy estimate because the snake was at peace and his bends were shallow. I made him out to be a 12-foot python. This gave me, if Oliver was right, two feet of grace—but even so, the snake looked alarming. I began to think that I really had no use for such a python—that I ought to wait for a three-foot specimen that would fit my collecting can. But this was only rationalizing. The python at hand was my first, and there was no way out for either of us.

I calmed myself a little. I took off my shirt and rolled it up and walked straight into the brush with the snake. He jerked back with a hiss and made a high pile of coils, pushed his head toward me on half a yard of neck, and blew softly, flapping his long tongue in the air. I moved one of my feet at him and he pulled his head in; then I did it again and he struck. Before his mouth shut I tossed the balled shirt in among his teeth and before he could spit it out I pinned down his head with the butt of the rifle, reached down and grabbed the slim neck, dropped the gun and ran my other hand back to the start of the second yard and squeezed hard there. I put my feet on what was left over, and then waited a little to see who it was who really had whom.

The snake took it well—as well or better than I did. His attitude seemed to be that, while he was big, I was bigger, or at least bigger around, and that the burden of the next move therefore lay on me.

It was a burden too. No plan at all occurred to me. Just temporizing, I let go with one hand, reached back, and pulled my collecting bag out of a back pocket. It was a good collecting bag, one of half a dozen my wife had made—eight-ounce duck and deeper than bag-shape, with double seams outside and with tie-strings sewn to the lip. It was a good bag for general collecting.

For the specimen at hand, it was just right for the head and first eight inches of neck; and I put that much of him in it, by pulling the mouth of the bag back onto his neck and tying the drawstrings snugly. After hauling the snake out of the brush and into the middle of a spread of clear ground, I let go and stood watching him for a while. He waved his sacked head about in an aimless way and made no move to leave. I saw that I had a little time to think.

I walked slowly back to the boat, groping for ideas. There was a tin tackle box in the stern and I opened it idly but there was nothing there related to pythons. There was nothing under the seats or up in the bow, and I was about to go back to the snake when my eye fell on the mooring line. It ran from a ring on the stem for a good 25 feet up the bank to the vine where I had tied it. It was half-inch manila, fat from use and wettings. I loosened the ends of the rope and took it out to where I could keep an eye on the white sack waving in the air. I had never heard of tethering a snake. I thought a while and then turned two half hitches together in the middle of the rope, walked over to the snake and slipped the hitches over his head and out onto his midsection, where I drew them together in a firm clove hitch. At headward intervals I rigged two more separate clove hitches, and then tied a couple behind the middle, leaving untrussed only the tail section and the bagged head. The rope was damp and the hitches held their form and pressure. I sat and studied the result of my random maneuvering. The snake could still move about, after a fashion. I looked at my watch and figured I had about two hours left for a walk, if I could get away. But it seemed likely that in that time the snake would work his problem out and be gone when I got back. There was a yard of extra rope at the

The Snake

neck end, and that gave me an idea. I cut off the piece, separated the three strands, and joined them end-to-end. Then I pulled the snake under a thorn tree, bent a low limb down by sitting on it, and whipped the snake's rope-loops to the limb with half a dozen turns of the pieced-out line. When I let the limb up, it raised the python part way off the ground in an awkward and no doubt annoying way. By this time I was pretty confused as to what I had been doing, and could only hope the snake was too.

I picked up the rifle and walked back to the trail. I found the slashed ground where the kudu had sprung away. For a minute or two I stayed there thinking about him, then I walked on, making up for the heedless noise of the half-hour before by not cracking a twig or rustling a leaf. The trail climbed a low ridge and I heard the clamor of guinea hens down the crest, but I was wrought up by the kudu and the python and had no stomach for stalking guineas with a nine-millimeter rifle. The trail left the ridge and broke up into a welter of walkways on a parcel of short-grass savanna. Some of the raveling trails made off toward the creek, some climbed the ridge in different places and cut back toward the river, and one led into higher grass that fringed an expanse of open plain. This last seemed to offer the best way for seeing, and I took it. I walked twenty minutes or so through grass higher than my head, sure each moment that I would come upon something to shoot, because it was hard for me to think of East Africa and grass without game.

As the trail veered away from the creek forest, the grass got shorter and there was promise of open country in the light ahead. I had gone beyond the range of any alarm my earlier shot could have spread, and had seen no human footprint and heard no dog or children shrieking in the distance. I had got back the lone feel of wild woods, the feel that you need only seeing-room to see fine things. As the grass began to open and a landscape and horizon seemed sure to spread just beyond the thinning screen, I felt for the safety catch of the gun and brushed grass seeds from the sights and from my eyebrows, and did what I could to get ready for any crisis the plain might offer.

And all at once the crisis came. It was only a little noise at first, as the noise of the snake had been. But that sound had been familiar, while this one was wholly strange. It was an eerie, singing, buzzing hum that grew as I wondered, and swelled into a petulant whine that bored straight in to where I crouched. It came so fast and was so without parallel among woods-sounds of my past that I could only crouch and wait, not knowing whether to be ready for meat or to run away. The whine rose to a peak and I jumped back to let it pass, but nothing burst into the trail, and the pitch of the sound started falling in Doppler retreat across the savanna. I jumped up and saw a brown object skimming away grasstop high like a harrier hawk. I ran forward half a dozen paces and broke into a broad track at the edge of the plain, and saw a boy on a bicycle racing off along the border of the grass-brake. The bird planing over the grass tips was his Aussie hat. He also wore khaki shorts and shirt, and I could see a leather-bound canvas pouch hanging from his shoulder.

For no good reason I whistled and the boy skidded to a stop and looked back at me, questioningly but not with surprise. I started to ask him where I was, but then I realized that, if this was a place in which my presence was no surprise, it did not really matter where I was. There was no sense explaining this to the boy, so I just waved him on and said: *"Palibe kanthu,"* which is not exactly "never mind," but almost is.

The Snake

The boy stood there a moment studying my problem and then said, "You wish nothing, bwana?" and I said, "No thanks, I'm sorry I stopped you." He stayed a little longer, thinking about me, then grinned and said: "Well, good afternoon, bwana," and rode away.

If that encounter had happened later on in my stay in Africa I would not have been astonished. We eventually got to expect bicycles almost anywhere. You can walk half a day away from the last road and see nobody for hours, and then all at once a bicycle will burst from the bushes. Even in the highlands, where trails are rocky and grades are steep, there are bicycles everywhere. Down in the alluvial sections of the Rift the villages are connected by networks of trails that follow the old game trails. In the dry season these smooth up like asphalt and open the whole Shire Valley to the cyclist.

It used to be the Singer sewing machine that deflated the explorer when, three weeks back in the wilderness, he got to feeling intrepid. He pushed on through incredible hardships and added inches to the map. His hired help got nervous and things looked rum, and then he came to a squatting of huts so rude and remote he expected to find everyone busily shrinking heads, and by God they were all sewing away on their Singers!

It is the same way nowadays of course with Coca-Cola, or worse; and down in Honduras it was for years that way with green peas. I can't explain it, but canned green garden peas, *petit pois*—Delmonico's mostly, as I recall—long ago spread clear through the most inaccessible parts of the Honduranean uplands. They sat on the shelves of the poor little shops and took dust from the years, a tired mule's journey from where anybody knew where canned peas come from. I remember a far-off little settlement there, where it was a common belief that blue-eyed folks ate people. They never saw any blue-eyed people out there, but they thought that; and when somehow or other a wild-looking girl from there was cajoled into coming to do the washing for my family, which has blue-eyed people in it, the girl suffered a lot of mental anguish till she got to know us. It seemed to me that a place as sequestered as that *haldea* ought to be worth visiting, and I spent a day in a truck and on a mule going out to see it. When I got there I went into the only cantina in the place and found canned peas on the shelf.

Well, as I was saying, in backwoods Africa, or in the parts I have seen, the thing that sets you back when you are getting to feel far away is the English bicycle. There are sewing machines, and Coca-Colas too, but they are confined to the abodes of men—however remote the abodes may be. But the bicycle is the means of its own dispersal, and anywhere people walk you can look for bicycles. The Singers and cokes, and the peas too, all shock you by their ethnic incongruity—standing next to the blowgun or among the poison pots. The bicycle on the other hand turns up when you think you are stalking a leopard, or being stalked by one.

The boy who scared me in the grass was probably a minor government employee on some fiscal errand among the villages. I knew of no villages there, and was certainly out of reach of their sounds; but the bicycle took the heart out of the hunt, and I turned and went back the way I had come.

Going back I walked fast, giving up my stealth. The distance seemed shorter. I came out in the late afternoon on the flat by the mouth of the creek, and though the light was weakening, it was strong enough for me to see across to where I had left the python tied, and to see that he wasn't there. I ran across to the tree and found the

The Snake

loops still hanging and the five hitches all empty, each still holding the shape of its section of python. I went out into the clear and looked anxiously around. Over at the far side of the flat I saw the sack weaving and pushing at the air. Laying the rifle aside, I walked toward the sack, and before I had gone half way I made out the form of an animal there with the python, between him and the edge of the woods. It was a big dun-colored creature, and it was making short charges at the snake and then backing off in stiff-legged retreat. At first it looked like a lion, but its tail rose stiff and straight and I thought of an old male baboon. Then it moved into a streak of better light and I saw that it was a wart hog. I yelled and it saw me and dashed off into the brush with its tail standing up behind, stiff as a stick.

I got between the snake and the woods, only a few feet away, and looked him over for damage. There was none, and I wondered why, because the scuffed ground showed that the hog had been making his foolish charges for a good twenty feet back the way the snake had come. I took the python by the neck and slid him over the grass to the bank of the creek above the boat. I ran back, picked up the rifle, and returned to the creek bank. Dragging the snake down the slant of the shore, I started helping him into the middle of the dinghy.

Heaving him piecemeal like that over the high gunwale, I judged he would weigh fifty pounds or more, all good solid snake, firm-fleshed and glistening with a new skin. He was really quite a tractable snake too, all things considered; and lifting him into the boat that way, I conceived a mild affection for him and tried to remember whether pythons fed well in captivity. Perhaps I was thinking of keeping this one in camp alive. If that was actually what I had in mind, it was the first hint of any purpose that had entered my relations with the snake up to that time. Till now I had just followed a formless urge to dominate this biggest snake of my career, and maybe get him back to the camp to be seen and photographed, and to scare the Africans. I arranged him in a heap in the center of the boat, a little toward the stern, then pushed off and rode the current out into the bay, keeping in the stream with the one oar I had along. As we drifted I watched the snake closely, trying to decide how he was going to take the voyage. He seemed irritated by the feel of the water in the bottom, but his moves were aimless, and I could see no need to tie him. I paddled and drifted till the boat was out of the bay and into the main stream of the river, then I turned and cranked the motor.

At the first flurry of power, the python began to weave and loop, tickled, I suppose, by the vibration of the planking or by the shiver of tiny waves it set up in the bilge. I thought I might have trouble after all, and scratched off my shoes to free my feet for hands. Then, as the snake grew more restless, I leaned forward and grabbed his neck. To get the trip over faster I gave the motor gas and the bow lifted as we skimmed downstream on an angling course for the other shore. We were just off the upper end of the village on the bluff, and I was keeping down the loops the snake threw over the gunwales pretty well, when I noticed the rifle in the bow slipping down into the water on the bottom. That was when I made a mistake and brought on the circumstances mentioned earlier, and ruined any chance of amity between me and the snake.

I let go of everything and jumped forward to keep the gun out of the water. I was only up there about three seconds, but when I got back, the python was part way over the stern, threaded between the frame of the motor

The Snake

and the transom, with his bagged head trailing and skipping in the wake. I grabbed him at his midsection and pulled, and he drew in his head and took another turn into the bracket of the motor and threw a coil of his after-section around my leg. I pulled harder and heard his scales crack, but I took in only enough slack to skin the bag off his head and free it for better-directed resistance.

With his eyes free, the snake seemed to hate the sight of the water, and he hurried back over the stern and into the boat. I thought he was attacking me and jumped reflexively away. When I moved back, he did attack me, but he missed; and for the second time that day I ripped off my shirt and let him hit that, and then grabbed his neck while he chewed. Then I started pulling on the snake again, right-end first this time, pushing the back part out to pay for what I was taking in. It was tedious, unrewarding work, but the crowd on the bluff was enjoying it, and I was getting in the inches pretty steadily when the middle part of the snake crooked and jammed, and I tried to stand on the head for a moment to free my hands for working. My foot slipped off and the snake snatched at my leg and got by the grace of God only trousers in his teeth but scared me so I fell on the motor, which raced up and stalled. Without unhooking the snagged jaws, I got a good grip and pulled very hard. This time the whole hind half let go and I fell on my back in the bottom of the boat with the snake on top of me and the people on the bluff, as I have said, roaring.

It was only a little way from the village down to the camp. By the time I had pulled out of the melee in the bilge and stood up in the bow to figure what could be done, the boat was passing the landing. There was no one there, and that was a mercy, but the growing spread of upstream distance made me uneasy. It would be no use trying to paddle the beamy dinghy against the current with one heavy oar, and the shore water below the camp was too deep for poling. To get back, I would have to use the motor, and that would bring more trouble with the snake.

Unless I might be willing to let him go. I looked at him again. He was still half coiled but clearly on the verge of action. I thought that he had not sought this predicament we were in together, and for a little I could have let him slide over the side, if that was what he wanted, or maybe would have helped him with a kick if he still should have shrunk from the water. But then I thought of the reptile collection I was trying to make, growing so slowly and with no sign of a python in it; and holding hard to the feeling that the python was only a snake, I raised the paddle and broke his neck with the end of the blade.

Then I stepped back to the motor and started it and tacked up across the current toward the camp. When I was half way over, Lewis and George heard the sound of the motor and came walking out to the bluff. They got to the edge and peered out my way, trying to see what I had in the bottom of the boat. The light was too far gone to show what was there. Lewis yelled, and though the noise of the motor drowned the question, I knew he was asking what I had brought.

I said I had brought a snake.

The Bird and the Behemoth

THE HERONS were out among the cows when I got to the Prairie. I saw *them* first, and then I saw the dragline working.

I slowed the car to creep along, irked by the sight of the dragline, bemused for the thousandth time by egrets and cows together. Then one of the herons got up and flew in under the swooping dredge-boom and lit on the spoil pile, all white lace in the slop and splatter. He was a snowy heron, and his coming in to stand there, though a small, ill-sorted thing to see, was for me a last chink stopped in a long daydream. It was a dream of birds and behemoths and of the smallness of the world, and its essence is this: the snowy heron remembers mastodons.

Not personally, of course. I don't know how long snowy herons live. Longer than a sparrow, no doubt—less long, perhaps, than a parrot. But racially the snowy is, I'll bet, a tie with times when, faunally speaking, Florida stood shoulder to shoulder with Tanganyika today. It is as plain as old bones, or coprolites, or rotten ivory in a Florida roadcut. Slim and impermanent as snowy herons seem, their race is old enough to recall a lot, and it does. The snowy remembers mastodons as clear as day.

Paynes Prairie is fifty square miles of level plain in northcentral Florida, let down in the hammock and pinelands south of Gainesville by collapse of the limestone bedrock. Partly it drains into Orange Lake to the south, and partly into a sinkhole at its northeast side. The sink used to clog up once in a while, and for years or decades the Prairie would be under water. The people called it Alachua Lake in those times, and ran steamboats on it.

These days the Prairie is mostly dry, with shallow ponds and patches of marsh where ancient gator holes have silted up but never disappeared, and with patches of Brahma cattle here and there, out into the far spread of the plain, like antelope in Kenya. The Prairie is about the best thing to see on U.S. Route 441 from the Smoky Mountains to the Keys, though to tell why would be to digress badly, even for a book that is already mostly digressions. But everybody with any sense is crazy about the Prairie. The cowboys who work there like it, and tell with zest of unlikely creatures they see—a black panther was the last I heard of—and colored people fish for bowfins in the ditches. There used to be great vogue in snake catching on the Prairie before the roadsides became a sanctuary. People from all around used to come and catch the snakes that sunned themselves along the road shoulders. When William Bartram was there, the Prairie wrought him up, and his prose about the place was borrowed by Coleridge for poetry in *Kubla Khan*. The Prairie has changed since then, with all the wolves and the Indians gone. The deer no longer mix among the cows; no wild gobbler is there to strut when the jasmine grows gold along the rims. But still there are things to make a crossing worth your while, to make it, as I said, the best two miles in all the long road south from the mountains.

I live on one side of the Prairie and work on the other side. I have crossed it a thousand times. Two thousand times. And always it is something more than getting to work or going home. I have seen the cranes dance there, and a swallow-tail kite, and 765 snakes on the road during one crossing. And there was an early morning in October that I remember. It was after a gossamer day, a day when the spiders go ballooning in the sky. Through all the afternoon before, the spiders had been flying, young spiders and old, of a number of kinds, ballooning to new places in the slow flood of a southwest wind. Some of them traveled no more than ten paces, riding the pull of their hairthin threads for the space between two bushes. Some went by a thousand feet up, streaming off to Spain on jagged white ribbons like thirty feet of spun sugar against the sky. By nightfall the whole plain was covered with the silk of their landings. As far as you could see, the Prairie was spread with a thin tissue of the dashed hopes and small triumphs of spiders, held up by the grass tips, draped over every buttonbush and willow.

We drove by in the early, mist-hindered morning. The dew was down, and the drops were like strands of beads in acres of silken webbing. The fog had flaws in it here and there, and the sun coming through turned the plain all alive like a field of opals, and I slowed the car to look.

Up toward the east from the road, a Brahma bull stood in the edge of the sea of silk, and as I stopped on the shoulder across from where he was, he raised his head to look our way. He was stern and high-horned and stood straight up from the fore quarters, like an all-bull centaur. Suddenly the sunlight touched him, and my wife and I fell to beating at each other, each to be first to say, "Look at his horns." The old bull had gone grazing in the night and now his horns were all crosslaced with silk picked up from the grass. He stood there with the sun rising behind him and his horns were like a tall lyre strung with strings of seed pearls, gathered in the mist, and burning in the slanted light.

There is no telling the things you see on the Prairie. The sun rises at one end and sets at the other. To a taste not too dependent upon towns, there is always something, if only a new set of shades in the grass and sky or a round-tail muskrat bouncing across the blacktop, or a string of teal running low with the clouds in the twilight in front of the winter wind. The Prairie is a solid thing to hold to in a world all broken out with man. There is peace out there, and quiet to hear rails call, and the cranes bugling in the sky. It looks like Africa, out on the Prairie, looking off through the tawny plain to far bands of cattle like wildebeests in Kenya.

But it was not just the African look of the place that stopped me half way across, and brought on my digression. It was seeing the dredge and the heron there together.

I slowed down, as I said at the start, just to watch the egrets with the cattle; and to fret at the mess the dredge was making, sloshing about the old ditch, slinging muck about, scaring the cooters and congo eels. It was a big diesel dragline, a Lorraine 81. It was scooping fill for another pair of road lanes. It crouched in the mud on caterpillar tracks, and the steel boom that held the bucket up slanted away for sixty feet against the sky. In the shiny yellow cab a fat man snatched and shoved at a row of levers, barely able, it seemed to me, to keep up with the churning rhythm he was making. It was imposing, in the way of ponderous engines, the big, live-looking thing turning on the groaning bull gear, casting the brutal jaw, horsing up six-yard mouthfuls of spouting muck, and twisting to drop them on the growing fill. It was a gross, unlikely thing to see, a metal Brontosaurus sloshed out to wreck the plain in vast quest of Mesozoic tubers.

It was that sort of fanciful thinking that slowed me down. But as I started to crawl on by, the egret left his cow and came flying in to the dragline. Straight in under the swinging tower he flew, and lit on the piled new muck. I quickly looked up and down the road for a bump on a black-and-tan car that would mean a state trooper was coming. Seeing none, I pulled out onto the grass shoulder and shut the engine off.

I was only thirty feet from where the heron was, but it paid no heed to my being there. Its mind was all taken up with the fine things the dragline was spilling. Each time the bucket sucked out and rose, there seemed no way the heron could keep clear of the spilling mud. Each time the bucket dropped I looked for it to paste the bird flat with the splash. But always it jumped easily away and back again and fell to jabbing about and throwing its head up to juggle some squirming little animal and swallow it with hurried zest. Close in to the clamor and race of the engine, to the slap of cables and chains and chatter of drums and sheaves, it worked away, completely single-minded in its gleaning. *Drag, hoist, twist, drop, twist, cast, drag;* and the egret flapped in under the soaring bucket, and took up the sad, succulent creatures from the mud, out of the midst of their disaster.

For a time I watched as if watching any unmeaning oddity. Then I caught a quick smell of half-burnt diesel fuel, and it took me back, the way odors sometimes do, to the deck of the *Piri Piri* and the same smell in the air of a hot African afternoon, and to a flock of white herons standing on another plain with cows. Thinking about in time and space like that, I saw all at once that a change had blurred the form of the dragline by the road. A sort of flesh seemed to be filling out the steel bones of the engine, and before my eyes it took a fleeting mammal form—not solid, skinbound shape, you know, but an eerie, momentary show of creature stuff, partly condensed about the metal frame. You can't think how weird it was. It made me look hard; and after a bit I seemed to make out in the mist of meat, still working away, still sloshing about in the ditch, the form of an old bull mastodon.

It was only for a moment. Then a car went by, headed south. The driver glanced the way I was looking but quickly turned back to visions of his own, to whatever draws the Yankees down to the end of Route 441. That made it plain that I was seeing untrustworthy things, and I looked back and sure enough, the elephant had all ebbed away. The dredge was working for what it was, the motor straining at the drag chains and chattering through the turns, the steel mouth gnashing the muck to froth. But short as the stay of the elephant had been, it made sense of the heron's presence there. It made one more little piece in a pattern that first took a sort of shape in my mind half way around the world.

It was down below Megaza, on the twisting last reaches of the Shire River in Mozambique. We were nearing the Zambezi, at the time, running between natural levees that stood three feet or more above the bottomland beyond. Ever so often there were clots of huts on the narrow moraine, perched there for dry-season fishing or to house the tenders of slim patches of corn or tobacco along the levee. Once in a while there were bigger clumps of huts back where the hills began to rise, and when these were not too far away, people came running in strings across the plain to see the boat go by, the children all screaming, the women hurrying with jars on their heads, and breasts bouncing or swinging according to their time of life.

The thing that made the world seem suddenly small—the thing I remembered later when I stopped by the roadside to ponder the egret and the dragline—was a herd of cattle strung out along the shore, and burning points of white where herons stood among them.

We had set out down this last stretch of the River Shire at seven that morning. We had no very valid reason for making the trip. It was mainly just a stubborn urge to see the river out to its end. After spending two months getting to know the Upper River, the rapids and the lake, to go away without seeing the final reaches of the Shire seemed unthinkable.

The last 75 miles of the river—the part from just below Port Herald to the Zambezi junction—runs through Portuguese territory. The trip we planned was to be by launch, from Port Herald to the Zambezi and then upriver to the Mozambique town of Dona Ana, where our driver would be waiting with the Land Rover to drive us back to Nyasaland. This seemed an unpretentious intrusion upon Portuguese soil—the river people said we could make the whole trip in one long day if we found nothing to stop for on the way. But in spite of the unobtrusive character of the expedition, the Limbe Office was a long time getting the necessary authorization from the Portuguese officials in Laurenço Marques. For six weeks we kept everything ready to leave, and the proposal was studied by the Portuguese.

Meanwhile our office engaged a Portuguese launch for the expedition. Her name was *Piri Piri*. She was all banged up, rusted steel, hull deck and deckhouse. She was 45 feet long with a nine-foot beam. She had a flat bottom and shallow draft and a crew of five Portuguese Africans, including a pilot who knew the Zambezi channel. The name *Piri Piri* means hot, in the sense in which Cayenne peppers are hot. The ship *Piri Piri* was hot in another way. Being all iron and half filled with a vast old Kelvin diesel engine, she heated herself up badly; and she ran on the Lower Shire where the air is hot to start with. So *Piri Piri* was a good name for the launch, as we found out on the trip.

We waited six weeks before the expedition received the approval of Portugal. When it finally came, we set off lightheartedly in the Land Rover for Port Herald, the southernmost town in Nyasaland along the river where the *Piri Piri* was scheduled to be waiting. When we got to Port Herald, the *Piri Piri* wasn't there. She was somewhere off down the Zambezi, and though everyone said she would be back any time, she wasn't there just then. We got permission from the railroad to put up at its resthouse in Port Herald. We moved in and started waiting for the minute the *Piri Piri* might arrive.

The stay at Port Herald was pleasant, on the whole, in spite of the fact that we were waiting. There was plenty of work for us to do in the district. The waterfront was a scandal of bilharzia snails and there were villages all about this lowest end of Nyasaland where we had not yet collected mosquitoes. And across from the rest-house

The Bird and the Behemoth

there was a little grove of big trees, and the trees were full of a number of kinds of nesting birds. I spent a lot of time sitting on the shady veranda watching the birds with binoculars that brought them almost into my lap.

There were six trees with nests in them. The birds were black-headed herons, cormorants, pink pelicans, and maribou storks. Some of the trees had nests of all four in them. The tree farthest to the right, for instance, to my right as I sat on the porch, had nests of twelve storks, eleven pelicans, five herons, and two cormorants. It seemed a curious mixture of birds, and an odd place for them to be, right there in the center of the town. But the birds appeared to know what they were doing. Nobody bothered them. There was the river to fish in nearby and garbage around the town; and there were acacia trees near the grove where twigs could be had in abundance. Still, the birds looked pretty queer up there. Not the storks so much. You get used to the thought of storks in town. But the others, the pelicans—it seemed peculiar to see them, especially, so far from the sea and so near the railroad station.

Storks and cormorants occupied the highest places in the trees. Herons, evidently by choice, were in the lowest branches, and pelicans built throughout the body of the tree. In most of the stork nests there were two or three young birds, some of them able to stand up and be seen. They were covered with grayish fuzz. Even when they had big young, the old birds still continuously puttered about the nest, repairing or rearranging it, flying out now and then to pluck twigs from the acacia trees or pick them up from the ground. When the parent returned to the nest, there was usually a great fuss, because the young ones jerked and hauled at the new twigs as if to help with the work. Really, they only hindered it. Some storks and pelicans and one pair of herons had young about ready to fly. Most of the herons and all the cormorants either were just building nests or had eggs or small young. In both cormorants and herons, the two sexes appeared to co-operate in building the nest. I saw a male cormorant fly in with a stick, give it to the female, who was setting or brooding, and stand on the edge of the nest while she installed it. Sometimes one bird brought in the twigs, while the other stayed at the nest to receive the stuff and fussily work it into the structure. Sometimes both birds came in together with nest material.

I watched one pair of herons trying to decide where to locate their nest. I was looking at a female on a limb when a male flew in with a twig some 18 inches long in his beak and lit beside her. Immediately the two of them started poking and fidgeting about in a space of maybe a cubic yard. They kept at it for six or eight minutes before lodging the twig in a place that pleased them both. That was the start of their nest. Then for three days they puttered about near that spot before doing any more work there. When they finally resumed work on the nest, that was the site they built on.

Despite the heavy traffic in the trees and the constant coming and going between nests and the river, there was little wrangling among the birds. Once I saw a brooding cormorant crane her neck to adjust a twig too near the nest of a heron, and the heron jabbed at her and she withdrew. The herons were generally the most pugnacious. I saw one take a perch away from a pelican. The pelicans and storks seemed completely compatible. I saw no case of dispute or fencing between them. One pelican built so close to the nest of a stork that the two nests touched and even the bodies of the brooding birds

The Bird and the Behemoth

brushed each other when the wind blew, and there was never any sign of irritation.

Besides the nesting birds, some white herons—a species like the common egret but with a line through the eye—perched about the trees from time to time, and a flock of about 150 openbill storks came in each evening to roost. There were a few white ibis in the trees from time to time, and a great galaxy of palm swifts swirled about two *Borassus* palms at the edge of the rookery grove. For some reason the pelicans did a lot of flying around during the night, even in the black dark with an overcast sky and no moon. On the whole it was really fairly exciting there on the veranda, for anyone who likes to look at birds.

There was also the drumming and dancing of the local Africans to enliven the wait for the *Piri Piri*. The people around Port Herald are noted dancers. One day Wilson came in to say there was going to be a "nice dance of women with nine drums" in a village on the Zambezi road. We quickly got in the Land Rover and drove out to see it. We found a great crowd there, in a circle under the usual baobab tree. The drummers sat, or stood, in a row that made a chord across the circle of the crowd, and the dancers stood in front of them. The dancers were two girls and two old women, dressed in blue sarongs, beads, and dozens of tight rings of brass and copper on their shanks. One of the old women wore a python-skin girdle, and held a spear in one hand and a hatchet in the other.

At each dance the drumming started in a desultory way, and then quickly built a complex pattern of interlocking rhythms. The dancers danced by turns. As each came out she would stand for a minute or more with an ear cocked, listening critically to the melee of the drums, moving her arms and hips a little, feeling for her cryptic signal to come out of the cascading rhythm. Each made several false starts and quickly stopped in disgust, to try again to make the mystical connection.

The old crone was evidently the mistress of the dance. She danced as hard as any of them, but ever so often she got bent and had to be straightened out by two buxom young women in the crowd, who from time to time jumped into the ring, grabbed her, and squeezed her tightly around the middle. This seemed to take the recurrent crooks out of her back, and for a while afterward she danced like new again.

The movements of the dance were stylized, jerky, and without much meaning to me. Besides the chiropractic attention that the girls gave the old lady, the most engaging action was that of another pair of female attendants, like seconds at a prize fight, who sporadically sprang to the side of the dancer and rubbed the top of her head hard and then sat down again. The four women danced in turn for about half an hour, then suddenly the drums stopped and the dance was over.

The next afternoon the District Commissioner, who was justifiably proud of the rhythmic talents of the people of the district, persuaded the Mfumu of another village to arrange a dance for us. This one was a dance by thirty little girls, who seemed to be mostly between nine and fourteen years old. Their dance was a frank and very athletic fertility rite, devised, I should say, to bolster group confidence in their racial future. It certainly bolstered my confidence in their future. Their future numbers anyway. It would take a real pessimist to watch those little girls dance and doubt the ability of their tribe to go on repopulating the earth. For two solid hours they danced, ten separate numbers, one after another in quick succession. Each dance was a slight variation on a single theme, and the theme was procreation.

Like the women's dance the day before, the dance of the girls was accompanied by nine drums, played by five men. Seven of the drums were tall and thin, with tapering bases. They were tied in a row, graded in size, to a bar between two stakes and played by three men using sticks. To the left of this battery, there was a tall drum shaped like the high-pitched ones, but bigger, and at the far left there was a fat, cylindrical bass. Each of these two was supported by a stake, and played by a man, with his hands. Besides the drums, the older girls all had pairs of hardwood blocks to slap together, and the younger ones had tin-can rattles with pebbles in them.

There was a lot of fussing with the drums at first and the girls stood around looking as self-conscious in their g-strings as the fourth grade in a Christmas pageant. While two men were setting up the stakes to support the drums, others anointed the drumheads with a mixture of oil and ashes and warmed them at a fire. After half an hour of solicitous attention, the drums were ready, the girls formed a half circle in front of them, and the first dance began.

The girls with the blocks gave the beat: *bap-bap-bap;* the rattles went *shuck-shuck-shuck;* then the string of treble drums took over the time and started to cut it up, first one way and then the other, sort of idly at first, but with growing purpose; and while they were doing this, the baritone drum came in, and then the bass. Then the full symphony swelled and a girl jumped across the half circle and yelled, and every girl began to writhe and jerk, and then the drums exploded. The sound bulged out into a single throbbing mass, solid throughout, but textured by the wild arpeggios of the high-pitched tom toms, the racing syncopation of the baritone, and the pounding obligato of the bass. The *shuck-bap* sound of the rattles and blocks kept the basic beat, but the nine drums ranted off together like demons in monumental conclave, clamoring for a while in the ordered chaos of their chorus, then turning to gibber and groan at what the girls were doing.

It is a humbling experience listening to good African drumming and trying to understand it. You stand there watching thirty dancing girls and a crowd of a hundred people, all in mystical rapport with five madmen raving on drums, waiting through chains and webs of intervals that must be programmed in their genes; and the cryptic climaxes all come and pass without your even knowing.

Before I went to Port Herald I thought it was only the West Africans, the Nigerians above all, who did the very fancy drumming. But both they and the Port Herald people so quickly swamp the Western listener, so hopelessly flood his senses with their demoniac virtuosity, that comparing the two is not really feasible. It is like judging the sizes of two oceans while you are swimming in them. The Yorubas are bigger and better-looking people, and they use a greater variety of percussion instruments than the Senas do. But it seemed to me they know no more of the magic arithmetic of the art, and have no more of the unimaginable skill it involves.

There were ten dances, each only a little different from the one before, as I said. The girls worked with terrific verve, and though every move they made was on the face of it concupiscent, their attitude was detached, even uninterested, as if they might be only reciting the Shorter Catechism. I judge these dances were not intended as erotic exhibitions at all, in spite of the signs. Certainly the girls were not feeling erotic. Their parents didn't act erotic either. They all stood around in the ring looking proud and gratified, congratulating one another on some special sinuosity or invention of a child of one or the other of their number. I have seen parents in the same mellow state at a baton-twirling contest of drum majorettes. For all I know baton-twirling by majorettes may be some sort of subconscious modern American fertility rite. If so, I wish they would stop it. We don't need it. What we need, and the Africans too, is a good sterility rite. To conjure up more people nowadays is very irresponsible.

Like most people to whom Africa is a land of dreams, I had always been stirred by what I had read about talking drums—about using stretched skin or hollow-wood percussion instruments to send messages around, not as code, but as partly articulated language. We heard an example of this on Lake Malombe, and I inquired about it at Port Herald. The word there was that the art used to be known, but is not any longer. But talking around about drumming, I came upon a curiosity of musical ethnozoology. This was the hippopotamus dance. Wilson told me about it first, and then our driver translated a local African's account of how it is done. After that I asked the District Commissioner about it, and found him a sort of amateur authority on the hippopotamus dance. He said it is still used along the Lower River as a way of catching hippos, and he was not by any means positive that faith in the dance was empty superstition.

Hippos are still fairly common along some parts of the river. Whenever they and people live together, they are bad for agriculture. It would be hard to measure the misery that has come to Rift Africans, chronically teetering at the edge of famine anyway, through the disruption of their farms by two very different animals: baboons in the open dry country, and hippos in the river gardens.

So although it is edible, the hippo is hated by riverside people for its depredations. Because hippos live in the water, they are often lost if speared or shot with whatever antique firearm may be available. The water table in floodplain lands is high, and pit traps are not practicable. So the people harpoon the hippos, and this is much like harpooning an elephant. Some way to stop the creature's run and flurries is required. One way is to use a buoy on the harpoon line as in whaling. Another is a dramatic technique described to us at Port Herald by a man who had seen it used.

In this kind of hippo-hunting, a team of four men is used. They carry short spears and a heavy harpoon with a detachable barbed head tied to a coil of heavy bark rope. The other end of the rope is fastened to a ponderous but portable stake that is sharpened at one end. The rope is tied just back of the sharp end. The hippo is stalked on land, usually when a report comes in that one is wreaking havoc in a garden. When the men get close enough, one of them throws the harpoon. The other three push the sharp end of the anchor stake into the ground. The hippo bulldozes away through the brakes toward the river and runs the line out, and if the hold of the barb is strong, the four farmers pushing down on the stake will plow the deepest furrow of their lives behind him. If the drag of the stake stops the hippo, two of the men dash up and try to finish him with spears. If not, he will soon reach the river, where the stake serves as a buoy to slow his swimming, tire him out, and show where he is in the water.

The hippopotamus dance I spoke of is a ceremonial ruse to lure hippos into harpoon range in broad daylight. It combines features of the Fiji sea turtle dance and a medieval recipe for hunting unicorns—the former because singing and dancing are involved, the latter because the performers are maidens. The dance is really just a rhythmic song sung by a chorus of young girls who are most effective at the work just before puberty. Apparently only the hippo knows why this should be. The girls line up on the bank of the river where a hippo lurks in the reeds and floating-island of the other shore. They sing, clap, and stamp out the rhythm on the ground. The hippopotamus hears them and, losing his native shrewdness in his admiration of the girls, he crosses the river to listen and watch more closely. Men lurking in canoes hidden in the reeds go out and harpoon him. This technique was described to us by various people, not as a mystic ritual of animal worship, but, as I said, as a means of hunting the hippo. Just looking at a hippo you would never think he would fall for such a thing, but you never know.

With those things to see and hear about, the delay at Port Herald was not bad, really. And finally, on the evening of September 23, the *Piri Piri* came cringing up the river to the landing, and the skipper sent word that we could leave any time we wanted to. We said we would leave in the morning.

Wilson made us a lunch, and at seven the next morning we went aboard. The *Piri Piri* nosed out into a fast current and we wheezed away down the river at good speed, with Wilson waving at the landing. We crossed the Portuguese frontier a short way downstream, and at 9:30 reached the river village of Megaza. We spent a long time at the tiny customs house while the official stamped our passports. He stamped only a few passports there he said, and had never had one from the United States. He put on a uniform coat and cap to do the job in style. When we finally got away from Megaza at 11:15, the customs official said he was sorry to see us go.

Above Megaza the Shire flowed between solid walls of

maiden cane leaning out over fast, deep water. Below the town the river entered a broad floodplain with short-grass savanna spread on every side. The only high ground between us and the mountains was the narrow flood-levees at the edges of the stream.

We reached the Zambezi at 6:15, with Dona Ana and the Land Rover still forty miles upstream in the bar-ridden Zambezi. I don't know who it was who told us we would make Dona Ana that night. Whoever it was, he was probably Portuguese. Scheduling things precisely seems to be a racial virtue, or vice, of the Nordic peoples. In the case of the *Piri Piri* trip, there wasn't much lost, though. The only troublesome part was missing three meals, and sleeping on the iron deck with the ship rocking in the night when hippos broached to ponder our being there.

The sun set as we reached the mouth of the river. The pilot tried to go on up the Zambezi for a while. He proved the next day that he knew the bars and channels of the river like the back of his hand, but in the dark that night we ran aground five times in quick succession, and he finally gave up and tied the boat to the bank. By luck a breeze blew to us across the river all night, and kept the mosquitoes that were swarming in the grass on shore from coming aboard.

The night was not as long as it might have been. The worst part was thinking of a day coming without breakfast. At dawn there was mist on the river. We tried to move on before it burned off, but three starts ended on sand bars, so we tied up again and waited. The minute the pilot was able to see across the river he yelled to cast loose and we set out up river again. This time there were no setbacks. How the old pilot knew where the bars were hidden under the muddy water of the wide river was a mystery. I sat with him for an hour trying to see what

The Bird and the Behemoth

signs he might be seeing, but he was an old witch doctor of a pilot and his markers were all occult. For forty miles he zigzagged back and forth across the river, working the old rusty boat through a perfect rat-maze of bars and cross channels and never once ran us aground again.

We got to the village of Mutarara at three in the afternoon, and docked alongside the rocks between Mutarara and Dona Ana a half-hour later. Some Africans on the rocks told the pilot that our jeep was parked at Dona Ana. I borrowed a bicycle from one of them and went to tell the driver we had come. The car was there but the driver was away somewhere. I gave some sixpences to a posse of little boys, and they soon found him visiting a family of Nyasas at the edge of town. We put the bicycle in the car and drove back to the *Piri Piri,* got our meager gear, thanked the crew and handed some shillings around, and drove away. Because we were all a little numb from hunger, we stopped briefly by a cantina and bought some sardines and a wheel of cheese, a box of biscuits and a bottle of wine. With these, the fifty miles back to Port Herald seemed not so many as they might have seemed.

As we drove the dusty road back into Nyasaland, it was mainly the rhythm of the *Piri Piri's* engine that was in my mind. But as we ran on, racing our cloud of white dust across the steppe, the wine took away those thoughts and I began to think instead of the wild animals no longer standing along the shore as they stood when Livingstone went up the river a hundred years earlier.

When we reached the Zambezi the night before, we had reconnoitered the whole length of the Shire, from its beginning as the outlet of the lake to its mouth. We had spent ten weeks almost constantly on the river, much of the time in country that to the eye seemed almost wholly untroubled by man. The wild mammals we had seen, not counting monkeys, squirrels, and bushbabies in the trees, were probably no more than half a dozen kinds. Days would pass with no beasts seen but birds or the small things we caught with our tea strainers, or layed low with aerosol bombs. Always, though, there was the thought that a bit of old Africa might be herded down into the nethermost part of Nyasaland and along the Lower Shire, and that we would see it there. But now even that hope had run out. We knew the river to its end; and the last part was, if anything, more lifeless than the rest. We had seen some monitors slide from the banks, and in the water itself a few hippos stayed to gape and glare as we passed. But in the whole last 75 miles of the Shire we saw not one land mammal, and not a single crocodile. I had never before seen deletion of a fauna so complete in country so thinly inhabited.

The only trace of exuberance in the Lower Shire country was its birds. The Zambezi bird fauna is rich, and though it too has no doubt declined from old levels of abundance, it still seemed imposing to me. As soon as we left Port Herald two kinds of kingfishers started flying away from perches ahead of the boat. One was a solitary mite of a bird, bright blue with a scarlet bill; the other was pied black-and-white and went always in small flocks. There were herons of at least three kinds. None seemed to be the black-headed heron that was nesting in Port Herald. Fish eagles soared in sight for most of the way. There were two kinds of cormorants, and a big black species of anhinga. Pelicans were perched in the ivory palms along the bank. Soon after we started down the Shire we began seeing flocks of geese in the air; and when we reached the Zambezi they were standing on most of the emergent midriver bars. There was a big dark species about the size of a Canada goose and another, probably the Egyptian goose, a little bigger than a brant. There were hundreds of geese on some of the flats, and with them there was a kind of black stork like an ironhead wood stork, and another ibislike bird that looked like a spoonbill. On the Zambezi there was a species of gull or tern with a dark head and a grating unhappy voice, and a few black skimmers cruised low over the brown water.

A pair of redpolled swallows with long plumes trailing from either side of their tails followed us down the Shire for hours—all the way from Megaza to the Zambezi. They flew along beside or before us and swooped in under the roof and even down into the forward hatch and out again. Maybe they had decided to build a nest in the boat when she lay tied up at Megaza, and had too much character or too little sense to abandon the plan when we moved away. Anyhow, they seemed disconsolate and I felt sorry for them. When dark came, they disappeared and I looked about the cabin and hold by matchlight, thinking they might be roosting there. But they must have gone on back to Megaza. The next day they did not show up again.

Once, somewhere down toward the end of the Shire, a wagtail came out from the bank, sat on the anchor two yards from where I lay on the deck, and sang in a piercing happy whistle for nearly half an hour.

So there were all those birds, at least, to see from the *Piri Piri*. And there were the white herons that I have mentioned, that stood on the floodplain with the cows. They were the birds that I thought back to when I stopped by the dragline out on the Prairie, to watch the snowy egret there.

The birds with the Morrambala cows were buff-backed herons. Buff-backs are called cattle egrets all about the Old World Tropics because nowadays it is mostly only cows they walk with. They are also known as "tick" herons, but that is a poor name. Another bird pulls ticks off rhinos and the like, but for buff-backs eating ticks is only a casual thing. It is grasshoppers they are mainly after, and, unlike the snowy heron, which can go and come between pasture and pond, the buff-back seems heavily committed to living among grazing mammals of great size. As we passed the mixed flock on the Shire shore, we could see the birds making their shrewd use of the shuffling cows. Some of the egrets stood poised by a cropping snout in a little trance like a pointer certain of a rise; some darted about to spike at the ground for fumbled game; others sprang into short flight after quick bickering among themselves.

I was groggy as it was, from the sun and the blood-deep rhythm of the engine, and the familiar look of the flood-plain, the flat wide country with grass and cows and white birds in it, made the thought that this was Africa seem whimsical. I knew, in a way, that close downstream the Zambezi was sprawling in the shimmer; but the thought was fantastic and hard to hold to.

Away in the distance the mountain stood higher than anything back home. Close in beside me the pilot was scooping out peas and rice with his hand from a china chamber pot that sat on the useless binnacle, and he looked pretty exotic, to be sure. But for all I could see, the whole spread of land in the middle distance might just as well have been a pasture at home. There were clues of course, the Kaffir cast to the cattle, for one; but Brahma blood gives a similar look. And, as far as I could see in any direction, there was no cowhand on a quarter horse riding out to check the hyacinth ponds for bogged-down heifers. The herons themselves, though white and set about just right for snowies, had a different knack in their hunting

—a sprier, more henlike lack of stealth than the snowies use. But none of these things were things I thought of. I thought only of the sameness of the scene, and that set me thinking; and before we had gone past the meadow, I figured I knew why the snowy egret had astonished me in my youth by leaving the frogs and marshes.

When I moved to Florida thirty years ago, the herons there were wading birds. The cattle roamed the unfenced woods or sloshed about wet prairies—puh-raries, the crackers called them—the marshes of maiden cane, bonnets, and pickerel weed. The herons stayed in what you think of as heron habitat, in the shallow lakes and pond-edges, and along the roadside ditches. They ate frogs and fishes there and little snakes and sirens. Even in those days there was a big cattle industry in Florida; but it was the hit-and-miss husbandry of the old Spaniards, profitable mainly because the stock was as Spartan as camels and land was cheap. In the old days the Cubans loved Florida beef because it was like game. It had the fatless, dark taste of tropical deer. In the early thirties of this century it was still about the same; the beef was lank and fatless and the herons were in the ponds.

Then all at once the land began to change. A new sort of ranching grew up, with fences and purebred stock and planted pastures. New breeds were coddled in stumped-out, smoothed-over lands. The hammocks were cleared of brush and the palmettos were bulldozed away to make the flatwoods into parks. Patrician Angus, Hereford, and Indian bulls were sent out to serve the skittish Spanish she-stuff, and pretty soon, all over northern Florida, fat cows were being gentled on a new kind of tended lawn. By the thousands of acres the old rough land that no sane heron would be caught dead in was made into *pangola* parkland and clover savanna, into manmade pampa and veld of Bahia and napier grass. It was a landscape made over; and as strange as the change in the land itself was the change in the ways of the snowy heron.

To see what lured the herons ashore, you have to understand that every Florida rancher, in spite of his dreams and of all the courses he had in the College of Agriculture, is not likely ever to find himself raising cattle in pure culture. He will inevitably turn out to be also a grasshopper husbandman. In fact, if he should stock his pastures with just the right number of cows, a number that eats grass exactly as fast as the grass replaces itself, a certain predictable weight of beef will be there, and a predictable yearly crop can be harvested. Of course, no rancher in his right mind works that way. He pieces out the winter diet of his cattle with protein and minerals and moves them to winter oats, and does all he can to supplement the basic productivity of the pasture grass. But if only perennial grasses supported his cows, there would be in the pasture a certain fixed ratio of grass to meat.

Well, it's the same with his grasshopper culture. Let the insects move in and breed and live there with the cattle—and there is no way to keep them out—and the weight of the insect meat will be predictable too; and the awful part is, it may not be a whole lot less than the weight of the beef. The herons of course know nothing of the rules of physiological ecology that make this so. But they know a good thing when they see it. And during the time between the two World Wars, the snowy egret in northern Florida changed from merely a water bird to a seasonally insectivorous associate of cows.

When I first began to notice snowy egrets walking with cows, it was black cows mostly, and the two together were a fancy thing to see. I got into a great state of excitement; and knowing no ornithologist in those days, I canvassed the cattlemen of the county to see what they could tell me. Without exception they had noticed the hegira of the herons and they dated it as "just lately"—lately being the early thirties, as I said. When I went on to quiz them further, some said it was the coming of the Angus cattle that drew the birds ashore, some queer attraction of Angus black for egret white. But those with a less mystic cast of mind said no, it was not the blackness of the cows at all, but the pastures smoothed out in the old rough hammock and palmetto land, the brand new bowling-green laid out for a stick-legged wading bird to walk in. I looked through the bird books I could find, and from them went to the journals, and always the snowy was cited as a water bird, more active in his hunting than the rest, but never reported as a cattle heron. Before the nineteen-thirties nobody spoke of snowy herons walking with cattle. By the end of the thirties they were doing it all over the place.

Looking back to those times you can see that several changes favored the hegira of the herons. These were the years when egrets were making their great comeback after plume hunting had reduced them almost to extinction at the turn of the century. And the new flocks were not surging back into the old Florida, but into a land less fit for herons, with marshes and gladeland everywhere being drained and made into farms or real estate. Then there were the new crops of grazing grasshoppers on dry land, fed up to teeming tons on clear stands of planted grass, and there were placid cattle there to stir them out of hiding. And as important as any part of the new outlook was the change from the cluttered hammock and palmetto pinelands to lawns of short grass as wadeable to heron legs as water.

It was a new opportunity, and it was not the snowy

alone that saw it. If you look around North Florida long enough, you see all his nearest kin out in the fields, especially the American or common egret, and the little blue heron. A common egret that had fished in our pond for months came up one day and walked around the pasture with the horse. He had a quizzical air about him as if he were testing some uncertain feeling, but he stayed by the horse's head the whole morning, and even followed it into the back dooryard. Then a dog came charging out and the egret flew back to the pond; and it was weeks before we saw his kind in hoofed company again.

It is the same with the little blue heron, both the white young birds and the blue adults. They clearly get the drift of the new bonanza; and they come out from time to time, singly or by twos or threes, alone or mixed with other kinds of herons. But something is lacking in their attitude. They stand off a little too far from their hoofed companions, just at the fringes of the good hunting, their technique and appetite evidently marred by lingering apprehension. I don't know that there is any connection, but one year in my own pasture I found the remains of two little blue herons in white plumage, where a hawk had given body to their qualms and a possum had come by later and left only patches of changing feathers. Snowies stay out in open savanna in hundreds, and buff-backs in thousands; and you rarely hear of such a thing happening to them. The very timidity of the little blue, the lack of confidence that keeps him from moving in to the protecting bulk of the cow, may raise his susceptibility to such a fate. In any case the little blue herons still stay mostly in the water.

Of the other herons, I have twice in seven years stopped by a pasture near my house to watch a Louisiana heron among egrets and black Angus there; and once in the same period my family and I saw our own great blue heron—one we had seen at another time near death for half an hour, choking over a rice rat he could neither swallow nor cough up—fly up through the woods to an acre of short bahia behind the house, and for half an October morning stand tall and wary among the cows.

So traces of the sort of mind it takes to go ashore and consort with behemoths can be seen in the snowy heron's relatives. But in them the venture has the look of aberrant behavior, of a timid, unhappy straying from the comfort of the normal. The snowies, however, came out in confident flocks from the start. They emerged with unawed enthusiasm, as if loosed at last among joys once known, and too long withheld from their bloodline. So nowadays the cattle quarter the mankept plains, the grasshoppers fly up, and the snowies snatch them out of the air. It was a rare thing they found, a feeding niche not occupied, a chance going begging. Any frog-spiking heron has the eye and the tools to tweak down a grasshopper out of the air; but only the snowy had the wit and the gall to go out and do it.

But "wit" and "gall"—what do they mean in a heron? What trait of mind was it, really, that singled the snowy out among his fellows and let him go out and use cows to harvest the new manna in the new landscape? Creatures as fancily rigged for fishing as a heron is, ought to stay stiffnecked and single-track in their roles, untempted by any chance their ancestors never had. Where did the flexibility come from? Why was the snowy so much the most ready when the new opportunity came along? It is no good just saying the snowy was brighter than the rest. Look closely at the cleverness of animals and you see that the most astonishing examples are not the intelligence of people at all, but the acumen of a rat trap knowing so smartly when the rat has come and how to grab him.

Why, then, was it the snowy who was so quick to make the change? You turn to the student of evolution, and he looks about for a term to comfort you with, and terms are never lacking to him. He comes up with the word "generalized."

"A generalized animal," he says. "Not drawn out by evolution to the point of no return as a tapeworm is, or a penguin. Ready for anything. Like a country doctor who will still deliver a baby or pull a tooth. An animal not in a rut."

But it seems queer calling a heron generalized, with his fancy fishing and wading gear and all, and you say so. And besides, the extraordinary thing about the snowy's behavior was not so much the use of the tools of his body for a new job but the "knowing" somehow that wading is wading, in either grass or water; that a frog-quick eye and beak will snatch a flying bug; and above all, knowing that it is safe to walk on dry land close by the nose of a heavy-footed cow. And another odd part was the feeling the snowies gave me, even way back in the early thirties in northern Florida, that they had been out there on land before.

You point this out, and your consultant on evolution sees it.

"All right," he says. "Preadapted. The bird was preadapted to make the change."

You wince at the word; but you let it lose its Presbyterian ring, and try it on the heron.

"Preadapted," you say. "Sure. But how did he get that way?"

"He just was. That's what the word means—just happening by chance to be equipped for a way of life when the chance to live it comes along. The heron was just accidentally ready when the chance came."

"Not in a rut," you say. "Ready for anything."

"Within limits, yes."

"But that's what you said being generalized was," you say.

By then you see you are only fussing over terms. Just feeling about for fit ones among textbook words is a slow way to tell how egrets were the qualified partners of cows. But I think I know, as I said before. What I believe is that they were cattle herons all the time. I think they got inured to behemoths by walking with the fauna of the Pleistocene. That was the notion that struck me on the deck of the *Piri Piri;* and I felt like a hero and looked about to tell someone. But Lewis was aft of the churning diesel, and the black pilot spoke only a lesser Bantu dialect and Portuguese worse than my own.

The theory was not very revolutionary, really. What show of fancy behavior of any kind is not, in part, a show of the history of the race? What things does any animal ever do—by "reasoning," by learning, or by simple reflex—that is not in some way preadaptation? What I was trying to do with the cock-and-bull hypothesis that snowy herons were the American game egrets of the Pleistocene was to get away from the cock-and-bull pronouncement that their superior readiness was just superior intelligence.

A thing I remember seeing that now appears to be background for the heron question was some buzzards that looked clever too, beyond the scope of buzzard brains. After coming upon the egret with the dragline, I went straight home and searched out the notes I had made on those buzzards twelve years before, when I was living in the mountains of Honduras. I found I had even worked the notes part way up into a little manuscript, with a title hopefully put at the top: "Opportunism in the Black Vulture." But I had put the sheets away, from then till now, because of my misgivings over what a buzzard really is when he seems to be opportunistic. What the buzzards did that day was the same sort of thing a heron is doing when he goes out undaunted to walk with a mammoth or a steer or a big machine.

The manuscript says that my wife and I were sitting on a fence at ten one morning of a blue, windy dry-season day. It was over by the slaughterhouse at Escuela Agrícola Panamericana, and we were talking with some boys who had just finished butchering a steer. As usual at slaughtering time, some black vultures were sitting quietly in a row along the low peak of a nearby building, waiting for offal the boys might throw them, or leave behind. This time the offal had all been eaten, the bones were already chalky in the sun, and the meat was piled neatly under a mat in the meatroom pushcart. The buzzards could see all this as well as we, and I judge they felt the party was over; but they waited on anyway, without much hope but with nothing better in their minds to do.

All at once a whirlwind, unnoticed until it hit the fence three hundred yards away, came tearing across the pasture. It was one of the testy little *remolinas* of those high hot valleys where the trade wind swoops down out of the upwind ranges and into the baking thorn flats, and sets the hot air twisting. It was a mean one this time, noisy, crooked, and black with rattling trash. It was enough like a real tornado to give you a turn and you would have thought it would scare a buzzard badly. But the moment the whirlwind got inside the fence, one of the buzzards left the roof, flapped heavily across the pasture and flew headlong into the brawling column. We thought he had made some mad mistake, and would quickly be plucked and broken up; and he was tossed about badly. But by strong, and what looked a lot like practiced, effort he kept on the whole upright. As the vortex took him upward its spiral broadened and the vulture's efforts to stay inside became less frenzied. When he had risen to 250 feet or so—to a level where the turning funnel no longer held up visible debris—the vulture started soaring, tilting this way and that, flaplessly rising on the rising air, almost with the grace of a turkey vulture.

It was a strange thing to see, after decades of knowing black vultures that did no such thing, and we were astonished at the sight. We had begun to debate loudly over the disorder when suddenly two more *zopes* left the roof and crossed to the spinning spit-devil. They dived right in, as the other had done, went through the same strenuous time to stay top-up inside the writhing stem of the wind, and then in the same way they rose high over the plain in the spreading swirl. Then, singly and in twos and threes, all the other buzzards flew into the whirlwind, each for a moment fighting to stay, then leveling out to ride into the sky without the need for further work.

After several minutes all the buzzards were high over the valley, closely bunched and circling slowly with the climbing rise of the thermal. At what we judged to be two thousand feet they began to peel off one by one, and some went to quartering our plain in the regular foraging patrol, while others headed out for the high pass to Toncontín in a neighboring valley.

By then our loud marveling had tolled in students from all about the busy fields; and Henry Hogaboom, the sub-director, came over from the corral, trotting fast to get into the thick of the talk. There was a boy from a high part of Ecuador there, and another from Coban in Guatemala. There was a coastal Colombian, who kept calling buzzards *gallinazos;* and a Guanacasteco from the Pacific plain of Costa Rica; and another Tico from San José. There were all these there, and not one had ever before seen buzzards dive into whirlwinds. When Henry joined us and heard the story, he looked up at what was left of the circling flock and said we all were lying, and we said no, and he said well he'd be damned. Then a cluster of Honduraneans came up. One was from Catacamas, and when he had heard the cause of the talk, he drew up with the imposing calm that goes before a Latin revelation. When he had all the eyes there, he said:

"Thus *are* the buzzards here—*así son ellos.* They always mount the whirlwind in that form—*es costumbre del animal."*

At that there was more uproar than before, with everybody sure the Catacamas boy was only charged up over the *zopes* being Honduranean birds. But later I got him aside and talked the matter out, and came away sure that this one boy had really seen the thing before. And now, thinking the incident over a long time after, the strange part seems not so much that the buzzards did what they did, but that it was only the Catacamas boy who had ever seen such a thing before. Because the vultures that rode the *remolina* that day were not the first of their kind to do such a thing. It was clearly a practiced operation, and the state of mind that doing it required was not the flexibility of smart birds, but the opportunism of a race beaten into a trick of mock intelligence by natural selection. But there were other knowers of *zopes* there in the crowd that gathered—why were they all surprised? Why was it only the Catacamas boy who knew about whirlwind-riding birds?

The Bird and the Behemoth

Well, take my own case for instance. I have lived around vultures all my life; and I was surprised. In all the places I have lived, buzzards abound, and they soar in thermals too, and no doubt they esteem rising air as they do a dead mule's eyes. I have never seen them climb with visible whirlwinds; but it may be simply because there are not many whirlwinds where buzzards and I live together. Among all the non-Honduranean buzzard experts in the crowd at the slaughterhouse, it could have been the same —the lack of precedent for what we had seen was perhaps a fault of the weather of the lands we came from, and not a deficiency in our buzzards.

I am a little surprised at the boy from Guanacaste. Guanacaste is not only fine buzzard country, but the Pacific day breeze there blows into a hot, flat land, with hills set all about it, and I should have said it was good whirlwind country, too. In fact I saw a whirlwind there one day. It came as a waterspout from the sea. It was a dark terror of a thing, and it knocked the woods about; but I am sure there were not any vultures in it. Maybe the *remolinas* there run too strong for the *zopes*.

In any case, in spite of our almost unanimous astonishment at what the Zamorano buzzards did, I'll bet there was nothing new in their feat. Like the egrets going out to walk with cattle, the buzzards were surely only loosing a stored-up pattern of possible action, built into their strain as a useful adaptation at some other time, and even perhaps in some distant place. All black vultures may carry the trick in their nuclei and neurons, resting hidden and unused there wherever whirlwinds are scarce, but ready for use when the right time comes back again.

All soaring is riding rising air, and there should be no great evolutionary step from the feeling about for the rising air, as hawks and vultures everywhere do, to seeing its sign in its trash-laden tip scurrying along the ground. The big step would be, I should think, to work up to the habit of entering the turning wind from ground level, where a wall of violent discomfort would lie between the buzzard ancestor and the bonanza of altitude to be got from the climbing air.

Or maybe the racial learning started higher up in the funnel and came down by stages, the learners finding by trial and error that a lift was always felt when the visible twist of a spit-devil went raving across the earth below. That way the buzzard would need no brain at all—no more cerebral cortex than a talented potter wasp—to work his way, through the ages, farther downward in his entry levels; each generation—or each thousand generations—would gain a bit more nerve to endure the initial shock for the sake of the fine free rise that comes just afterward.

In any case the black vulture is shortwinged and awkward, and altitude costs him dearly. It makes no sense to think he would go down through time not stumbling upon the visible sign of an asset so rare and negotiable.

Any evolution is likely to demand some sacrifice at first, some abandonment of comfortable ways. In fact, that is exactly what evolution is. In the case of our own special adaptation, that of conceptual thought, how many proto-men were lured by their growing brain into discomfort and danger? But always the good of the innovation outdid the damage, the slightly brighter chaps outlived or outbred the rest, and the brain grew on to think up poems and satellites. And so with fish coming out on land, and reptile-birds floundering in the air; and so with tornado-riding buzzards and herons that walk with behemoths.

The thing is, you see a heron under a dragline and you

can't just drive away. You ransack your mind for clues as to how he came to be there, standing the dreadful clamor for the sake of the easy feeding. It is easy to say his species is simply clever. But in this case the word is only a figure of speech. What it stands for is only a little more like personal genius than the fleetness of cheetahs, or the food-begging gape of a baby crow.

The vermiform appendix was once a useful section of the gut of our ancestors. We find it superfluous now, but suppose a change of environment made it suddenly good to have an appendix again. Bearers of the least degenerate appendixes would all at once be blessed among men. It is the same with a long list of relict devices or traits that once were used and are now obsolete but have not yet been wholly scrapped by retrogressive evolution. You see your first buck over the sights of a rifle and your hackles rise without your leave, without your even having any hackles. You get the goosebumps of rising hackles a million years after all utility in hackles going up has gone. So is it any wonder that buzzards and egrets should hoard away plans and circuits of lives they lived perhaps only centuries ago?

But then one thinks of the heron that fished with bread. It was not a snowy egret that fished. It was not even a near relative but a quite distant one. It was a little green heron, a solitary kind, that says "scow" and defecates when you scare him off a snag. The green heron that fished was told about by Harvey Lovell in an article in *The Wilson Bulletin.* Mr. Lovell saw the puzzling thing in Lake Eola in Orlando, Florida. When he came upon the heron, it was fishing normally from a retaining wall a few feet back from the edge of the lake. Idly Mr. Lovell threw the bird a piece of bread, which landed on the ground beside the wall. The heron picked up the bread and put it in the water. When it began to float out of reach, the heron retrieved it and put it back where it was. Pretty soon a lot of little fishes began to come in—mainly pusselguts, I judge, which always come to bread—and the heron at once began to snatch them up. When the bread disintegrated, Lovell threw another piece. This time it fell a good way back from the edge of the water. The heron went straight to the bread, picked it up, ran back and dropped it in the water, and began to fish some more. Some coots swam up. The heron picked up the bread, drove off the coots, then dropped the bread back and resumed his fishing.

Keep in mind now, that Lovell is a reliable man, a responsible observer; and that there was another man with him who saw the whole thing. The anecdote grows more bewildering, too. In fact, to be sure we get it straight, I am going to quote the next bit from Lovell's text:

"A clear indication," he says, "that the Green Heron knew what he was doing, was furnished by the following incident. When he was standing by some floating bread some small fish broke the surface of the water several feet to his left. The heron immediately became excited, picked up his bread, and moved it to almost the exact spot where the fish had appeared.

"We observed the procedure for several hours on three consecutive days. Several people present agreed with us that the Green Heron was using the bread for fishing."

To me that is about the nicest smart-animal story I ever heard; the neatest, cleanest, most demoralizing case history the dilettante dabbler in lower intellects could hope to hear. It is ten times as subtle as my buzzards; it is clear out of the league of what the snowy egrets did. For Mr. Lovell, whom I never saw, I hold envy and admiration. He was witness to a fine thing, and he told it well and fairly. He will confound many an armchair ethnologist with that tale. He already has. But with one slight word in his story, with the overtone it carries, I have got to take exception. Mr. Lovell shouldn't ever have said the green heron "knew" what he was doing.

Lord knows I am not one of those naturalists who live in fear of incriminating themselves with anthropomorphic judgments about animals. Animals *are* anthropomorphic. A dog we've got is at least as anthropomorphic as I am; some we have had have been a good deal more so. But when I see a specially fancy bit of living by an animal, one dashing into a whirlwind or one coming out with cows, even a heron using bread to fish with, I can't help looking for ways it might have got into the *racial* intelligence of the beast—into his inherited set of fixed behavior patterns or of tendencies to acquire such patterns easily. The little green heron is simply not that bright. He is not intelligent enough to have done what he did through intelligence. And because the sharp thing he did involved food-getting, any student of adaptation would quickly look for the grounding of the trick in fixed behavior handed down from forebears that fished too, not with bread but with something.

When custard apples fall into a West Indian pond, the turtles and fish come up, and it is easy to catch them there. The same in our pond in Florida—when the corollas of cow-crazy drop, the cooters live avidly off them and the bass and warmouth will rise and strike up at the floating flowers. The anhinga on the limb can't help but notice. I never saw him cross the gap to haunting oak trees with cow-crazy vines over water, but give him time. How could his strain help get the point, in the long run of generations? Well then, once a bird feels out the connection between things falling into the water: fruits or flowers from overhanging trees, food he himself fumbles while carrying, his own excrement even, let loose so fish-fetchingly at every takeoff—once the bird's bloodline is exposed to chances like these, it would be strange indeed if no use were made of the chances.

I am not belittling Lovell's heron. I think he was wonderful. I am only using him in a rambling rationale to prove to myself that snowy egrets remember mastodons.

Formal discussions of learning and instinct are not easy to follow. The shading of adaptive behavior from simple and conditioned reflexes through trial-and-error learning to what is plainly insight, are very fine. A whole vernacular must be learned to keep track of the talk, and I don't know it. But in a way the tornadoes and cows of the buzzards and egrets I spoke of would fall in pretty close to what students of behavior call "tools." The word is more clearly applicable to such adjuncts to anatomy as a monkey wrench, or the fire and pounding stones of early men. Among non-humans the false beak of the woodpecker finch of the Galapagos Islands shows the tool idea plainly.

When the Galapagos came up out of the sea, finches got over there somehow, and found themselves the only land birds on the islands. It was a dreary landscape but there were opportunities in it for an enterprising sort of bird, and the finches proceeded to evolve along lines that let them get what blessings the place offered. To fit the new roles, they changed in ways that were makeshift but in some cases admirably clever. Most of the changes involved shifts in the old finch anatomy—just enough change to let a finch live like a hummingbird, say, without actually being one. But when the woodpecker finch I mentioned set himself up in the specialized business of

The Bird and the Behemoth

woodpeckers, he did it by using a tool. To serve in place of the long, probing tongue that woodpeckers have, the finch gradually got the knack of plucking a cactus thorn, poking it into cracks and spaces in dead wood and bark, and grabbing the flushed-out bugs and spiders as they fled. That is a solid, classic example of a tool.

But tools don't have to be sticks or stones in the hand or beak of the user. To break out the meat of hard-shelled clams, gulls fly up and drop them on rocks or roads; and the road or rock is the tool, in a manner of speaking. There is a sort of reverse English there, though, and if it offends you, think up to it through the Australian black-breasted buzzard that drops, not shellbound food, but rocks on shellbound emu eggs, then dives down to eat the contents. The tool idea is involved in all these, without any sensible doubt. But insight is not.

Life has lived with the principles of mechanical advantage for two billion years; and with the force of gravity. Always under pressure the way they are, living beings cannot be expected to have missed the good to be got from these things, and the using of them is not a sign of insight.

It is the same way with the marvels of animal orientation. Since the backboneless ages when animals first became something other than simple spheres and got two sides to their body, they have found good in going ahead. Once you start going ahead, you find good places and bad, and a choice to be made between them. For short runs you grope your way, or peer through the murk, but to get about the planet cleverly, you need landmarks that are better than a tree to be kept on the right side, or the edge of a reef to follow. For all this time the landmarks were there. The skies were burning with information. The cycles of the sun and moon all ran on schedule;

the constellations went wheeling with the sweetest regularity; even the polarization patterns of sunlight were as predictable in the sky as a road map of Kansas. Living with these landmarks through the ages, needing them desperately, and being all the time under the iron hand of natural selection, how could protoplasm have missed the chance, any chance, to keep from getting lost? It is no wonder that some traveling animals are guided by information they get from the heavens, that they inherit the craft to use the sun or stars to hold true courses, making always the right allowances for the time of day or night, for the shifting of the seasons, for the slanting help or hindrance of currents or wind. This is marvelous all right, but it is not the work of intelligence. It is not even a step in the direction of intelligence.

You seem to get closer to what some people call insight in the string-pulling tits—the Great Tit, the Coal Tit and a number of other kinds—of the British Isles and Europe. It is surprising how much has been written about tits. One thing they do that endears them to animal psychologists is pull strings to get food. I mean this literally—not in the vulgar sense of pulling strings. It seems that Englishmen hang seeds by threads at the edges of bird tables, as they call feeding trays, and tits come and study the situation for a bit and then do just what the Englishmen themselves would do if some delicacy were hanging down there—they pull in the string and get the seed and eat it. This is satisfying to the bird-man and momentarily so, no doubt, to the bird itself. I must say, though, I have worried some about the tit flying off in satisfaction, only to be jerked head over heels when it comes to the end of the anchored string. But that, of course, is pure sentiment, unscientific thinking, and irrelevant here. The science of the thing is that these tits

The Bird and the Behemoth

are exceptional in being able to think the matter out. Other birds are nonplused by the complication. They come to the table, and they show clearly that they know a seed is swinging down there by a string; but according to all reports, they never can visualize the profit to be got from pulling the string. This makes the tits doing it a creditable thing indeed.

But calling what they do insight, or even a stage in evolution toward insight, puzzles me; because if the tits are working from insight, then it must be that my string-pulling spider was too, at least as far back as his third cephalothoracic ganglion.

The string-pulling spider I refer to was one I found on a low bay leaf, over the edge of a lake in Umatilla, Florida. I was down there one afternoon long ago, along the shore hunting spiders for H. K. Wallace, who was then a fellow student of mine working toward a Ph.D. in spider biology, and is now my boss at the University. My family lived by the lake, and so did the spiders Wallace wanted; and I was down there peering among the wax myrtles, button-bushes, and sprouts of silver bay at the edge of the tea-red June water for diving spiders when I came upon the spider I spoke of. It was a kind I didn't know, a jumping spider I suppose, but with a longer body than they usually have. Anyway, I was about to pass on down the shore when I suddenly noticed that this spider was creeping up on a naked measuring worm that was resting quietly at the edge of the leaf. I stopped to see the outcome, sure it would be the usual faultless charge, with the poor worm ending up a thin sack with all its juices gone. But this time something went wrong. The spider jumped, and the worm dropped off the edge and drew up swinging by a thread, two feet below the leaf and a foot above the water. You have seen measuring worms do that, I am sure. I don't know whether they anchor their lifeline at the instant of crisis or keep it fast all the time to what they are walking on, for safety's sake. In any case, when the spider missed his charge and the worm fell free, it was not just to be snapped up by the little stump-knockers in the dark lake water below.

I looked close, to see how the spider would take the reverse, somehow feeling he would not simply go away, or settle down in melancholy. I was right, too. The spider clearly perceived that the loss was not complete. He walked rapidly back and forth for a moment waving his pedipalps thoughtfully about, then he reached down with a front leg and felt along below the edge of the leaf and quickly found the strand that held the worm up. I am sure he couldn't see the worm itself. The spider was on top of the leaf, you understand, and his eyes were all on top of him; and there was no way for him to see a thing two feet down toward the water. But in spite of this, the instant his foot touched the taut silk he began to pull it in. It was a worm-silk strand, remember, for all I know spun of wholly different stuff from spider threads. But the spider grabbed it as if he had reeled it out of his own spinnerets, and began to haul it in hand over hand, and to pass it back to the pairs of legs behind. The second legs took the loops with deft ease and handed them back to the third, and they in their turn gave them back to the fourth legs and then reached forward again for the new loops coming. It was skilled work but wholly orthodox for a spider, and in only a short while the worm had been drawn up almost to the edge of the leaf. Still not looking down, the spider suddenly stopped pulling, moved out to the edge, and shifted about for a stance that would let him get at the prey. Feeling around for what to do, he ran one of his feet down the shortened line. It touched the worm lightly, and instantly the worm drooped down a foot and bounced to a swinging stop in the safe space between the leaf and the water.

Again the spider began to take in line. He did it with a little less sure stealth this time, with what I took for a tiny taint of worry. Again he was able to raise the worm to within millimeters of the platform, and this time, too, when he groped for a position from which to snatch or stab or do whatever he had in mind, the worm took fright and fell free, and swung there slowly above the water.

Up to then I had only marveled at the sense of the spider—at his knowing, as Mr. Lovell said, without seeing, that his quarry was hanging below the leaf, and seeing so quickly how to fish it up. But when the spider again began to pull in line, I could see the incident taking a different turn. I began to understand that the shrewdness of the spider was not sufficient to show him what to do with the worm thread he was drawing in. There seemed, in fact, to be in him a sort of gradient of shrewdness, going back from his front end, which had thought up the project, through the substations in charge of the four pairs of legs. As the line was passed along back, it was the fourth pair of legs that had to decide what to do with it. One might say, why not just drop it, and perhaps that is what the front end thought would be done. A bird fishing up a hanging grain of corn simply pulls with his beak, holds down the taken-in slack with a foot, and reaches for another beakhold on the line. The string piles up on the tray, or falls loose from the edge, and there is nothing to get the bird in trouble. But the spider was not pulling man-made bread string, or familiar spider cables either, but a more ethereal sort of silk, the wispy filament of an infant lepidopteran. By the time he had begun to draw up the worm after its third drop, grave trouble was mounting. The second legs still shared the optimism of the first. They took the thread with confidence, and passed it to the third. But the third legs quite clearly showed diminished verve in handling it; and on back at the fourth pair the insight anteriorly was beginning to build disaster. Already the fourth legs had received more thread than they knew what to do with. The stuff was too light and flimsy to be thrown off the edge, or even to lie still where the frenzied combing of the hind feet tried to drop it. Instead, it piled and tangled and clung to whiskers and spines of legs and feet—and still it came looping back in more air-thin bights and hitches. Before long, the last legs had lost all semblance of ability to cope with the clinging stuff and their uneasiness began to flood forward in the spider. The third legs were stirred to reach back and try to help with the harassing tangle. But the silk kept coming, and because the last legs were unable to take in any more, the third were soon in as bad a state as they, and the second pair started reaching back to help in the growing crisis.

By then the worm had been pulled up almost to the edge of the leaf again. When its hind end showed at the rim, the spider launched a short jump, but, with most of his legs trussed up with worm silk, he missed. The worm let go and fell again, and dangled as before. Still clinging stubbornly to his insight, the spider, the front part of the spider, fell to snatching in the worm-string in a way that bordered on hysteria. He dragged it in over the edge with unnecessary vigor. He handed it back in heedless abandon, showing no concern for the chaos back there, where six of his legs had lost all their initial enthusiasm, all thought of group action, and were only scraping miserably at themselves, helpless in the toils of parochial anxiety.

I give you my word, it was a bad business. There was this poor spider with his front end still filled with insight, hauling away at the hanging worm with all the cunning of a British tit, and his after-parts taken hopelessly aback by the versatility in the front, and all their reflexes shot to pieces. And still the forefeet hauled in line, more frenziedly, even, than before; dragging it up, pushing it to the rear, and leaving it lying there untended by even the second legs, which by now were distraught with the gravity of their own predicament.

I don't pretend to know how realization comes to a spider, how a dawning doubt that starts at the back end moves forward through the subdivisions of his nervous system. But in this case I'm telling of, when the tangle, and the apprehension, had spread forward to the second legs, and they had begun to help the third and then to turn back and claw at their own snarled quota of the worm's thread, you could see desperation mounting in the spider as a whole. One moment he was pulling frantically. Then all at once you could feel him sensing back through the grades of panic behind—and then suddenly he stopped his pulling. With one front foot he reached back as if to assess the disorder, testing with a single nervous touch the tangle about each hinder pair of legs. The appraisal done, the calamity sure in his mind, he stood there for a moment and waved his pedipalps. Then sadly but quickly he drew the thread up to his jaws and bit it off.

The worm fell into the black water of the lake with a plink too tiny to be heard. I picked him up before the stump-knockers could get there, and put him on another leaf. As I went away the spider had turned to the work of chewing and clawing free from the silken bonds the worm had left him.

That is a peculiar sort of tale, I realize. But I hope the main moral is clear. What the spider did of course required no insight at all. Spiders live by pulling strings. They weave and trap prey with string webs, and throw nets and anchored bolas at bugs. They hang up egg sacks and swing from lines or walk on them, and truss up victims and haul them here and there. They pay out cable, rig guys, take in slack, and eat up spare line to save it. Scare a spider and he does what the caterpillar did —he drops and hangs by a quickly fastened safety thread. Knowing about strings is built into spiders. It surprised me to come upon a spider that could think so quickly across the gap between pulling his own string and pulling that of another creature. But the gap was pretty narrow, really, and the need for insight was little or none. The spider just made a slight adjustment in fixed behavior his ancestors had long before acquired.

And so, I venture to say, it is with tits. I know little of the life of tits and less of their ancestry. But if all the facts were in, I bet they would show tits facing string-pulling problems through the ages. Not in just the ways arranged by the English ethologists but enough like those ways to take the shock of novelty out of the hung-seed situation, to suggest to even a bird's mind a course of action, to call out the string-pulling pattern, though it might have lain unused since last required in some earlier way of life left a thousand centuries behind.

I do not mean to depreciate the tits. There just are two very different types of complex behavior. It can be the real invention-on-demand kind, as ours is; or it can also be stored-up programs of response. And like any vestigial trait, the stored patterns may be no longer useful equipment, but the remains of patterns appropriate to ancient situations now dissolved. They may be inherited as chemical traces in a billion cells, waiting through generations for the old need to arise. Then it comes, and whoosh . . . And there streams out string-pulling by a tit or a spider. Or a buzzard rides a whirlwind—or an egret walks with a cow.

I got started with this line of thought, as I have said, on the deck of the *Piri Piri*. Most of my thinking there was very idle and not to be trusted, with the reek and beat of the engine and the brain-baking heat of the one-o'clock sun. There where David Livingstone saw elephants, lions, and buffaloes, there were only cattle for egrets to stand with. I watched them, and an idea dropped into my shifting daydream that I have not been able since to reason away. The idea was this: the snowy heron is, as the buff-back is becoming, an old game heron with the game all gone. Both of these small, white herons are today walking with cattle as a compromise with the grand living of the past, as the best they can do in a world all changed around them. The buff-back is becoming a cattle heron because the savanna fauna of Africa is being wiped out— the snowy because the Pleistocene herds are gone.

Continuously, since Africa became a refuge for the Ice Age megafauna, the buff-back heron has lived as a working part of the savanna community, the companion of elephants, rhinos, zebras, giraffes, wild asses, and a whole world of antelope. For the snowy egret, there have, for a few hundreds or thousands of years, been only frogs and fishes. But for him too, not so very long ago there was ponderous company to keep. Through millions of years Florida was spread with veld or tree savanna much like the Zambezi delta land today. Right there in the middle of Paynes Prairie itself, there used to be creatures that would stand your hair on end. Pachyderms vaster than any now alive grazed the tall brakes or pruned the thin-spread trees. There were llamas and camels of half a dozen kinds, and bison and sloths and glyptodonts, bands of ancestral horses, and grazing tortoises as big as the bulls. And all these were scaring up grasshoppers in numbers bound to make a heron drool. Any heron going out among those big animals—any small, white bird able to make use of a glyptodont to flush his game—would have to have guts galore and a flexible outlook; but he would get victuals in volume.

Back among the ice ages and before, there must have been times, thousands of years at a stretch, when marshes and swamps went slowly dry, and frogs and puddle-fishes grew scarce. At times like those, the crotchbound kinds of herons could only mope and squabble about the dwindling water holes and starve there, or go away some place. But any heron strain with even a mite of extra flexibility would not need many generations to work out a way to live out in the grass.

Most kinds of herons eat insects, if they can get them without extraordinary exertion. But mainly, herons hunt by freezing in a dead-stiff seizure and standing for hours on end like a heronlike snag till a victim comes within reach of a snatch or stab. Such a passive technique is no good for insects. Ambush is all right for fish or snakes or cruising rice rats; but a grasshopper will spend the morning clipping in one bunch of grass. Wait for him to walk by and be grabbed, and you'll likely pass a hungry day. You can liven up the hunting a bit by walking about yourself, and herons do that, too. But there seems to be no real opportunity for them in that kind of feeding. Grasshoppers are hard to see, for a man at least, and I daresay for a heron too. They are colored all wrong to be seen, for one thing; and they have an unfair way of circling a stem of grass and sneering at you from the off side, as a squirrel does on a tree. A grown man with a good bug net and a Ph.D. in entomology can waste a lot of time catching a few grasshoppers.

But it is different when you walk down close to the nose of a cow. The game can't hide from a creature that is eating up its cover. Out in front of a cow, or a gnu or a giant tortoise, the grasshoppers are unable to use their cunning. They have to spew out into the clear like quail flushing ahead of a crazy setter. And for a fish-fast, frog-quick heron, picking them out of the air on the rise is no trick at all. The only hard part would be the daring to move in close to the head of a creature a thousand times your size, the restringing of thin herons' nerves for consorting with behemoths, with cattle or mammoths or draglines.

There is no telling when the snowy got this other string to his bow—maybe as far back as the Pliocene, maybe farther. In terms of geological time, climate has always been unsettled, and animals have changed with the climate, or gone away, or simply died. Again and again marsh has baked into adobe plain, tadpoles have withered, swamps have dried into forest and then into chaparral, and then through slow milleniums have become swamps again. But even with all this going on, the snowy would only have to shift his ways a little to survive—this way in the times when the fishes flourished, that way when the frogs became mummies in the cracking mud.

My thoughts were pretty roundabout on the *Piri Piri* trip, as I have said; because Africa looked like home until a hippo broached and yawned, and because the senile pulse of the Kelvin was beating at my belly; and out at the far seaward side of the plain, Morrambala rose dim and solid to the high blue cool. The only thoughts I had that lasted were about the herons—the cows and white herons, back at home, and here in Mozambique; and about Livingstone seeing wild animals walking with the ancestors of the egrets I was seeing. The game was gone from around them, but the buff-backs were still out there on the floodplain making the best of the change, with grasshoppers leaping like upward rain in front of the mowing muzzles of the cattle. With that thought to measure by, it seemed no distance back to Florida, and no time at all from snowy egrets walking with steers and engines to their forebears walking with ice age elephants.

In America the snowy egret had to go back for a while to living only in the ponds before the cattle came. The buff-backs went over directly into the pastoral scene. But it was a wonder of a coincidence, all the same—these two white birds on two continents, with no blood tie and no scheming between them, both changing their ways of life in the same way, both becoming cattle herons after ages of being mainly something else. It was odd and unreasonable. Hot as my skull was, I could feel the marvel of it. But what I saw that day was only something less than half the story. The rest makes the twin tales of the two herons seem almost unbelievable.

I knew little or nothing about the African heron before I went to Nyasaland. But during the very time the snowy was invading the pastures in Florida, the buff-back was extending its own living space on a world-wide basis, in a series of unprecedented jumps that took it at last across the Atlantic and into the very Florida fields where the snowy is. After who knows how many thousands or millions of years of living with oceans between them, these two thin, white, but only distantly related herons were coming together face-to-face in the grasshopper-Angus pastures of northern Florida.

The Bird and the Behemoth

What was it that drew the African birds to America, off of the elephant's back, out of the yards of Ankole cows, and across the sea to a land they had never seen? To say they sensed opportunity there, or got word of it somehow, won't do. To say it was pure coincidence that made them come sounds silly, too. Yet the fact remains that during the nineteen-fifties the buff-back came to Florida and took up the same way of life that the snowy was leaving the marshes to live. Out on the Prairie these days a splash of white by the head of a distant steer can equally well be either one. In a pair of stick nests a yard apart in a black gum tree at the Lake Alice rookery on the campus of the University of Florida, two snowies may be nesting, or two buff-backs, or one of either kind.

Birds are by nature a footloose lot. Ornithologists have to get used to all sorts of zoogeographic laxity in birds. But ornithologists have been stirred to marvel at the great trek of the buff-back heron. When you look through professional bird journals for the past ten years, you can see the excitement spreading in the numbers of notes and articles telling of new localities in the buff-back's invasion of the New World.

What could be going on in the mind of the bird? Is he only being blown about by winds from which he was shielded before? Or is it possibly, as James Chapin thinks, a snatch of evolution we are seeing, an event that might divulge much about the origins and causes of bird migration generally. Chapin says that in Lower Egypt and Mauritania the buff-back is a sedentary bird; but in the Sudan when the dry season comes, it picks up and flies far southward across the equator, through ten degrees of latitude. That may be the beginning of some kind of restlessness in the race. Chapin believes that it is ground for tracing the dramatic migrations of birds back to a groping escape from drought, converted later on to the spectacular cold-zone-warm-zone journeys of the modern global migrants.

There seems to be good evidence that the restlessness of the buff-back is really a recent thing. Once unknown in South Africa, it is now common there. In the New World it was first noticed in 1930, in British Guiana, suggesting that it may have crossed the Atlantic where it is narrowest, between the bulges of Africa and Brazil. Its spread was local for a time, and then a few years ago it began to turn up all over the place. In the United States it was first seen in 1941 at Clewiston, Florida. In 1956 over a thousand nests were counted at Okeechobee, and meanwhile buff-backs had been reported in places from Maine to Bermuda, the West Indies, and the far interior of South America. They were nesting in South Carolina, Puerto Rico, and the island of St. Croix.

Some people watching the buff-back spread figured that when it and the snowy came together in Florida there would be hell to pay. The buff-back seems tough and cocky, and coming in like that where the snowy was just getting back on its feet after near extinction by the plume hunters, some people were afraid that the snowy would be squeezed right out of most of its range. It may happen yet, but I doubt it. The snowy has his fishing craft, and frogs still fatten in the ditches. The snowy is still open-minded, with no inflexible commitments in either marsh or pasture. If his place is taken with the cattle, he can still make a living in the water for so long as there are any natural ponds and marshes; while the buff-back, for all his verve and energy, seems almost wholly at a loss without his behemoths.

In an article in *The Auk*, Dale Rice suggested that the snowy heron unwittingly helped the buff-back exploit his

The Bird and the Behemoth

beachhead in Florida and colonize the hinterlands. In both birds there is a strong flocking tendency, a disinclination to be alone or to do anything at all without company. They journey in flocks and nest only in numbers. The buff-back, especially, never breeds alone. The urge comes upon him only when enough of his fellows are about to make a party of it. If there had been no other slim, white herons around, Rice thinks, to stir the community spirit of the first few buff-back pilgrims, they would likely have skulked about with the Collier County cows and never thought of spreading, or of increasing their kind and founding a lasting colony. Certainly the two kinds of herons do move about in mixed flocks, and it seems possible that Rice was right. It may be that the snowy has taken a viper into his bosom, but the two often fly and feed and nest together. To an outsider, like a man, there seems to be as yet no serious friction between them.

You can sit in your car at the Prairie—any prairie, in the Florida sense—and see, as I said, both kinds of herons among the cattle. The buff-back is out there doing what he never stopped doing. In his home range his relationship with big mammals is so close that some people have called him an "obligate commensal"—a partner by necessity—of game and cattle. He has even been called an "obligate symbiote," to suggest that he gives, as well as receives, benefit, like the alga and the fungus that live together so necessarily and well in a lichen. What the heron is supposed to furnish is a warning system for his grazing partners—a sharp eye for danger and gleaming white plumage to flash out the alarm when he springs into flight. The oxpecker almost surely furnishes such warning service for the rhinos and antelopes it polices for ticks.

That part of the association will be hard to prove. Most

egrets nowadays live with cattle—not with harassed wild game—and cattle have few enemies to be warned of. Even when the egret goes with elephants, one wonders how many of the dangers imagined by the bird would seem important to the warned partner. Jittery as herons are, you'd think any elephant relying on his herons to announce a crisis would get more harm than good from the deal. He would keep getting warned about heron dangers wholly innocuous to elephants. The egret would get his grasshoppers, but the elephant would only get thin and nervous.

On the other hand, any two creatures that stay together for as long as buff-backs and their hosts have, are bound to interact and, in time to be changed by the relationship. I used to talk about these herons with my class in ecology every year, and the people in it always reacted with more or less interest or with an outraged sense of science, as their natures dictated. The context of our heron talk was the subtle kinds of co-operative ties that develop between living species. The lichen is a classic example of this, and another is the gut of the termite, with its little animals able to live only in the gut of a termite that is wholly dependent upon their living there.

One year I had Dan Belkin in the class. Belkin is an extraordinary fellow, very bright and ingenious, and versatile to a fault. With Belkin I had some exciting talks about the white herons. Finally, though, he finished the course and got his degree and went into physiological work across the campus in the Medical School.

After that I didn't see Belkin much. One stretch of weeks went by without my seeing him at all. When he showed up again he had a beard, a Volkswagen, and a very lovely two-year-old peregrine falcon that he had

The Bird and the Behemoth

caught two months before and had trained himself. Belkin came by with the falcon one afternoon and asked if I would like to go out with him the next morning to do some hawking for cotton rats. I said sure, but how do you hawk for cotton rats? I said I didn't think duck hawks ate rats anyway. Belkin gave me a look of cunning or contempt, I couldn't tell which, blurred the way it was by his beard, and said I should leave that to him.

The next morning I drove over to the University about nine o'clock and Belkin was there waiting behind Flint Hall, standing beside his car with the hawk on his arm. The hawk's feet were tied with leather straps but she had no little pointed gnome cap over her face and eyes, and it was a disappointment to me to see her so untechnical that way. But Belkin said she didn't need a hood so long as nobody made any brusque movements near her face.

Besides the falcon, there was a physics student named Kay Eoff with Belkin and a biology student named Wayne King. Eoff and King got in the car with Belkin and the hawk, and I followed alone, because I expected to have to leave them after a short while and go back to town.

We went out the Newberry Road and stopped where wide pastures spread on either side. Belkin got out with the falcon on his arm and stood on the road shoulder, and the falcon bobbed her head and looked hard into the pastures, first one way and then the other. She looked at some black Angus cattle that were there, and having the eyes of a falcon, she no doubt looked at other things that we didn't see at all. When she had looked around a while, Belkin loosed the straps from her legs and she flew straight up to the top of a telephone pole and sat there bobbing her head and looking out first to one side of the road and then the other as before. For two or three minutes she stayed there, peering off into unknown distances the way those birds do. Then suddenly she seemed to see what she had in mind to look for. She hunched her shoulders and fell into the air, caught herself up and started off at the easy clip of a thrown boomerang toward a far corner of the field, where eight young cows were grazing.

The heifers were black and shiny on the short green grass in the sunshine, and they were not alone. By the head of one of them, there was a single splash of glowing white, where a cattle egret stood. I quickly judged the slant of the hawk going out from the pole and saw that it led straight to where the egret was. I climbed to the top of the car and focused my field glasses on the heron and saw it darting about and stabbing at insects the cows were flushing. I looked again at the falcon crossing the grass like the lazy lightning her flight seemed to be, and then turned back to see whether the heron would be struck on the ground or in the air.

But when the hawk was still maybe fifty yards away, the heron caught the meaning of the menace. He gathered somehow that it was no mouse-hunting harrier that was there, and he did a thing that could hardly have been more sweetly connived to bring point to my talk of birds and behemoths. He neither stood there numb nor rose in panic to meet destruction in the air. Instead he dashed straight in among the legs of the nearest cow. The hawk pulled out of her stoop, rose high over the backs of the cattle, and came in again; and once more the egret kept down frenzy and dodged into more shielded cover beneath another cow. Back and forth the falcon sliced, coming in low in short sallies, skimming over the cows only inches away. At each stoop the heron dodged to some safer place among the sixteen legs.

After a while the heifers, in their slow way, seemed to

suspect that things were abnormal somehow. One by one they started looking around with the ewe-necked look of alarm cows get, and then all together they began to trot away. When they ran, their legs, of course, no longer stood there stiff and still as a thicket of cow legs for a hard-pressed heron to hide in. The thicket moved away beneath the anxious cows, and around the dodging heron. The refuge of the forest of shanks translated itself across the Bahia lawn like a Birnam Wood, not coming to Dunsinane but moving nonetheless, and throwing hooves about that seemed bound to smash the heron, or to flush him finally out to the slashing terror.

But then, watching to see the heron struck, I saw instead a final solid proof of the inborn meaning of ungulates to egrets. As the thicket of legs moved away, the heron moved with it, in it, among the pettishly prancing hard feet of the heifers, now dodging to evade not just the falcon but also the swinging hooves. For a hundred yards across the pasture the dreamlike vignette held steady—the cows trotting away, black, shining, and unhappy; the sparkling white of the egret dashing about beneath them, and the foiled falcon still swooping over the backs of the trotting cows.

It was a Sunday morning and many cars were passing, mostly with children in them, no doubt on their way to Sunday school. A few of the people going by seemed to sense some excitement in the two cars stopped beside the road. To keep a crowd from building up, I got into my car and moved a little way west to the top of the next hill.

By the time I had parked in the new place, the cows had stopped running, and were pausing now and then to nose tentatively again at the grass. After one last irritable swoop, the falcon left them, climbed in a long spiral, and circled back high above the road. I could see Belkin looking up and watching her anxiously, because this might be a crisis in his relationship with her.

A man came out of a lane that led up to a house in a grove.

"What's the trouble," he said.

"No trouble," I said. "They're waiting for that hawk to come down."

The man looked up at the hawk and said, "What's the hawk doing up there?"

"Hunting cotton rats," I said. "Or so those fellows say."

The man looked at me as if I might be joking.

"Cotton rats?" he said.

"That's what those guys say," I said. "The ones down by that car."

The man shook his head slowly, and no doubt was about to say there were no rats in the pasture; but suddenly the hawk stopped her high turn and struck out in her slow-seeming rush, straight into the pasture across the road from the one the heifers were in. I looked to see where she was going this time. The line of her flight was a true course toward a single black bull that stood by a hedgerow of young live oaks. He was over there alone, except for three clean, cattle herons like three white holes in the green grass beside him. As the falcon came down, one heron jumped beneath the bull, but the two others sprang into the air, as if to plunge among the oaks. Before they were six feet off the ground, the hawk was upon them and instantly one lay in still dishevelment on the grass, with the hawk beside it, the two a confusion of white and gray in the climbing sunshine.

The man beside me watched it all and thought about it for a while. Then he turned and walked away down the lane. I looked out into the pasture again. The bull had moved away, and the heron and the hawk were a jumble of white and gray on the grass beside the live oak hedge.

From that it is plain that the buff-back's ties with behemoths are no casual thing in his life. So whether one likes the idea of the warning service—the mammal associate also getting good from the partnership—the fact is it almost surely does exist. The extent to which that part of the pact has influenced evolution in the two blood lines would be hard to assess. But obviously, you cannot live though long ages with a shining white bird that springs into the air at your head whenever company comes, and not be warned. You will be warned in spite of yourself.

When I was about to leave Kenya at the end of my second visit, my amateurish slides of game showed no good kongoni, one of the species of hartebeest. In a last-minute effort to fill the gap, I tried to stalk a herd of mixed kongoni, gazelles, and wildebeests. Each time I set the camera up, the cattle herons with the antelope took fright, and instantly the whole herd started to move away. This happened several times. While it was no proof that any really useful warning by the heron occurs, at least it was obvious that the egrets were seeing me before the antelope did, and that the antelope took alarm from their flying up.

Even in the brand new relation that the snowy egret has with cattle in Florida, you have only to find a heron with wild Indian cattle to see the system work. I remember trying to take a picture of a snowy heron that was foraging with a young Brahma cow, a sleek, capricious heifer, as Bartram would say. It was out on Tuscawilla Prairie. I had a big tripod and a ponderous long-focus lens, and I kept sneaking from one separate clump of cover to another, setting up the tripod behind a bush for a blind, fumbling for field and focus, and each time scaring up the heron before I could take the picture. For over an hour I kept at this, and each time I parted the bush to clear the way for the lens, the egret sprang into the air and the cow went charging off like a wild stallion, looking back over her shoulder for what there was to be scared of. Again, there was no shred of doubt that, usefully or not, the heron was warning the cow. Through no sweet spirit, to be sure; with no end or ethic in mind; and in this case without any real help to the heifer. But suppose there *had* been malice in my stalk. Suppose I had really been after beef, as the cow pretended to think. As in the case of the Kenya kongoni, the bare fact of my failing to get a picture shows how the arrangement would work.

Of course it takes more than emotion-ridden observations like these to prove that warning raises the life expectancy of game, and still more to prove that the warning function has been shaped and held up by natural selection. But if egrets jumping into the air do, to even the slightest degree, increase survival in their partners, then their partners clearly become more successful animals and stir up more grasshoppers more consistently; and the herons get back the bread they cast upon the waters. That is to say, everybody knows that a heron and a zebra taken separately are products of natural selection. Each is crammed full of adaptations, traits of body and mind that are there because in some way they increase the fitness of the bearer. If living together, as heron and zebras do, can be shown to be an advantage to both, then it should come as no surprise that each has traits it acquired, not just for its own sake directly, but for the sake of its partner, for the sake of the partnership that enhances the life expectancy of each of its members.

I freely admit that the idea of the game getting benefit is not to be swallowed docilely like a small pill. But look at it this way. The game herds of Africa today are not pure cultures of one species of hoofed mammal. As anyone who goes to the movies knows, they are mixed assemblages of antelopes of different kinds, usually with zebras or ostriches or something else thrown in. Insofar as lions or leopards or cheetas or aboriginal men are an adverse factor in the survival of the animals that compose the herds, anything that tells of the coming of these dangers brings longer life. Moreover, even the mere comforting confidence that sentries are on the lookout cannot be discounted as a factor in survival. Grazing is hard work; you have to keep at it to keep fed. When an animal grazes, his eyes are down at the level of the grass, his horizon is what he sees from among the legs of his fellows. In such mixed company, such edible company, when warning of danger comes to a wildebeest it may come from a Grant's gazelle, a zebra, or an impala—or it may be an egret in the air. It doesn't matter much, just so the warning is true and timely. So taking the herd as a unit—which in a real sense it is—and the egret as a factor in its survival outlook, and the herd as a factor in the survival of the egret, you find that the herd becomes somewhat attuned to egrets in its midst because the unattuned individuals were each generation a little more likely to die a little younger.

Well aware that I may go too far and mislead the young, I want to suggest that the whiteness of the buffback and the snowy heron, increasing, as it does, their effectiveness as a warning system, may be one more sign of long-time evolutionary interchange between herons and great grazing mammals. Or, to be safer, say that the whiteness of game herons owes some of its hereditary stability to the partnership of the heron with game. I mention this only because nobody else's explanation for whiteness in herons seems very convincing to me.

Whatever the main or original reason for herons being white, the whiteness is ideal for signaling. I remember a flight from Nairobi to Khartoum when we passed over Lake Rudolph so high one needed field glasses to tell buffalo from elephants in the herds of animals along the shores. But even that far down we could see the little egrets, flashing white points of heron white, scattered among the gray bulks of the behemoths.

Of course, a few other kinds of birds are white and not partners of anything. Arctic animals are white because whiteness conceals them in the snow. Sea birds are often white, and that may be because their main dangers come up from underneath, as a kingfish might come up at a floating tern. The bell bird of the American tropics is a dead, solid white and it lives in deep rain forests. No one will say why that should be. But the bell bird is an eccentricity anyway, a paranoiac creature with an ear-tearing voice to match the blatance of its whiteness. It seems for some reason determined to draw to itself the attention of the world by any means it can.

Among other Florida herons whiteness occurs in the little blue, the American egret, and the great white heron. It is only the first-year young of the little blue that is white. This can be taken to mean that being white is a primitive trait in that strain; and since the little blue is, of all the snowy's kin, most often seen walking in the pastures, one is bound to suggest that in some past age the little blue was both white and a mammal associate, too. Perhaps this was even before its stock and the stock of the snowy split apart. Or maybe its interlude on the plains came and ended at some earlier time and place, without reference to the snowy at all. It doesn't matter. The point is, the two traits, whiteness and tolerance of big terrestrial companions, show up together again in this other kind of

The Bird and the Behemoth

heron. And they show up yet again in the common egret, which as I said earlier, can sometimes be seen walking among cows, walking musingly, as if—as *if,* I said—ransacking his slim mind for what it was that some remote set of forebears learned to get on shore.

Don't think I mean herons are white only because they warn more effectively that way. Any adaptation is constantly being both coddled and battered in many ways by natural selection, both positive and negative. The fact, for instance, that a white bird would heat up less rapidly in the sun than a colored one is bound to affect the evolution of the bearer, though I haven't the vaguest idea how. It has been suggested that white egrets are concealingly colored—that, seen from below against the sky, as egrets are by prey and sometimes by predators, too, white is simply the best color for them to be. One writer even says that the fine, lacy plumes of egrets are not decoration at all, but a further concealing device. He says they come out at precisely the points in the silhouette where, without them, shading would reveal the form of the bird. This last seems pretty esoteric to me; but it's silly to quibble, when the fact is, plumes are surely and inescapably to some extent both revealing and concealing, and in the mind of female egrets both devilishly attractive and a dreadful bore. Whatever the other implications of whiteness may be, wild game under pressure from predators cannot afford to ignore warnings. White egrets, inadvertently or by evolutionary design, furnish warnings. The good they do this way may fail by far to match what they get in return, but if they do any good at all, the deal becomes a two-way one.

Some sound ornithologist ought to look about among the white herons of the world to see if they aren't significantly more inclined than the colored kinds to take up with mammals. Just dabbling around among regional bird papers, I seem to see that this is so. The thing is, white is such an outrageous color for a wild thing to be that it is hard to imagine a creature being white with no utility in it to outweigh the damage it does. Time and again, since grasses evolved, vast mammal herds have spread through the earth and stirred timid creatures out of hiding, and then have died slowly away when blizzards or rains made steppe or forest of their range. Perhaps herons of different kinds have come ashore many times, and independently have exploited the white mutation as an obvious step toward the life on land. By such reasoning, the buff-back may be simply the game heron to which this niche has remained most continuously available. The snowy is simply the most atavistic heron in his present range—the last to leave the mammoth pastures, the first to have taken up with cattle when landscapes were remade by man.

It is wild, though, isn't it, the way I go on over this small thing. There's no end to where it takes you, really.

Consider this other twist for a minute. Suppose you walked habitually with hard-footed behemoths, and were little and light and had breakable bones. One of the hazards of your life would be the possibility of getting stepped on. One way to avert the calamity would be to keep your partner aware that you are there. He has no wish to tread on your twiglike toes—he may even have evolved an inclination not to. Ungulates by their one-track nature shrink from a scene. They would hate the disruption of their peace that your squawking and flopping would bring. But ungulates are not very bright, and they must always be shown plainly where you are. To keep you in their eye and mind, what color is more suitable than white?

And lord love me, how I enjoy lying on cropped grass to

The Bird and the Behemoth

watch a snowy egret or a buff-back sidestepping the stumbling charges of an infant calf. I see the calm good humor of the bird as another way he is adapted to his partnership. A heron that got scared by the charging of a calf would be hopelessly hampered. And come to think of it, this fun for the cudless child must be reckoned as a blessing for the mother, as another bond of give-and-take in the egret-ungulate lichen. It may only be one of my irresponsible spells coming on, but I'm thinking how often I've watched a calf—a cowcalf, a little gnu in a Disney movie that nearly everybody saw, or an elephant's child deviling its mother's herons with stiff-legged ferocity—and have wondered what peace of mind for the mother it brings, what confidence for less distracted grazing, to make more milk for heron-deviling calves, to know just where the baby is and to have him entertained.

When the pterodactyls, the flying reptiles, mysteriously quit the world for good in late Cretaceous, there were aspirant bats to fit the living space they left. When dinosaurs dissolved away during the same calamitous times, mammals were on hand to take over their roles and skills and to think up many more besides. But in the more recent great extinction, that of the Ice Age grassland fauna, there has been only the most spurious replacement of what was lost. A whole life-form has dropped out of the old land-life structure. Throughout North America the whole grazing-browsing savanna community is gone or going. There is a rent-out space in the life-web where only a little while ago five kinds of elephants were; and camels and horses, bison and shrub oxen, pronghorns and cervid deer, making mammal landscapes which, you can see in even the dim evidence of bones, were the equal of any the world has known. It was in northern and central Florida that the great savanna fauna probably persisted the longest. Paleoecologists now say it might have held on down to no more than 4,000 to 8,000 years ago. It has been no time at all since they were here, when you think how wholly they are gone, how empty of them the days are under the same sun and rain, how recently their horn flies dwindled, the condors mourned over the last cadavers, the dung beetles turned to quibbling over piles of rabbit pills.

In Africa it was 1854 when the *Ma Robert* wheezed up the Shire and Livingstone saw elephants where Lewis and I saw Kaffir cows. The calamities on the two continents were comparable. The one in Africa simply happened faster. It went on there at a rate that only man can raise destruction to. So it might have been this sudden shrinking of its habitat that sent the buff-back questing about the world. How he came to probe across the sea, to join the snowy heron that was invading the new pasture-veld in Florida, cannot be told—at least not by me.

Whatever it was that took the buff-back to America, it surely must have been the disaster in the landscapes of Central Africa that pushed it down to the temperate tip of the continent. All through the gameless populous south of Africa I looked for buff-backs when I was there on a recent trip. I saw them, too, all about the place; in range as new to their species as the lands they have reached across the South Atlantic. I saw them stalking the bleak high-veld with range cattle, and in a corn patch, a patch of mealies, they say down there, by the head of a Holstein cow. In the gray cold of the Cape winter, I took a train out to Stellenbosch, and three times saw egrets through the rain-streaked window. The first was in the cluttered edge of Cape Town, where five herons stood in a pen of Poland China hogs. We left them and went on through the rain, reached Lynedock, and went by it. Just the other side a toy red tractor was harrowing in the wet wine fields, and behind it a whole flock of buff-backs was following in turmoil, jostling each other in their greed for the grubs and worms turned up in the cut earth. And then, as if to leave me with an essence of these days of herons and men, there was a sleeping mule slouched in the rain at the edge of Eersterivier, and on the high ridge of his scapula a buff-back stood, dour as the mule he stood on; waiting, one-legged, without evident hope, for things to be different from what they were.

There is a growing emptiness around us, and we fill it with noise, and never know anything is gone. But the buff-back remembers other times, with great game thundering through all the High Masai. And back at home you come upon a raging dragline with a wisp of a snowy heron there, dodging the cast and drop of the bucket as if only mammoth tusks were swinging—and what can it be but a sign of lost days and lost hosts that the genes of the bird remember?

The Lion Song

AT FIRST it was hardly more than a feeling in the ground, from out in the night somewhere. Then there was a bass cough, and crumping sobs gathered and went rolling about the dark, one by one, like barrels tumbling. It was the lion song, and I sat quiet to learn it, as you learn the trill of a tree toad, or how an alligator goes. And though there may have been little real song in the sound, it came in strong and lonely through the whisper of the mist; and to me, at the time, it seemed to tell of an age being lost forever.

I had reached the park gate ten minutes earlier, uneasy over what might be in store for a visitor an hour late in leaving. An African ranger was waiting when I got there. I dropped into low gear and crept toward him. By the light of the headlights I studied his posture for signs of indignation. I hoped his English would be up to the words of my excuse.

"Carburetor" ought to be all right, I thought—organs of engines everywhere go by English names. Or maybe just "car not start," leaving out the part about illegally driving off through the grass to get behind a thicket where three giraffes were browsing. There was no sense saying it was out there that the engine had to cool for half an hour before I could get it started. It must be a common situation, I thought; and no great offense either, really. Except for that one bad point—its happening off the road—it was clearly a blameless accident. Stanch from such figuring, I leaned out to face the ranger.

"Engine trouble," I said. "Sorry I got in late."

The man said nothing. I peered at him in the dark. He was listening, out the way I had come from.

"Simba," he said. "Lion—roaring."

I had never heard the voice of a free lion. But I could not bring myself to shut off the engine inside the park. Maybe the ranger was just forgetting that by rights he should berate me. It would be a fine thing to hear a lion roar, but the moment seemed in balance, and I said: "I better go outside to listen. O.K.?"

The ranger walked over to the gate and opened it, grinning and saluting absently, still listening to the lion. As I rolled past, I scratched in a pocket for some shillings and held them out to the man, half afraid the move would remind him of his duty; but he took them gladly and never stopped his listening.

I drove a little way along the road, stopped the car on the shoulder, and shut off the motor. I opened both doors wide to let in the sound of the lion. But there were only wet crickets to hear, and the rustle of windless rain. I reached behind the seat and felt in a basket for a bottle of beer, opened it, and settled back to wait. I was glad of the chance to close my eyes and sit, with no plain out front to search for antelope, no ire to feel over a stalled engine. A little while passed like that, and then the voice of the lion came back through the hanging dark.

At first I listened, as I said, just to learn how a lion roars. But soon there seemed more to the ponderous call than its sound alone, and it came to me clearly what a lion stands for. I thought of the lionland fauna of the Pleistocene harried through a changing world to a last refuge in Africa; and of the herds and prides safe here at last from floods and drought and fickle ice, and from everything else on earth but the Age of Reason. I thought how little of the old world remains anywhere, and how unlikely it is that a creature as petulant as man will let these last bits of Africa stay fit much longer for the lion song.

I remember the time, long before I heard the lion, when blood came into the Ice Age for me—when it seemed all at once to be more than text in a book with pictures by Charles R. Knight, and I thought for the first time of dyings of the Ice Age grading in with the ruin of the Age of Man.

It was noon of a clear July day when it happened. I was riding the run of a Florida spring, floating face down and searching the bottom through the pane of a homemade face mask. There was nothing special I was looking for. In those days it was enough just to ride down with the stream and look for things to see and never see a single beer can from Ichtucknee Springs to the Santa Fe. The sun was hot on my back through the wet lap of water and I hung belly down in the air-clear stream and looked at the bottom slipping by, one moment a waving yellow-green of Sagittaria ribbons and the next, a black-green of a naiad bed or a sudden red of water purslane, or moving

The Lion Song

soft horns of pink-tipped coontail set with slim cones of spiny snails.

It is a fine sight down through new spring water. One of the sad parts of my lot is that goggling needs more drama than pretty plants to stir my slight metabolic fires and keep off the dire sickness of the skinny skin diver—the ague we used to call the "big shakes."

There was that day, for instance, a long run with no break in the water gardens—no bone-strewn riffle or shards of Indian pottery, or Suwannee chicken cooter shying at my passing—with nothing there but the man-killing cool and the sweetness of a spring run at summer noon. The zeal began chilling out of me, and I thought how welcome a fire on the bank would be, and a chocolate bar; and the bottom got to looking like only wet plants. Then an eddy swung me over a bed of stonewort and I felt the prickle of the little leaves, and the smell made one of those queer smell-imprints that stick hard forever; so that now, to me, the faintest scent of stonewort or even of some sorts of onion soup brings back the sight of the big molar tooth lying there on swept sand beyond the stonewort bed, with all its roots and cusps, and its enamel still shining as if a big man had lost it the day before. It was the tooth of a mastodon, and the heat came back in me at the sight. I worked back along the edge of the sluicing channel, dived, and grabbed the tooth and rode the current down to slack water. Then I stood there knee deep in more musk grass, turning the fossil in my hands, looking back plainly to a time when real giants lived in the Suwannee Valley land.

The tooth was half the size of a football—too big for the bag that held my match-bottle and chocolate bars—but I had warmed up from its being so ponderous and so sure proof of different times, and I dropped back into the current to ride on down, with the four-pound tooth held tightly in one hand. There was a quarter-mile of smooth travel, with now and then a Suwannee bass rolling his red eye from under a jutting log, or a sprinkling of silver minnows all nose-upstream in the channel edge, or a moss-thatched stinkjim craning his neck to scramble from under my slipping shadow. Then suddenly I slid over another swept riffle and in a litter of meaningless pieces of brown bone saw bulk like a shaped lump of coal half out of the dark sand bottom. I clawed back to a point upstream from the object, dived, and rooted out the chunk of shiny black with one free hand. Then I kicked away downriver to feel for shallow water and see what the new find was. When my feet found bottom, I gulped air, scratched the mask off, and stood there studying the object.

It was clearly a piece of another tooth, but it was very different from the first. It had an undivided root, and the crown was crossed by repeated low, wavy ridges instead of high cusps. One end was broken off, and I was barely able to summon the lore to know that this, too, was a bit of a proboscidean, a relic of some elephant-kind of another sort. It was the grinding molar of the big Columbian mammoth. I thought the matter through, and then stood there in the suck of the current with bits of two Florida elephants in my two hands. I was so fired up by the coincidence and the triumph that the water stayed warm as new milk for the whole mile down to the landing.

That was a long time ago, but it gave me a lasting feel of the lost times as real days. Later I got to know keen bone men like Walter Auffenberg, who scratch out clay-filled cracks or pipes in the limestone, or sling on an aqualung and headlight and crawl a hundred yards back into the feed-tube of a big spring and bring out sacks full of the Ice Age fauna. You spread out on the bank the bones that Auffenberg can bring up in a morning's diving, and get him to name the pieces for you, and long before you reach the end of the row of bones, you see how an arm of the sea of savanna-lands swept down into the jut of Florida, and the complex grassland life trooped in from the interior of the continent where mammal time was at its climax.

These old animals of the spring runs and filled-in sink traps, the beasts from the asphalt pits in California, and the dwindling herds of the Kenya plains, are all relics of the great tropical savanna fauna of the Pleistocene, a fauna that had taken shape earlier, when grasses arose and spread over the open lands of the world. The Ice Age was not by any means one long even run of cold, but rather a changeable million years when weather cycles rose and fell and seas came over the land edge and went away again, and glaciers piled and spread and rotted down. Ages of long drought made plain, veld, pampa, campo, llano, or prairie of much of the land of the earth, with short or tall grass set in orchards of thorn or hard-leafed monsoon trees, or with snaking galleries of scrub—or with nothing at all but the beasts to break the sweep of the green or gold of the grass itself. Nowhere on earth have the mammals so clearly shown the evolutionary vigor of their line as in this terrain. Nowhere have there ever lived together so intimately—so finely subdivided in life-theme and elegantly woven into the warp of the landscape—such diverse and fancy gangs of big, warm-blooded, grazing, browsing, predaceous, scavenging creatures as make up the waning brotherhood of the warm savanna country.

There was a time when the spring-run fauna of Florida was live elephants of four kinds, sloths bigger than steers, sabertooths and jaguars, and a dire wolf the size of two German shepherd dogs together. There were camels in it, and horses in herds and glyptodonts like armor-plated Volkswagens; and to show the endless bounty of the grass, there were even tortoises in slow shoals there—herds of giant tortoises that grazed among herds of mammals. Through a million years of change, these animals of the open lands spread over half-continents and drew back before cold or flood or drought, or savanna-turning-into-forest, or desert or steppe; and when the Ice Age ended, if it has, the grand old fauna was in shreds. There were camels left on the Gobi Desert and in the Andes; and there were asses here and there. The pampas had an ostrich of a sort and the flat insides of North America had bison, pronghorns, and prairie dogs left to eat the grass. There was one place left in the world where the fauna had the many-faced look of the old lost times, and that was the African savannas.

So the spread of beasts that today we call the African veld fauna is not from a long view indigenous to Africa at all. As an ecological organization it is really a version of the grand plains community of the Ice Age. It grew into something like its present form on the plains of Asia not very long ago, and in good times spread down into Europe, leaving France, for instance, with bones of such creatures as waterbuck, kudu, wildebeest, and zebra. Later on tolerable times in Asia waned. Spain spread smoothly into Africa, which had green corridors into it from time to time, and the lionland animals took this only highway to survival and found the vast savannas of the African plateau. Now, the only place where you can see how it was in the old wild times when men became human is there on the African veld.

I have been to Africa four times in the last decade.

The Lion Song

On the first two visits, in no way connected with big game, I was astonished and depressed by how much of rural Africa you can cover and see less wildlife than you would kick up in an equal amount of Georgia. The trips took me back and forth across the continent several ways. Between Kenya and Cape Town I looked at animals in National Parks and reserves and managed areas, and looked for them in other vast empty places where animals used to be but are no longer. Everywhere I stopped, I talked to naturalists and wildlife officers and hunters. I came away with my first clear realization of what is going on in Africa.

I saw for the first time that the trouble is not just that tractors and highways scare animals over there, or that new dams are drowning them out of a few valleys. The finish is looming for the old savage world of mammals at peak grandeur. And to save it as anything more than a row of cages—to save for even the next generation after ours a few fragments of primordial earth—will be a feat that only the will and resources of a world more stirred up than it is now can bring about. Every year that passes brings losses, and new sources of loss, at a rising tempo. The way things are moving in Africa, the time will soon be past when even a good fight can save anything more than scraps.

This was new thinking to me. I had read little on the subject since Theodore Roosevelt and Carl Akeley, and in their time such talk was prophecy. Today the game men show you figures, empty land, and unanswered questions of game ecology. They trace trends that make you see that it is already almost too late to save much outside of the parks and preserves. I came back from Africa puzzled at how little I had known of the urgency of the problem there. I began sampling the temper of my colleagues and countrymen to see if Americans in general have been lulled as I was by the new game parks you hear about.

I learned that the New York Zoological Society and the Conservation Foundation had invited the articulate English ecologist Fraser Darling and Noel Simon of the Kenya Wildlife Society to come to the United States and try to make Americans understand what the world is losing in Africa. In *Animal Kingdom* and in *The Atlantic Monthly* I read articles by George Treichel that gave clear outlines of the tragedy ahead. A little later the International Union for the Conservation of Nature reinforced the slowly mounting campaign with its African Special Project. The World Wildlife Fund was established, and Prince Philip made a stirring speech at its New York meeting in 1962. Project Noah, the dramatic rescue operations at Kariba Dam where animals were being trapped by rising water, got wide and helpful publicity. Exciting pictorial articles on African animals began to appear in popular magazines.

But in spite of these good signs, I saw that even among Americans who carry a chronic head of steam over the passing of the wild, any show of concern over Africa seemed pretty visionary. A damned shame, of course, they seemed to feel, but a sort of academic shame. One trouble is that the North American adult with a predilection for nature finds his own losses at home so cruel that going far away to cry the blues seems irresponsible. It was a big land Americans were born in. It is still so near pioneer times that people over forty remember wilderness to spare. But talk big to your boy nowadays about your own boyhood in the woods and you suddenly realize that you're stirring him up with urges less likely to profit him than knowing how to shrink heads or to build himself a sound harem.

In Florida these days, you can still hear, under the mindless, glad din over industry coming in, the voices of the old ones—or of the young ones who have listened to the old ones—grieving over the passing of the wilderness. They are no longer watching landscapes wasting away. That happened long ago. What is going on now is just a lot of little cleanup operations, little scratchings-out of small tag-ends and patches of the past overlooked in the first waves of ruin. Outboard motors are washing the water-plants clear out of the spring runs; the last evergreen hammocks are falling in chopped-out confusion; the airboats are cornering the wildest sulphur-belly frogs in the farthest coves of bonnet marsh.

There is a little pond I know—Jonah's Pond we used to call it, until that seemed to some less elegant than "Lake Alice"—a few priceless acres of marsh and swamp and pond water at the edge of the University of Florida campus, where any spring morning you can to this day have a glimpse of how Florida used to be. There will be five kinds of herons nesting there in the good seasons, croaking and chuckling over the sharing of the home space; gallinules and boat-tailed grackles running the pads, over and around basking turtles and alligators; white ibis, glossy ibis, anhingas, swamp rabbits, and people coming and going; and fat watersnakes that do not bother to whip off when cars full of children stop and gibber ten feet up the fill from the edge of the pond. The flooding sun, the bullfrog talk, the song of redwing blackbirds—it is all there still, saved somehow almost as it was when I first saw it thirty-two years ago. It is a little island of old times. It is slowly edging back before the closing circle of necessary progress. Everyone is sorry to see it shrinking. But the war babies are coming to college now, and having babies of their own, and little can be done.

It is sad in Florida these days. But it is worse in some other states. Ohio, for example. Think of Ohio.

And Missouri. A sad thing happened in Missouri a little while ago. The Nature Conservancy made a reserve of a 160-acre tract of Missouri prairie. It was the last piece of undisturbed prairie left in the United States. Not the last virgin prairie, mind you—there wasn't a bison or Comanche left on the whole place—just the only remaining unplowed, primitive plot of grass and gophers in the whole flat heart of the continent. But it had never been planted to corn and it seemed worth saving as a relic. Then no sooner had the deal been closed than the Road Department claimed a right of way and could not be dissuaded from its rights. The great American Plains will accordingly go down to posterity, not as 160 pristine bisonless acres of grass, but as 80.

With that sort of clutching at straws going on at home, I suppose it is no wonder the plight of the Pleistocene seems far away in Africa, where an unreal aura hangs anyway, part gin, part cordite smoke, part sex on a canvas cot. And anyway, you can easily see from the movies that animals are all over the place out there—the ground is crawling with fauna. So with plenty to worry about at home, and with no real understanding of what is happening in Africa, the usual American says, oh, what the hell, the British will look after the animals.

And as a matter of fact, to the extent that good will and stewardship will do the job and that the remaining time will allow it to be done, the British will take care of the animals—and the French, Belgians, and South Africans will too. They have known the value of the resource they are tending for a long time, and it was their concern over its deterioration that finally began to stir the world a little. The British recently sent Fraser Darling out to spend six months studying the situation in Northern Rhodesia. His book *Wild Life in an African Territory* gives a clear picture of the land use and management problems there. In the newly organized Nuffield Unit of Tropical Animal Ecology, the University of Cambridge, Makarere College at Kampala, and the National Parks Authority of Uganda are beginning a series of careful studies of the ecology of the larger herbivorous animals.

Beginning with the visit of Dr. George Petrides to Kenya in 1953, a series of American Fulbright Scholars has been in East and Central Africa to study problems of range ecology and to test the applicability of American methods of big-game range management in the tropical savanna landscapes. For the future of wild Africa outside the parks, the most hopeful advance to date has been a realization that in most of the important game areas a natural mixed association of herbivorous animals produces more meat per acre than the cattle that are driving them out. The mixed fauna of many kinds of ungulates was molded into the landscape by natural selection. Its use of the range is more complete and less injurious than that of cattle, which graze selectively and degrade the landscape. Game is also immune to ngana, the endemic sleeping sickness carried by tsetse flies, which is fatal to cattle; and many of the antelope can live with a water ration that would kill a cow. This favorable outlook for game cropping bolsters the preservation campaign with another economic asset to be added to that of tourism in the parks. It thus is another selling point with the Africans who will one day take the whole thing over. I believe it was George Petrides who, in 1954, first suggested substituting game husbandry for cattle raising, although John Emlen of the University of Wisconsin was saying similar things about the same time. In any case, the productivity of the veld in antelope meat is now envisioned as the only hope for the permanent—and I should put the word in quotes—maintenance of anything that looks like wild lands outside the inviolate preserves.

But this is just a tactical expediency. It is in a way a desperate recourse, too, because it will only make life even more feasible for greater quantities of man. And in any case it has little to do with the problem of maintaining the parks, the museum-piece areas, where the obligation is to save bits of the primitive earth in as unruined a state as possible. Everywhere I went in Africa during the fifties the people were puzzled over how little the world outside seems worried over these matters. They figure they have charge of a thing that is sure to be treasured a thousand years from now—a thing likely to be lost in spite of all we do to save it, but not, thinkably, to be abandoned through short sight, ignorance, and provincialism.

The world has never come to grips with a preservation problem of the stature of this one. Nobody ever set out on a conservation project that could be compared with the job of keeping intact a delicate, rowdy, perishable relic like the plains-game landscape. It is a problem that puts both the humanity of man and the skill of the ecologist to test. Even if the good will and compassion of the world are won, there will still be the towering problem of understanding one of the most complex of all biological communities—and then of controlling and preserving it, both in separate, walled-off sanctuaries and in land where growing numbers of Africans must share the habitat with the game. Anywhere one starts to plan, the unanswerable questions loom. How much land, for instance, is the right amount to make a permanent preserve? How much is needed to build a self-sustaining unit, not just for now, when bordering wild lands feed in new stock or take off surpluses, or furnish restless herds the room they need at roaming season, but for times when, all about the preserve, progress or destruction have skinned the wild off down to dirt, and the antique wilderness must live at last within its limits?

Some day, to exist in the world coming, every big game wilderness reserve will lie behind fences—real, varmint-stopping fences, leopard tight and eland high. And in those times, as now, the urge to migrate will still stir some species; and drought will come in, or unfettered fire; or grasshoppers will rage down and wreck the grass, and the herds will have to find shifting room or starve. How big must a preserve be to weather times like those?

There is probably at present in Africa no area in which an unabridged grassland community is living wholly within set limits. Kruger is the oldest of the National Parks. Its 8,000 square miles perhaps come fairly close to self-sufficiency. But Kruger, in spite of its magnificence, is far from being a natural area, and is, moreover, in broad contact on its eastern frontiers with wild country in Mozambique. Nairobi National Park, beginning just four miles from town, is the most-visited park today, and one of the wonders of the world. But how good would it be without the broad reserve lands behind it? All the other big refuges for mixed plains animals, living in more or less natural balance, touch primitive lands broadly at their edges, and give-and-take is going on all the time.

The prospect of the fences brings up another question: how nearly natural can you hope to keep a wilderness preserve with a varied fauna in it anyway? The ideal of an absolutely undisturbed sample under fence is probably not realistic. One doesn't simply wall off a diverse community of live wild things and protect it from hunters and expect it to stay the way it was. The mere presence of a wall there brings about changes inside; and then, to keep track of the changes, rangers move in, and they need houses, and roads to range on. There will be visitors, too, because it is people the relic is being saved for, really. Only the endless enthuiasm of people will make the venture work at all. Visitors need game-viewing trails, and guides, safari lodges and gas-pumps; and these must be mixed in tactfully with the trees and beasts and grass. With all that going on, it soon becomes clear that the job at hand is in most cases not simply one of protecting wilderness, but of managing it, which is a very different thing. You run for the rule book, but you find there are no rules—no manuals, and very little in the learned journals —to help the people running an African wildlife reserve to plan for the days when their grandchildren will pave the world over, clear up to the park fence.

So now, when population explosion and nationalism are bringing the crisis in Africa to a climax, the laborious studies on which to ground control techniques needed to save the most complex mammal community in the world are only barely getting under way. There are people who for a long time have known how to manage forests—some kinds of forests—in the sense that they can keep more or less the same kinds of trees growing there. Watersheds can be managed, too; and trout streams, after a fashion. Stoats still chase hares in English hedgerows after a thousand years, and Pennsylvania has more deer than Pitt ever saw there. But out in Africa the thing to be managed is a host of kinds of big herbivores, carnivores, and unseen beings in the soil—all built into an intricately adjusted organization with a teetery balance inside. To save such an organization you have got to keep tampering with its adjustments, and no one really knows yet how to predict results of the intervention.

A pint of hay tea set to fester for a spell will work up into an exciting small sea of wild things, a wet little wildlife reserve more complex in its affairs than a guided missile, I guess, or than New York City. Looking down into a drop of such frantic soup, a man cannot start to say how the life of each microbe, alga, and protozoan bears upon the lives of all the others. But few biologists deny that there is something more there than a formless grouping —than the simple sum of what he sees.

Any stable natural assemblage of beings living successfully together is bound to be an organized system, with energy coming in through vegetables like grass, trees, or algae, and then passing along chains and through webs of feeding relations, till the last dead buzzard or toadstool gives it back to space as heat for the cold. It is not that way in the zoo, but in the jar of hay broth and in the sea it is; and in any wilderness preserve that can claim to have saved anything at all. How many elephants, for instance, make a lasting sample of the wild? Too few, and the landscape changes and nobody sees an elephant— bush grows into the water holes and the water trails close over, and the antelope die off on the baking plain in the dry season. Too many, and they wreck the woods that feed them. What is a lion, really, you will finally need to know. What is the real role of this seemingly simple machine for killing, once he is shut in for good with the last hosts of his natural prey? Now is the time when you need to know more about lions than just how they feel about tourists. The place can be made or broken by lions. The problems of predation are always subtle ones, even if it is only deer or quail you are raising. But lion-management in a faunal preserve in Africa has the makings of a nightmare, with the grass-eating lion-bait out there in thousands, straining to overbreed and trample into the clay more grass than it eats; and with leopards, cheetahs, servals, civets, hyenas, and hunting dogs doing partly, but not exactly, what the lion does to help the herbivores live right, and themselves all fecund in their own right, all susceptible to rabies—all separate parts of a system that any little push might send snowballing to disaster within the unyielding walls around it.

It takes a sound organization to support lions under fence. Keep your lions in good fur and your place is doing all right. Let them get out of hand and the zebras will soon show it, and the impala; and all the herd animals that give sweep to the landscape will go to making lion, the undergrazed grass will go off into scrub, and the lions will end up with the mange, or even with a taste for tourists.

And fire. Who knows what to do about African fire? One thing is sure—you can't simply keep fire out and have the place stay the way it was. Most of the vast grasslands of the tropics are to a greater or lesser extent fire landscapes. They grow where half the year any spark can catch and run for miles. Wherever dry grass spreads, men, lightning, or volcanoes can set yearly fires that whip up their own winds and race across the plain before them, blotting down the fire-shy plants and holding the land in a state of hung-up change they call a fire climax.

In Florida, a hundred years ago, you could drive a wagon across the whole midsection of the peninsula, they say, through rolling parks of longleaf pines. The trees, set spaciously on the sand hills, rose a hundred feet to their crowns, and made a majestic landscape not often seen today, and not at all in Florida. The trunks of the longleaf pine are not hurt by passing fire; the high rise and wide spacing of the crowns in the primeval hills kept them from catching fire, or from lighting one another. The crawling groundfires shaved down the understory to duffless wiregrass; and the backbone ridge-lands were held that way—by fire—as a stately orchard of big-cone pines and gophers and fox squirrels. The hills are all cut over now, all in turkey oak and citrus and watermelons and people. But back in the Indian times the whole central ridge was clean groves of high pine, kept steady in their way by fire.

And now ecologists are trying to learn, before it is too late, how much of the savanna land of Africa owes its look to periodic or sporadic burning. Once in the dry season I flew from Nairobi to Johannesburg—straight down the long middle of the continent—on an evening flight. Looking down by the hour into the dark heart of the land, I saw for hundreds of miles no patterned twinkle of town lights anywhere, but there was never a time when the country was not burning. For as far as fires would show, dozens of separate thin-lined red arcs or circles were down there eating at the crisp monsoon country, keeping it as it was when the handaxe men were there—keeping it fit for grass and a grassland fauna.

Much of the good game land is an interrupted stage in the sort of landscape-evolution that ecologists call succession. Succession is the natural progression of steps from however a landscape is first colonized by plants and animals toward whatever kind of vegetation the climate of the region would finally mold and hold there. There have always been natural forces to set fires. For ages pastoral men and hunters have been burning the veld, too, and gardening men have cut back the forest edge, burned and tilled, and left grass behind when they moved away. No one can say how the plateau of Africa would look if it stayed free of fire for a century. But there is little doubt that much of the land is fire landscape, and that without it savannas would go into forest, thorn scrub, or something else very different.

The only thing to do is learn how to make of fire a tool to maintain the landscape, to keep the kinds of habitat the fauna requires. But if fire is a factor in building landscapes, it is also one that can degrade them. Fraser Darling thinks that in some parts of Africa, fire is being used with too great a zeal in the management of range. So an important line of investigation seeks simply to determine when to burn, whether early or late in the season, whether every year or once in two years, or once in three.

Down in the quail country of southeastern Georgia they used to say that Herbert Stoddard could take a piece of country and, using fires set just so, at just the right time of day and year, shape the woods like a boxwood hedge, making it fit the taste of any finicky sportsman. Setter dogs work better in one kind of cover than in others, and so do pointers; and people use odd sorts of creeping spaniels, with special sets of cravings and horrors. A woman is scared of snakes, say, or a client is short or very tall, or shoots a .410 gauge gun or shoots only from horseback or out of a mule-drawn buckboard—or so skillfully that only rises in tight thickets put sport in his chances. For each of these, the Stoddard system of burning can make quail woods, and they turn out as tailored to the figure of the owner as his hunting pants.

In the Belgian Congo, a few years ago, the plague locust came and blasted the best of the antelope country in Albert Park. To get green back into the land as quickly as possible, it was kept free of fire. But what came back was not the old grassland and the antelope that the place had been famous for. It was dense scrub instead. There were elephants and buffalo in it, but they stayed mostly out of sight in the rough bush, and visitors went away disappointed.

So there will have to be people who know how to fight fire, and how to use it, both in the lands in which Africans share the habitat with the animals, in the wholly inviolate relic tracts, and in the islands of plants, animals, and tourists that the game-viewing parks will be. Somebody will have to know how to lay out and keep a clean sweep of short grass, with ten thousand ungulates of ten different kinds to be seen at once, and lions to tend them, and, around the pans and waterholes and in the stream bottoms, elephants under fever trees where the casual safarist just out from Boston or Brussels with his family in a hired car can take a picture. Fire is bound to be a part of maintenance. It is no good planning to keep the Ice Age relics free of fire.

And it is no use making plans that exclude people. Like other saved-up bits of wilderness everywhere, any African preserve that lets visitors in will, from the start and increasingly as time passes, have people to contend with. As distances shrink and more people get about to look at the world they are losing, the parks will succeed only if they are built to stand the admiration of the chains of human generations.

In the United States, the National Parks, which are not nearly as fragile charges as the wildlife preserves of Africa, are right now, as a park official says, being "loved to death" by the hordes of visitors goaded by a growing vogue for outdoor recreation. The vogue seems bound to swamp the wilderness it cherishes. Not long ago, lunchtime caught me in one of these parks. I was driving a car full of my family at the time. When my children are traveling and lunchtime comes upon them, it is a crisis, and something has got to be done at once. There were victuals in the car that day, and all we required was a place to park and eat. For miles, with the tension growing, I kept trying to draw up beside the road where it ran along a little river; but every turnout was filled with cars. Picnicking people were clotted in every slight break in the rhododendron. With hysteria looming in the car, I raced out to the camp ground and threaded a maze of car-lined roads for ten minutes before I could find any way to leave the crawling queue of vehicles. Finally, by sheer courage and good fortune, I fought my way into a space a car was leaving.

As the children struggled over the food, I sat there looking out at what the world was coming to. For acres of what had been, the last time I saw it, silent forest, I could now see no way to walk, for the clutter of tents, cars, and people. There were queues at the fireplaces, and out where once there were only ruffed grouse, a man was selling, for fifty cents each, bundles of firewood brought in from somewhere else. There were trees there still, but more people than trees; and over along the creek that sang unheard in the clamor of the lovers of wilderness, there were dazed frogs still, but more babies than frogs by far. The scene in that wonderful old place of my youth was only a little more sylvan than downtown Cincinnati. And yet, when you get to thinking about it, there is no sense in sneering at one's species for flocking to the woods. Sneer at the abundance of people—deplore it more than any other human attribute—but not at their wanting wilderness. Only the hankering that makes man clutter and track the parks will ever make it possible to save any wilderness, anywhere. I don't mean that the African fauna preserves have to be turned into recreation areas. But there is no sense kidding yourself that, being away off in Africa, they will stay safe from the clamor of humans. Forty thousand visitors went through little Nairobi National Park last year, and at some seasons you have to get reservations months ahead to be sure of accommodations in Kruger Park. The visitors are not just local folk, and American tourists who are going everywhere. A new European lust for Africa is spreading, and a new interest in natural history. German, French, and Italian people are showing up in droves with telephoto lenses, and building up traffic in some of the parks to a critical level.

But this problem of too much love can probably be solved—somehow—because it proves the economic value of wilderness; and economics will loom large in the eyes of the new African governments, and will help get their support for conservation generally. Meantime, there are other people in the preserves who are doing more damage than the tourists, and not for love. These are the poachers. On my arrival in Nairobi one day I opened a copy of the *East African Standard* and read big headlines that rejoiced over the destruction of a poaching gang in the Tsavo National Park. The gang had, in a period of two and a half years, killed 3,000 elephants, the paper said. Tsavo is a big place, to be sure. It covers 8,000 square miles and there is vast wild country around it. But even so, 3,000 elephants seemed a lot; and I walked down to the Game Department to see what the men there thought of the paper's figure. They thought it was a careful estimate; and they said, moreover, it was only the number of elephants killed for ivory, and did not include the unknown hundreds of calves that must have died because they lost their mothers.

Policing a place like the Tsavo preserve is a hard job; and it is the same in all the best game areas, because the best terrain is likely to be the most remote and the most devilishly easy for poachers to work and hide in. Out in those tough, thirsty places you are working not just against hungry tribesmen but against rich old Chinese with talented concubines and rundown vigor, whose agents pay well for the new potency they figure they get from rhino-horn shaved into a cup of wine. The old mandarins of past times killed the rhinoceros out of much of its Asiatic range that way; and with a little more time they can kill it out of Africa, too. That is a strange thought to me: that the big slow-grown rhinos and elephants, only barely left over from Tertiary time, are rotting finally away for a snout horn, or for two teeth; while the most technological ape tinkers about in space before he improves on ivory of elephants, or on aphrodisiacs of Kubla Khan.

There is also cash from curio dealers for the backland tribes that bring in tails of wildebeests for tourists to take home as exotic fly-swatters. The bodies are often left to comfort the vultures and jackals. The wire-strong sinews of giraffes make good bowstrings, so long as it doesn't rain; and always there are the people craving meat, and biltong brings two shillings the arm's length. So with Arab and Indian traders goading them, the tribes follow their old arts of the snare and poison arrow, and kill far more animals now than they did in the days when they hunted for themselves alone. Some of the poaching is done with guns, but the real craftsmen like gang snares and arrow poison, which make no noise about their mass murder and require no driving of game or moving about that might draw the rangers in.

Of all East African game country, the land most celebrated, for half a century past, is the great Serengeti Plain in Tanganyika, once a famous hunting ground and now a

National Park. But Serengeti is cruelly arid. During the dry season, there is no water in hundreds of square miles, and big herds of antelope move westward then to river bottoms outside the park. The routes of these migrations make ideal poaching stands for the tribes living about the western boundaries of the park. These people are archers. They poison their arrows with tarry stuff boiled out of the bark of a leguminous tree. They smear the gum on the arrow for several inches back of the barb, leaving the point clean to keep an accidental scratch from killing the bowman. There is fast traffic in this poison. Ten shillings will buy enough for a dozen arrows, and these will last a hunter for a year, because the arrows can be dug out of the dead animals and used repeatedly.

Parties of hunters build blinds at the water holes and wait there for the herds to come to drink. When animals move into range, arrows are pumped into them as fast as they can be let go. A good bowman can get off twenty arrows before the game has stampeded out of reach. After that there is plenty of time to walk about and quietly locate the fallen animals by the circling vultures above them. If finding them is slow and the meat spoils in the hot sun, it doesn't matter much. The tail of the beast is likely all you're after anyway.

Snares are good, too, as quiet as a snake—and they work while the hunter drowses in the shade, clear of the scattered wardens' sight. There are surely more snare loops hanging in Africa today than anywhere else in the world. They set snares there for giraffes, and they set them for mice. The worst scare I got out of backwoods Africa was when I personally stuck my neck into an antelope snare.

It was a silly thing, looking back on it; but it was harrowing for me at the time. It happened down in Nyasaland. One afternoon of my first week in Africa, I took a walk on a flat-topped mountain back of Limbe, only a short way—a mile-and-a-half, maybe—from the hotel where Lewis and I were staying. I climbed the slope at the edge of town, through the clean-stemmed planted blue gums there, and came out where head-high grass covered the ridges and slopes, and bits of forest filled the swales. The clouds were down around the mountain, and the look of it up there, with the Scotch mist swirling, made it seem like a real wild place where any wild creature might be.

As I stood just out of the blue gums at the edge of the high savanna, an uncouth squalling set up over toward the highest rise of the mountaintop. There was a rockfield there, between the far edge of the grass and a slash of black forest. I thought how leopards were said to wander across this mountain; and wondered what monkey might make such sounds; and, going on down the list of my book-learned animals, I hit on *hyrax*—and started stalking the noise to see if it was really a hyrax there.

Hyraxes, small as they are, were a kind of beast I wanted to see in Africa. Most people know, nowadays, that, although it looks more like a little woodchuck, a hyrax is really a sort of elephant, or vice versa. I had read that looking about inside one will prove to the most stubborn person that hyrax parts, despite the way they look when assembled, are not the parts of a rodent at all but more nearly like those of a little elephant. Or a sea cow. There are those who say that hyraxes are even closer kin to sea cows. There seems no limit to the wild conclusions learning can lead to. As far as I am concerned, however, it is going far enough to say that it is elephants that the hyrax resembles most inside.

In any case, when it came to me that a hyrax might be doing the yelling in the rock pile, I pushed my way into

The Lion Song

a trail that made a tunnel through the eight-foot grass, and started sneaking forward, head down and quiet as I could, through the packed-back stems. I could see only the grass; but the trail appeared to be bearing the right way, and I ran along it in the close trench.

The ground was misted wet and quiet to walk on. The trail kept heading toward the sound; and after a while I thought it was time to stand high and look toward the rocks for the singing cony. But all at once the thought was blotted out by an odd small feeling of resistance across the base of my neck. Even in the split second before momentum could take me on forward, the force there seemed too hard and even to be dragging grass stems, and I stopped in my tracks. I raised a slow hand and felt that it was a ring of wire around my neck. Stiff-necked, I rolled my eyes toward one side and saw there an acacia sapling bent down over the trail, holding up the noose my neck was in by a line of the same steel wire. Too scared to judge what move might be least sure to throttle me, I thought back to when I was twelve years old and, after many trials, rigged a snare just right, with a trigger to trip and let a bent sapling snap up straight, and finally one morning found frost on the fur of a dangling cottontail.

I wondered where to feel for the trigger of this snare that almost had me dangling. I cautiously fingered back and forth around the loop to the line that held it up, and suddenly the fright eased out of me. The noose was hanging loosely, and I could see then that the tree was not set tense to spring and close it. It was bent over the trail to suspend the loop, and to anchor it while the victim lunged and garroted itself in its own wild misunderstanding. It was a clever trap for little antelope no doubt. But I was a man, and probably had about as much sense as the man who made the trap. I backed my head out of the ring of wire and, leaving the hyrax singing, I headed straight back to town.

I doubt if any trapping of animals in Africa has ever equaled in volume the wholesale snaring operations of the East African Negroes in the recent steel-wire years, with the big game dwindling, the price of meat rising, and tourists coming in and paying tourist's prices for souvenirs. The snares used to be made of sansaveria fiber; but now, with better times, trickles of cash reach into the farthest hinterlands and steel wire is bootlegged through the countryside at five shillings or so the eight-foot trap length. The snares are hung in rows from double lines. Sometimes a village party will build miles of thorn fence across the ways to water, and in a gap every ten to twenty yards hang an anchored loop of wire. Or two loops—a high one for big game and a small one down low for duikers and the like.

The traps may be visited once a week. When a hunting party returns and finds animals still alive after their long thirst, the excess is hamstrung and let loose to find water and await its turn for slaughter.

Although snaring has no doubt been going on for ages, it has only lately come to be a factor in the survival of the fauna. So long as the Africans, lions, and antelope were out there alone together, they were only working out an age-old natural give-and-take. But now the wild is fading out of most of the continent, and even among the primitive tribes the outwash of modern medicine is saving lives. The protein ratio is nowhere growing the way the population grows. When you add up the mounting hunger for meat, the better techniques of killing, and the new ways to get the products of poaching to better markets, it is not hard to see how just the one job of policing the preserves and managed areas can keep a wildlife staff at work.

It sounds at first like a simple matter of cracking down with a rough regimen of enforcement; but it is not a straightforward job like that. The hand that crushes poaching nowadays has got to crush softly. The poachers are Africans, and they are doing what Africans have always done; and nowhere in all the spread of the continent can any system of control of foreign origin do any good just barging ahead as it would at home, heedless of the thought of Africans restless everywhere, sure to take their land in time and meanwhile oversensitive to any sign of European force. You set one arm of the government to doing things to keep the tribesmen from dying in customary ways, causing them to swarm where once they were scattered, flooding the land with a sea of need for meat and shillings and with a flood of new drive to raid the shrinking herds of game. And then you call the wardens out to stamp it down—but softly, old chap, we mustn't make a real nuisance of ourselves, you know, and feed the trouble in the land. Because even if the world's indifference is overcome in time, the research done, and the problems of an unborn craft of veld management are faced and solved, there will still be the Africans waiting to take back Africa and to set the final limit to our hopes—to say what of the wild world of the past their sons and ours shall be allowed to see.

It is not usually sensible to generalize about races of men—especially about the African race. But it has to be said that the usual African citizen, the dark-to-light man of varied phenotype, with round-to-long head, short-to-tall stature, straight-to-peppercorn hair—this hamitic, nilotic, negritic, australoid or forest-type fellow, of blood group O, A, B, or AB, who beats hell out of drums and out of white men in a lot of their own athletic games, will distinguish himself in various ways in the world to come, but not for a while for any passion for preservation of the wilderness. To Africans generally—not just to the tribesmen, to many of the educated Africans as well—the thought of putting energy, money, and hard planning into the saving of nature for its own sake seems perverse. Even the African doing a superb job as a game ranger is often just turning his woodcraft to work that a white man's whimsy will reward with shillings. The African has only lately come from out in nature. Any program to keep animals in a primordial landscape seems a mad, impractical endeavor. He may halfheartedly co-operate in a preservation venture, just to keep the peace, but unless it can be graphically shown him that the saving brings economic gain, he will give it up as soon as white men are out of the way. It was only a little while ago that the leopard was at his goats, the hippo trampled his garden, the crocodile dragged his women off the washing rocks, the baboons sniggered at his scarecrows, and the hyenas, in and out of his villages, showed how little separated his lot from the common lot of wild things. For all the time the African was living with animals, good things were few, changes came seldom, and it was tough and violent for a thousand years on end. The only innovation that for ages brought anything better was civilization. The thirst for civilization is abroad in the land. But it is self-rule, penicillin, and victuals in plenty that seem to Africans the good parts of the new way, and not the mystic bother over saving up mementoes of the dark time behind them. These things will be kept if they keep the tourists coming; but not, this generation, for any other reason.

A sense of stewardship for nature is a mellow virtue, a sign of sophistication that comes long after shoes and vitamins and bicycles. It is coming slowly enough in

The Lion Song

other parts of the world. In Africa it may come too late to protect the fauna in the troubled times ahead. Very recently, since much of this chapter was written, officials of some of the new African governments have shown a heartening recognition of their obligation to preserve the natural landscapes in their charge. The stand of Mwalimu Julius K. Nyerere of Tanganyika is beyond reproach, and his country's youth hostels and program of conservation education are exemplary. Prime Minister Jomo Kenyatta of Kenya, a country independent after December 1963, has issued a proclamation on wilderness preservation that may prove to be one of the important conservation documents of these times. But despite these good signs, there is little cause for complacency about the situation. The voices of these men are almost lost in the clamor of concern over material progress. Only a massive campaign of moral and material support from outside can help build these beginnings into a group conscience, and persuade the rising, multiplying peoples of Africa to save their land.

Not long ago I went to Ghana after spending a week in Johannesburg. Giving up the tension of the Transvaal was easy in Ghana, with the sun shining on the sea. No matter what you may hear of Ghanian politics, there are big black people there in flowered robes, free on their own streets; laughing on corners as black people laugh seldom anywhere nowadays, except in quick snatches down back lanes in Yamacraw and Port of Spain on Saturday afternoon. I stood by the front of a church and listened to them singing hymns inside. It was a Presbyterian church. What I thought was that Presbyterians singing that way shows what Africans can do for the world.

But there is one way in which the peoples of Ghana are no different from the Kikuyu and Nyanja and Yao. They see no shred of sense in saving nature. You can tell it by the mouseless sterility of the places they live in; by the glad convergence of boys to stone down a strayed-in cony; by their innocent rejoicing when any wild animal is killed—an antelope to be eaten or a lizard that was simply there.

So while some of the people interested in saving African wilderness are groping for sound techniques of management, others are working with an even more difficult problem: the devising of propaganda—of programs of education, persuasion, and, if necessary, bribery—that will save wild landscapes from ruin during periods of political change. One of the states of mind to be overcome was shown me by a North African in a group I spoke to lately. I was talking about some of the ecological problems of keeping landscapes wild. After a while I worked around to wondering how, when the Africans come to control their lands, they can ever be cajoled into keeping the parks and preserves. As I spoke the man I mentioned rose, very indignantly, and said he begged my pardon for the interruption, but my talking that way—proposing to tell self-governing people what to do in their own country —was exactly the sort of thing that makes Africans want white people to leave as quickly as possible. And besides being offensively presumptuous, he said, it was not practical to talk of wildlife preservation in places where men live in squalor and misery. It was hopeless and perverse to think of saving animals where babies are big-bellied and rubber-legged for lack of milk. He said that, as an African, he could tell me that I was right about one thing: Africans could not be expected to worry about National Parks; and any meddling in the course they might choose during the delicate days ahead would only bring on

The Lion Song

trouble. It is good to be seeing signs that this man was at least partly mistaken.

But the job of saving the lionland fauna will be long and complex and costly, and we need to have clearly in mind why we think it has got to be done. All along the way there are going to be people who will scoff at the work and say, oh, come now, why not junk this worn-out lust for wild space—let the difficult old beasts go into fossils, or keep them on for a bit in clean pens to please the children. Those are the practical ones, or so they call themselves, and they have in mind man's making much of his progress to date by getting away from the rest of animate nature. You think along with them and sure enough, there is smooth concrete out to the edge of the sky and every single man has an antiseptic Cadillac, knows all the pharmacology of happiness, and thinks back to these years of ours as we think back to the plague-time in Egypt.

It is no good trying to compete with visions like that. You cannot argue the case for saving African wilderness, or any other wilderness, on grounds of practicality alone. There is nothing practical about the labor of tending the unwieldy wonder in the plains. There will be no hard saving done out there by people who mutter about material resources being hoarded, or about grass or meat or timber we are laying by, or even about species being kept from extinction. Those are all necessary things, but doing them will not discharge our obligation to save samples of wilderness simply for men to see in centuries to come. The world will never be tolled in for the job if it is only to bring tourists to Tanganyika, or to feed more people. That is only treating symptoms. We have to do better than that. And we ought to stop talking vaguely about "space for man to breathe in," too. You can hardly breathe at all at Ol Tukai in the dry season. Anyway, a man breathes his very best in an oxygen tent.

If this difficult saving is done, it will only be for motives that make men keep paintings and dig ruins and write about their time for other times to come. It will be because man is the creature who preserves things that stir him—who will even pause in war to save such things in caves—who looks out from below Kilimanjaro at the crest of vertebrate life sinking away on the plains and knows with a sure knowing that if any art or history or monument or unpriced value is valid, this is valid and must be saved.

It would be cause for world fury if the Egyptians should quarry the pyramids, or the French should loose urchins to throw stones in the Louvre. It would be the same if the Americans dammed the Valley of the Colorado. A reverence for original landscape is one of the humanities. It was the first humanity. Reckoned in terms of human nerves and juices, there is no difference in the value of a work of art and a work of nature. There is this difference, though, in the kinds of things they are. Any art might somehow, some day, be replaced—the full symphony of the savanna landscape never.

What would be the worth, to men of dreams, of a prime dinosaur swamp railed off to gape at? The dinosaurs are gone these sixty million years and there is nothing to be done, and no one to blame. And now, at the edge of the Age of Reason, the last great fantasy of evolution is running out in Africa and we are about to let it happen. If we let it go, this most fantastic relic of organized life on earth, no cunning can ever bring it back. The bars will be down. The rest of non-human nature will surely follow. And we shall head out into the rest of our time, masters of creation at last, and alone forever.

1993 Preface to the 1952 Letters

IN THE summer of 1952 when Archie went on his wonderful *ulendo* there was only one fly in the ointment—I couldn't go with him. There was no possible way I could go. We had *five* young children ranging in age from nine years to six months. We lived in a barely completed house on ten acres of land on the shores of Wewa Pond. Our piece of woods was ten miles from Gainesville and two miles from the little old town of Micanopy.

We had two cows that Mimi and Chuck milked twice a day, a horse, Cricket that had a colt named Kate, two dachshunds, and a German shepherd.

At the time of Archie's first *ulendo* he was forty-three years old and I was thirty-seven. Our children were Mimi, nine years old; Chuck or Choco, seven; Stephen, or Steve or Titi, six; Thomas or Tommie or Bucho, four; and David, six months.

Of course it was a lonely summer, but the young were a good pack. We went swimming each day; for a while we had a baby raccoon and the garden produced the biggest Beefsteak tomatoes I have ever seen, before or since, in Florida. Archie's letters, written on little thin airmail stationary, were anxiously watched for and read and reread. And time did pass and he came home.

Marjorie Harris Carr

Letters from Archie Carr to Marjorie Harris Carr, 1952

Grosvenor Hotel, Victoria, London
June 20, 1952

Dearest: We got in yesterday about noon London time and God only knows what in your time. The trip was very pleasant. After writing you of co-urinating with Trygve Lie in the airport we found that he was travelling with us and so a very impressive delegation including Eden and others met the plane. They ignored us.

Yesterday afternoon we just rode busses around and walked about Piccadily and went to the Aquascutum place on Regent street and bought a coat, as you ordered—an olive beltless, allweather affair that seems OK.

Today we called on Scott at Sir William Halcrow's. He told us Nyasaland is a pleasant place but *chilly* at this time of year. He also says we are to have a Land Rover, a kind of jeeplike car, and access to the RAF air survey planes for our own survey. Had steak pie and ale and Devon cream for lunch. Kidneys have disappeared.

Later went to the British Museum and talked to Parker and the others there.

Now we are headed for the London School of Tropical Medicine to talk with the director.

Tonight we are going to take a three hour boat trip up the Thames. I love you. Tell Mimi tomorrow we're going to watch them change the guard!

Love to all. A.

London
June 21, 1952, Saturday

Dearest: Tell Mimi we just got back from the changing of the guard at the palace. It was even more colorful than I had anticipated. I took some color pictures.

Yesterday and last night we went for the boat ride down the Thames under London Bridge and past Westminster Abbey and all the rest. Went to a lot of pubs to quaff ale, including the White Hart Inn where Shakespeare and a long line of more recent characters used at.

Went also to Greenwich where they make the time and stood with a foot in each of the two halves of the world, astraddle of 0° longitude.

London is so chock full of historic and literary implications for the literate gringo that he tends to be surprised that folks still live here. The people though are very pleasant and so frightfully polite that it make one feel boorish at every encounter. But not as boorish as the worst of the tourists you see.

This afternoon we're going out to visit some people in the country.

You would like London even more than I and I feel very guilt ridden—as last summer.

I love you. Love to Mimi & Chuck & Steve & Tommy & David. A.

London
June 22, 1952, Sunday

Dearest: Spending yesterday in the home of a doctor working under the socialized medical system here was very interesting to me. It's a curious arrangement which except for a few bugs seems to work all right but I can see how it would horrify a US medico. The doctor in question lives out at Uxbridge 20 miles W. of London, and he drove us to Windsor and Eton—where they were playing cricket, believe it or not.

Kew is wonderful and the tropical house there is like the gardens at Lancetilla, Honduras squeezed into the University of Florida gym.

I'm about sick from eating English strawberries and cream. The strawberries surpass anything you could imagine.

So does the climate. This is "flaming June" and Lewis' and my sinuses are already shot. 38° the other morning. I miss you.

Love to all. A.

New Stanley Hotel, Nairobi, Kenya, BEA
June 24, 1952

Dearest: Lord, lord! Just got back from a 3½ hour safari in the Nairobi National Park. It's a limitless grassland running from the very outskirts of the city to the horizon and there are roads where cars may go, of which no one can get out. It is what you go to Africa for. In order, and in most cases in great numbers, we saw ostriches, wildebeests (gnus), 5 kinds of gazelles, kongonis in profusion and lots of zebras. Then we went to a little deep river and saw a hippo, then we saw jackals, a herd of impalas, elands and two wart hogs. We drove up to a parked car of Indians looking at them in the tall grass thinking they were lions. We then looked everywhere for lions and found none; but a huge beautiful leopard rose in the grass and looked at us and then jumped the width of the road in crossing at not 20 feet in front of the car, which scared our driver who says they jump into cars. Both Lewis and I took pictures madly all the time. As we were about to leave a herd of 7 giraffes came out of the woods and posed magnificently.

Now I am ready to pass on, replete. I thought of you all the time.

Stopped last night at Khartoum where Arabs in robes and turbans serviced the plane.

We're spending tonight in Nairobi and tomorrow go on to Blantyre by way of Dar es Salaam on Central African Airways (we came from London on South African Airways).

This is a big modern town, the hotel we are in—the New Stanley—is very good. Right across the street is one of the big outfitters of safaris.

While way out in the park this afternoon we saw a tall black striding across the plain. Our driver told us that he was a Masai and no Masai is afraid of lions (you remember the group of them that Akeley modelled spearing a lion) and none eats food, just blood and milk and none works, only watches cattle. They are allowed to live in the park.

I saw a dik-dik too.

Love to you all. A.

Limbe, Nyasaland
June 25, 1952

My dearest: We left Nairobi about 8 this morning, stopped for a spell in Dar es Salaam and arrived at the airport here (which is a few miles the other side of Blantyre, which is only four miles from here) at two PM. We are in a fairly good hotel, the Shire Highlands Hotel which has swarms of white-togaed serving "boys," dim lights and somewhat recalcitrant plumbing. Limbe is an utterly British and unpicturesque little town with a few hundred English planters and agents, a lot of Indian shopkeepers and a huge number of Africans most of whom speak no English at all. Some of the Indians are Sikhs with beards and turbans and some are Hindus.

This region is very thickly settled, but this morning, flying over Tanganyika and Mozambique we would cover a hundred miles without a sign of a human. We'll get into wild country some places along the river.

Incidently, we flew by Zanzibar, which always sounded pretty fancy to me.

Mr. Richards, Sir Wm's agent here, seemed distressingly vague about our gear that was sent out a long time ago, but will probably find it somewhere.

It's cold as hell here and no heat.

I love you. A.

Limbe, Nyasaland
June 27, 1952

My beloved: We are still putting up in the Shire Highlands Hotel and groping around trying to get gear together preparatory to going on our first field trip Monday. We expect to go to Ft. Johnston on the upper river just below the Lake. We have planned out our jaunts so as to hit the river at about eight points between the lake and the Portuguese East border. The first trip will be mild because Sir Wm has a shack there and the region is well settled.

Staying in this hotel is bringing us in contact with a

rather uninteresting kind of English colonial—lower middle class folk who have more than they ever had and don't know what to do with it. It's very like some of the Fruit Co. atmosphere. There are two principal tribes of Africans here, both very pleasant but completely unsophisticated and anxious to please. I learned how to say "no" today. It's "ee-ay." Silly, verdad?

We had a talk with the chief medical officer this PM. He wants to send one of his medical inspectors along with us on the survey to learn some entomology.

There's a big dance here at the hotel tomorrow night. Practically the whole European population of the two towns (Limbe and Blantyre) has made reservations. The hotel manager asked me today if Lewis and I would be there (admission 10 shillings for residents of hotel, 1 pound for outsiders). I plead lack of formal attire and he said, well if you only had a *slightly* darker suit . . . I may go anyway and sit in the shadows.

I'll sure be glad to get into the woods. Write. Kiss Mimi and Chuck and Steve and Bucho and David.

I love you. A.

Shire Highlands Hotel, Limbe, Nyasaland
June 29, 1952

Dearest sweet: I have barely recovered from the brawl last night. As I mentioned, the whole European population turns out for nearly anything and it was all here last night. Lewis and I went to bed at three but there was a lot of yelling after that. On the whole, though, there was less rough stuff than there would have been in a gringo group sucking up that much alcohol.

Tomorrow we leave for Zomba to spend the night with Dr. MacKenzie and to proceed thence to Fort Johnston, as I guess I told you. It's really taking us a hell of a while to get all the loose ends together but it doesn't matter much I guess.

One of the men at the Halcrow office is lending me a pistol and a rifle. Don't know how much game there is at our first station but I guess there'll be lots of mosquitoes and that's what we're supposed to lust after.

The best part of our stay in Limbe has been the chance to get acquainted with all kinds and classes of Englishmen and women and see for the first time how their outlook differs from ours and varies according to their own station.

Many of them, especially the females, seem a flighty lot and there are some utter asses among the men as everywhere, but it is beginning to be easier to see how England got where she did.

Incidently the blacks here (this is a protectorate, not a dominion or colony) are dead against the Federation (with the Rhodesians because they feel it will bring up the S. African racial attitude) and they are threatening a roughhouse for the last of August. Hope we're in the bush.

Kiss Mimi, Choco, Titi, Bucho and David.

I love you. A.

Fort Johnston, Nyasaland
July 2, 1952

Dearest: We are spending the week at the engineer's bungalow on the Shire about three miles out of Ft. Johnston at the edge of the little native town of Ntundu. As I write this the black folks are drumming themselves into a fit over something or other. They're a mixture of Mohamedans and heathen and have all got together to raise hell tonight.

This afternoon we went in the company launch down

the river to the traverse camp on Lake Malombe where two of the engineers are running a line. We collected mosquitos and schistosome-carrying snails in the lakeside marsh there and got a lot of stuff living in hippo tracks which makes better breeding places than cow tracks.

Last night I astounded the entire personnel here by catching a crocodile in the front yard (they had never seen one there in 14 months living here) and by being seized by the left hand by the bastardly thing's jaws so hard that it took three of us to get me loose. My left hand is stuck full of holes and two fingers don't work well but I don't think it's going to amount to anything. I stupidly grabbed the croc by the belly when it seemed he would slide out of reach in deep water.

We arrived here yesterday PM after spending a very pleasant evening at the home of Dr. MacKenzie, the chief medical officer.

Kiss Mimi and Choco and Titi and Tommie and youthful David.

> I love you, A.

> Fort Johnston, Nyasaland
> July 5, 1952

Dearest: It's 7 PM Saturday here (about 1 PM there?) and we were just ready to have a drink before supper when a boy came running up yelling "Bwana mvuu," which turned out to mean get your gun and come quick, there is a hippopotamus on the road. I tore tail up and the hippo had gone into a heavy reed marsh. But it just goes to show you.

This morning we drove up to Monkey Bay and collected mosquitoes. We saw lots of baboons and monkeys along the way. When we got back to Ft. Johnston at one o'clock a party to welcome Hore-Belisha was in progress, everyone roaring drunk and they dragged us in with our filthy field clothes on. H-B was so tight he didn't give a damn, and so was his wife and we had a long and finally somewhat heated discussion about the relative merits of our respective countries. H-B seemed proud that he went with Churchill to get his honorary degree at Miami. (This letter interrupted here by supper and another party for the Hore-Belishas at Palm Beach, a little Inn ten miles from here at the very wave washed edge of Lake Nyasa.)

Next day: Coming home from H-B's party last night a hyena ran across the road and stopped short way back in the bush. This morning I got up at 5:30, took the dinghy and outboard motor and one of the Africans who knows the region and went hunting—this being Sunday and a non-collecting day. Walked 7 miles or so and finally got out of the burned-over land and shot an antelope which the boys are now cleaning for dinner. Saw little else in the way of game but lots of sign showing that fires drove it away.

Caught my first side-necked turtle.

The puberty ceremonies are being celebrated in the villages round about and the drumming and dancing and singing is nearly continuous. I finally realized an old yearning when I heard signal drumming down on Lake Malombe the other day. Very stirring.

Tonight our local village of Ntundu is putting on a big sing and dance and we're going. I wish you were here. I love you. A.

Limbe, Nyasaland
July 9, 1952 PM

Dearest: We're back from Ntundu (Ft. Johnston way) after a very successful trip despite the interlude entertaining Hore-Belisha. We got about the upper part of the river, the southernmost tip of the lake (Nyoba) and the upper half of Lake Malombe and collected a lot of stuff and ideas and are now identifying mosquitoes and reading Protectorate medical reports in the hotel. We'll do the same tomorrow and I'm then going down to the Lower River on a quick trip to see how good a camp site there is at Chiromo where we'll probably go next week. Across from there on the Portuguese side there are some lovely wild people.

We're slowly beginning to pick up a usable pittance of Chinyanja, the local Bantu language, but the job is complicated by the admixture of Yao people, who look much like Nyanjas, but used to help the Arabs catch the Nyanjas for slaves and are mostly Mohammedan.

Did I tell you that even in camp full course meals are served and every thing stops even on a traverse line for morning and afternoon tea?

The lake fish are superb—the best freshwater fish I ever ate not excepting the bass from our pond.

We went over to Blantyre this afternoon and had a haircut—a very English one despite a lot of wrangling with the Greek who did it.

Did I tell you that some of the tribes here use big-headed ants to suture wounds with, pulling off the bodies and leaving the heads with jaws locked, *just as the Indians in Nicaragua and Ecuador do!* Isn't that something.

I'm over my crocodile bite and can move my fingers.

The people here carve ivory but aren't much good in wood. I've been trying to find some decent ebony sculpture. Located some moderate masks.

I love you all the time. I wish to hell you were here. A.

Limbe, Nyasaland
July 13, 1952, Sunday

Dearest: Yesterday we went down to the Empatamangu

Gorge in the middle Shire, just below the bridge on the Rhodesia road. It's a beautiful spot in the rapids section of the river and you would never recognize there the same Shire that we messed around in up at Ft. Johnston. Murchison Falls, which should be on your map, is a short distance below the gorge. We're going out to the gorge to camp a while after we get back from a week or so on the Lower Shire at Chiromo and Port Herald. While there we will try to arrange for a Portuguese farmer's steamboat to take us all the way down the Lower Shire to the Zambezi in Mozambique, just to see the stream out. Chiromo and Port Herald are low, just a hundred or two feet above sea level, but at this season are surprisingly cool. Every time we come back to Limbe we freeze.

I was very excited to discover in some circular potholes high on the granite cliff above the Empatamangu falls, a lot of clawed frogs (pregnancy test frogs). You remember that they are completely aquatic and spew out eggs any time they may be injected with pregnancy urine. What I never knew is that the tadpole looks like nothing on earth. It has a low flat head and wide mouth like a catfish and like one also it has two long whiskers that stand out an inch in front of its mouth. The belly is silvery and the tail drawn out into a long, thin flagellum. I seined 4 with my undershirt (we had gone down just for reconnaissance) and one lived overnight. He's still alive in fact. I'll try to bring him home to tell the next time you get pregnant.

On the sixth of August we are due to meet the steamer *Ilala* at Kota on the lake shore to board it and take a two day trip down the lake to Monkey Bay, where our Land Rover will pick us up to haul us to Ft. Johnston for another spree there. We'll drive to Kota Kota via Dedza and Lilongwe, where we'll spend the night. There's some real good wild country between Lilongwe and Kota Kota.

Letters from 1952

Arthur Hedges, head of the survey party we'll be with down at Chiroma and his wife came upon 4 lions on the Blantyre road the other night. A male, a female and two big cubs.

Today is Sunday and nearly all the survey parties are in from the bush to play, or watch, cricket. Ray Taylor, our host at the Intundu (Ft. Johnston) camp, is one of the stars and is in the middle of a two-day "test match."

I'm sorry it's hot there, but I'd rather be hot than cold. Kiss Mimi and Choco and Titi and Bucho and little David— or is he big?

I love you. A.

Limbe, Nyasaland
July 14, 1952

My dearest: Your third letter arrived this morning. It was full of news, what you say you'll send no more like, which I regret. Indeed I implore you to continue with such offerings as an antidote to my nostalgia. They are exactly what I want to hear.

To show the young how we came out here get a map of the world and draw them a line from London to Paris, then straight to Rome, then straight to Khartoum on the Nile, then straight to Nairobi in Kenya, then angling to Dar es Salaam, then to Chileka near Blantyre.

Don't know whether I've told you but our Land Rover wasn't here when we arrived and we've been using a huge Humber "Super Snipe" about $50000. worth of car that I wouldn't give $5. for. The engine falls partly out very often. Even though it hasn't fallen clear out it undermines your morale. Today the Land Rover came up from Beira. It's lovely. A kind of jeep with a bit more room, and in this newest model, with foam rubber seats and seat backs. It will make our travelling a lot easier—or at least a lot surer as to outcome.

The other day a new grave here was found disturbed. Suspicious relatives of the corpse dug it up and found only hands and feet. The cops came in and found the body being peddled as goat meat in the streets to the natives. Conceive!

Talked with Mr. Mitchell, the man who had the spears thrown at him on the lower river the other day. He thought it was a damned outrage.

Tomorrow we'll take a short but very rough jaunt to the middle river at Matope. The next day we'll move down to Chiromo and Port Herald, where we'll be for a week or two depending on opportunities for collecting.

Love to all. A.

Chiromo, Lower Shire
July 17, 1952

Dearest: Yesterday made one month away from you; and it seems a lot longer than that. I love you an awful lot and want to see you bad.

We are camping on the Lower Shire and I like it a lot better than Limbe. It's warm. Not hot but just exactly right like El Zamorano. Also the gals don't wear any shirts or black missionary sarongs around their chests and they are all tattooed—face and arms and chest—most gaudy. I've been trying to get some of the more statuesque ones to pose in the sun, with their huge clay jars on their heads but they run like deer if you look at them fixedly, much less photograph them.

The canoes here are made of bark sewn together with inner bark of saplings and they're very light and easy to handle.

We are on the edge of the great unmapped Elephant Marsh, located on a little knoll overlooking the marsh and the Shire valley generally.

There are three of Sir Wm's engineers here: Hedges from Kent, a soft spoken Irish lad named Ross and Fuller from South Africa. They're just as pleasant as the crowd on the Upper River, even 'tho our presence is really a hell of a disruption for them.

Found a chameleon today, the first I've seen. Unfortunately I ran over it before I could stop, but I pickled it.

We're going to spray native houses tomorrow to catch mosquitoes.

The Land Rover is a great comfort.

I love you a hell of a lot. The time is passing. Be happy. A.

Tengadzi Bungalow, Chiromo
July 22, 1952

Dearest: Yesterday we drove down to Port Herald to see the District Commissioner about hiring the launch of a Portuguese farmer to take us down the last part of the Shire from Port Herald to the Zambezi. We plan to go up the Zambezi the short distance to the nearest town in Mozambique, where the Portuguese Administrador has invited us to spend the night with him. We drove on 50 miles from Port Herald to the above-mentioned Portuguese town and talked with the Administrator about our plan and were very cordially received in a gleaming white building high on a cliff overlooking the Zambezi. All our conversation was between me and the Administrador, with me talking Spanish and him Portuguese and we got along wonderfully. It seems very queer to cross the frontier and find blacks that you can talk to. They do better there with their Portuguese than these here do with English.

On the way over a huge black cobra reared in the road ahead and spread his hood gorgeously, at least five inches across, and swayed there just like riki-tiki was after him. I got more of a thrill out of him than nearly anything I've seen here. On the way back we caught a puff adder, which is a handsome fat viper, but nothing to compare with the cobra.

Two youthful recruits have arrived in camp—both Scotch lads with the most incredibly thick burr; and very white and tender. It won't take them long to change color. There are 10 of us here now and the place is crawling alive. Besides Lewis and me and George Hopper, the Englishman who goes everywhere with us as liaison with the medical department here, and the two Scots, there is an Irish boy two years out of school, a South African who flew a Spitfire during the war, a riotous chap from Somerset with a flowing moustache and the jefe of the camp, a bird about my age named Hedges. A very gentlemanly crowd and astoundingly polite with each other.

Night before last I badgered Lewis into doing something you would have loved and I thought of you all the time. We got Paddy, the boy from Eire, located a dugout opposite a little village on the Portuguese side, sneaked over, propelled by two infant blacks, and went to the only pub in a hundred miles (and I discovered it)—a trading post run by a very pleasant fellow from Lisbon—where we bought a two-gallon demijohn of red wine for $1.50 and drank on the house till the crocs nearly got victuals on our way back. Or did I tell you of this before? No matter, we had a swell time in a most improbable way and your not being there was the only defect in the set up.

Give my love to Mimi, Choco, Titi, Bucho and David. Got your letter #4 today.

I love you. A.

Letters from 1952

Chiromo
July 24, 1952

Dearest: We have moved from Tengadzi Bungalow down to the rest house at Chiromo. It's a thatched, thick walled house right on the bank of the Ruo River, a quiet slow stream a hundred yards wide and with Portuguese East Africa on the other side. A very pleasant spot and I wish I had time and tackle to go tiger-fish fishing in the front yard.

This afternoon we walked over the footbridge across the Shire to collect in some pools in the marsh. We got a lot of the kind of snails that carry Bilharzia (Schistosomiasis) and on the way back we saw the prototype of the marimba. It was made of seven sticks laid across two sections of banana stem and staked apart by pegs. The players sat on opposite sides and hit the ends of the keys with hardwood sticks. The melody was simple but the harmony was marvelous and the rhythm soul stirring. They played for us a long time and a crowd of Africans gathered and it was weird because the instrument actually looked like a few sticks of stove wood piled on some decaying banana stems.

We haven't yet heard from the Portuguese government sanctioning our expedition to the Zambezi, nor from Lopez agreeing to take us in his boat but we're planning on going Sunday anyway.

Today all of us gathered at the little station to meet the weekly train between Beira in Mozambique and Blantyre. We had 10 minutes to drink beer in the diner before the train left for Beira, the beer is Portuguese and is very much better than Nyasaland. This simple diversion is one of the high spots in the week for Sir Wm's boys here. Some of them came in from camp 15 miles down river for 10 minutes drinking cold beer.

Kiss Mimi and Choco and Titi and Bucho and David.
I love you. A.

Limbe
July 31, 1952

Dearest: We got back to civilization last night after a fortnight in the barbarous Lower River the only thing I prefer about the emoluments of Limbe is the fairly decent victuals of the Shire Highlands (our hotel you gather) and the cold beer. We got right in the middle of a chiperone—one of those hellish Scotch mists that swirl down from the Portuguese mountains and envelope the whole southern highlands in fog and keep the temperature down in the fifties. The forester in Van der Post's book was killed while they were in a chiperone. Remember?

We have finally met the last of the engineer group working on the project and they have done a lot to raise my estimate of English personality. The big bwana, Scott (Sir Wm's first in command) came out from London for a look at the project and we were invited out to the Richard's last evening for drinks. Scott's a clever pleasant sort who sort of commutes between London and the Gold Coast, Canada, the Persian Gulf and Nyasaland.

Our boat trip down from Port Herald to the Zambezi had to be postponed, probably 'till about the 18th of August. I think I told you we drove way down into Portuguese East and talked (Spanish) with the D.C. at Mutarara about the expedition. We haven't yet received the sanction of the Governor in Beira.

Chiromo was a delightful place to stay. We put up first in Tengadzi Bungalow 13 miles back this way, and after a week there moved down to a resthouse on the bank of the Ruo River 300 yards above its juncture with the Shire. The river is only a hundred yards wide there and we could sit on our couch and hear the birds singing and watch the bananas wave on the other side.

The elephants came up on the other side one night and

Luis Ariano, a new Portuguese friend of mine, went over and shot one for biltong. He gave me the tail (which I'm drying for one of the young) and some meat and tried to make me accept a foot, offering to have it skinned out and made into a "bloody fine wiss-pipper beskit."

Ariano is an old Portuguese biltong hunter who lives on the 65 year old steamer *Empress*, now permanently moored just down stream from our resthouse. Ariano is the world's authority on tiger fish fishing, and makes a lot of money shooting buffalo and elephants and hippos and selling the meat in Beira as biltong for feeding "boys." He's a very wicked man but I like him.

Our next trip is to Kota on the lake, way south of here. It's the biggest native town in Nyasaland. We spend a night in Lilongwe on the way.

Be happy. Break the colt. Love to the young. I love you. A.

Lilongue
August 3, 1952

My dearest: We just pulled into Lilongwe and put up in the hotel for the night. Tomorrow we go on to Kota on the lake and tomorrow night and the next sleep on the *Ilala*, the steamer that makes the 10 day circuit of the lake. We'll be aboard for only the Kota-to-Monkey Bay part of the voyage. We brought an African along who'll take the Land Rover around from Kota to Monkey Bay by land and pick us up. Lilongwe is high, cool and frightfully dry—like Choluteca in April.

I had a wonderful time this weekend—the kind you and I seem better able to enjoy than most people, and perhaps the pleasantest unsuccessful elephant hunt anybody ever went on.

Saturday I got in the Land Rover and bumped the eighty miles down to Chiromo where my elephant hunting Portuguese friend Luis Ariano and his huge son José live on the old *Empress* (as I told you) tied on the Nyasaland shore. They gave me a bunk and at 3:30 the next morning Luis thrust a cup of coffee under my nose and told me to drink it quick and get in the dugout. The three of us and two blacks paddled over to the PEA [Portuguese East Africa] side where Ariano keeps his '28 model A Ford, which we pushed off, mounted and rode for 10 or 12 miles back in the jungle to Ariano's corral—a palisade of ebony logs sunk in the ground in a big circle and fencing against lions 250 fat African cattle. The only habitation anywhere around is the pair of straw huts of the two black cowherds but Ariano has a little round grass pavilion with two reclining chairs in it and three big rocks for a fireplace to heat coffee and a ten gallon demijohn of red wine. In this the two of them sit and wait for lions to come to the corral. They've killed a dozen.

We got out of the car, collected an African hunter with a horrid looking spear and set out on the trail of a big herd of elephants which had literally wrecked the forest for miles. We walked six hours and when lack of breakfast began to grieve us and we hadn't caught up with the elephants we walked back along the lagoon shore where long lines of geese were flying and egrets and huge black ibis stood in phalanges and two beautiful species of plover, one tern-like, fork tailed and maroon in color, the other strikingly done in black and white, were nesting and fluttered about our heads and played hurt on the ground. After some miles of weaving among two-foot deep hippo tracks in which you could easily break your leg if you want to, we got back to the corral and Ariano forthwith set about making breakfast. He fried a bushel of portuguese sausage and bacon, a hatful of eggs and broke out some crusty Latin bread and a huge Portuguese cheese. We ate and swilled wine out of the demijohn till I couldn't move. As we ate the cowboy's wife pounded *ufa,* maize, i.e. cornmeal. She pounded in the usual way by raising and dropping a huge pole in a log mortar. She was naked except for a breechclout and a fat little baby was strapped to her lumbar region. As she raised and brought down the pestle she yodelled a work-song in time in a wild, high and wholly unbelievable voice and her "tucks," which were easily a foot long, flopped up onto her shoulders and down against her belly as she completed each stroke. And all the while the baby slept peacefully.

After a while we got in the hot rod and crashed along the salvaged elephant trail Ariano uses for a road, stopping a couple of times to look for koodoo when there were tracks, and at length getting back to the dugout. Back at the *Empress* we had lunch—magnificent Portuguese thick soup, spaghetti and sausages, salad with a flood of olive oil, some more of the best bread in Africa and another demijohn of wine. About 4 PM I bid my odd friends goodbye and lurched up the scarp to Limbe.

Nothing very exciting but see what I mean? I love you. A.

Ntundu (Ft. Johnston)
August 8, 1952

Dearest: Just before dark this evening I borrowed the engineers boat and kicker, went up the Shire a couple of miles and walked through the wilderness with the rifle. As I was walking I heard a rustle in the grass and lo, I was confronted by a huge python (he proved to be 11½ feet long). I pinned him down with a sapling and after trying various schemes for getting him back and running the motor and not turning over in the croc infested river I gave up and conked him with a frail pole and cached him on an ant hill while I wandered off looking for bucks. I didn't find any thing till I got back and stepped out from behind the ant hill and damned if there wasn't a repulsive looking wart-hog trying to make up his mind to eat my snake. He ran like a deer when he saw me and it was so dark that I missed him.

We made the cruise on the lake and our connections worked out well. We got on at Kota at 6 AM Wednesday and got off at Monkey Bay Thursday morning. Our Land Rover was there, brought around from Kota by an African driver and we were glad to see him.

The high point of the cruise was the immense clouds of midges rising from water a thousand to 2000 feet deep and taken up by the thermals in dense columns that looked exactly like water spouts or tornadoes and which were so big they could be seen 20 miles away.

I got hold of some of the cakes the natives onshore press from bugs and had the cook make up some for me. I can do without the stuff but I'm going to take some home for you to make canapes with.

Tomorrow we go by boat down river to Liwonde, and return here by car to stay till Wednesday when back to Limbe.

I'm beginning to count the days. Kiss the young.

I love you, A.

Ntundu
August 9, 1952

My beloved: Yesterday George Hopper and I drove 12 miles down the lake shore and met the *Jeannie*, the engineer's launch with two African boatmen. We set out for

Liwonde some 20–30 miles below Lake Malombe; which we had to navigate first. Guess I have told you that I caught a 11 foot python the day before. I took this snake with me and trussed it up on the *Jeannie's* tiny foredeck to skin during the lake run. A few minutes out a hell of a squall came up and for two solid hours I skinned the python with seas breaking over the bow and next to drowning me. George lost his hat and it was too bad for us to come about to pick it up. A two-hour run saw us in the outlet, the Shire again, and after enjoying the peace of six miles of river we came upon the first real plethora of crocs we've seen—dozens upon dozens piled like logs on four bare patches of bank, lots of them 14 feet long and one I'd swear twenty. Then 10 miles more and we cruised right into a school of hippos rising and sounding and snorting and blowing spray and gaping and having a hell of a time. Hope I got some good pictures.

We got to Liwonde at 2 PM and came back to Ntundu by Land Rover.

This morning I got up at daylight and with a native outboarded up to my favorite creek to look for bucks. Saw fine bull Koodoo but looking into the rising sun my companion persuaded me it was an ant hill and I let it get away. We found a dead hippo though, swollen and floating side down in a thrashed out place in the riverside reeds. Went home for tools and returned. After superhuman effort we dug out the two huge tusks—18″ long I guess to send home for the young. They're really handsome and polish just like elephant ivory. I made the long suffering African get on the bloated beast and pose for a picture. The stench was awful and maggots wandered about and every so often fell off into the water where a school of big black catfish lay under the hippo waiting to pick them up. I'm glad its over.

One more month tomorrow. I love you. A.

Limbe
August 13, 1952

Dearest: Just back to Limbe at 3:30 PM after 10 days away. I'd had no mail from you in all that time but found three letters here when I arrived which was pleasant to say the least. I'm delighted to hear about your progress with Kate.

Yesterday back at Ntundu Derek Davis from the survey camp across the river from us showed up at breakfast after having left for his camp the night before. It seems that about 2 AM he was awakened by the chief of the village by which he's camped, asking him to carry to Ft. Johnston a man which had been mauled by a lion. A bunch of Africans returning from a funeral dance got tired and went to sleep on the edge of the village. A lion grabbed the outermost in the heap by the head and dragged him off letting go only when the rest woke and raised pandemonium. The man was nearly scalped but is doing all right. Twenty eight lions were killed in the Ft. Johnston district last year and literally dozens—nobody knows how many—of people were hurt.

We just heard that the Portuguese have approved our voyage through Portuguese East Africa and up the Zambezi. We'll make the trip a week from Saturday.

I went with our native assistant to his village to try to buy masks (dance masks carved of light wood) yesterday and was much entertained at the awful secrecy of the deal. The masks were surreptitiously fished from the lake bottom and out of trees, hidden under black cloth and delivered with anxious looking about for female watchers. The masks are used only in men's dances. They are very crude but we may bring back one or two anyway. Kiss the babes.

I love you. A.

Limbe
August 15, 1952

My own Margie: We're working out of Limbe for a while. Today we went over to Zomba Mountain. It's a bit over 6000 feet and has cloud forest which is so much like our cloud forest that it was really hard to believe your eyes. I didn't know any of the trees to speak of but that didn't matter they were all twisty and proprooted and draped and padded with moss and filmy ferns, and Selaginella was all about and huge fat treeferns. The one tree that I knew was Podocarpus which looked just like Uyuca ones as far as I could tell. From the depths of the woods I heard the woodwind notes of some sort of thrush that might just as well have been a jilguero in Honduras or a nightingale thrush in Jamaica. A lovely clear stream tumbles down from the plateau through the forest where the treeferns and bearded trees lean together over the white water dashing among the boulders and streaming into deep blue pools where trout with spots and stone crabs walk about like in any high brook in Central America. About the edges of the woods the wildflowers were like slopes above the prison camp only more unbelievably beautiful gentians and yellow composites and something like asters and a yellow flowering tree like a locust and raspberry and blackberry blossoms and an impossible plant in head high clumps weighted with heavy masses of pink blooms like cherokee roses stuck tight together and a red flower in heads of tubes—like the thing named after Doris Stone.

Winding about among the natural woods is a forest of planted Mlange cedars—huge drooping black cedars that look something like the religious firs in Toluca. They don't grow naturally on Zomba but thrive there and on Mlange they replace the broad leafed association in many places.

The same thing occurs in Central America where cloud forest is often found alternating with coniferous woods. Why?

Tomorrow we're going back to Zomba and down to Lake Churwa. Find it on the map.

I'll see you in the predictable future. Kiss the young. Be happy. Break Kate.

I love you. A.

Port Herald
August 26, 1952

My darling: Yesterday was full. In the morning Lewis and George drove Edmond, the African who had taken the jeep to the Zambezi to meet us back to Chiromo camp where he belongs. I stayed here and got out the 15 power binoculars and a stand for them and an *upholstered* chair in the shade and spent two hours mapping the position of nests of four species of birds—pelicans, marabou storks, black cormorants and plumed herons—in 7 big trees in front of the rest house. There are literally hundreds of nests (haven't made a total count) and the birds are completely unafraid.

Then I went collecting snails along the whole Port Herald River front, which is a festering place and a disgrace, where bilharzia snails live in abundance in the very marsh pools the people use for drinking, washing, bathing and defecating. No wonder the schistosome thrive and infest practically 100 per cent. The Portuguese wouldn't put up with such a mess.

At 4 in the afternoon I had one of the real kicks of the trip. The DC who's a hell of a good guy, went out to an outlying village and brought me the very best drum and dance chorus in the Pt. Herald district which is probably the fanciest and most completely unspoiled place for dancing and drumming in southeast Africa. I can't even begin to tell you what went on—words and space are inadequate and I've made copious notes anyway and have lots of pictures. It's enough to say that there was, as last time, a battery of seven conical open-end drums played by two blacks with two sticks each, then a long tom-tom played fast with the palms, then a fat bass to furnish the groundwork. The intricacy and drive and capacity to stir that this percussion section had was indescribable. Then there was a ring of 30 strikingly dressed virgins, 17 to 19 years old, the older in sarongs of wild primary colors, those with budding tits or none in wrap around skirts of the same. The older girls had each a pair of ebony blocks, the middle sized, square oil tins full of pebbles; all the rest had hands to clap and all to the very last had the magic African power of harmony. They did 11 dances the music and rhythm of which were a minor miracle and the movements nothing other than a casual unselfconscious exhibition of the contortions of sexual intercourse. It was really an incredible thing. Tonight they're bringing a marimba (indigenous) around.

I love you. A.

Chambo Plateau, Mlange Mountain
August 30, 1952, 9:35 PM

My dearest: I'm on Mlange. I'm in a cabin the forestry department built up here, with a cedar forest around it and a cold creek running behind, and I've got a pure hell of a fire of cedar logs and am just sitting here by myself writing to you and wishing you were here more than anything.

Not wishing you'd had to climb up here though, because it was rough—worse than Uyuca or Chile or Blue Mt. Peak. I drove over here in the jeep this morning. This mountain sits by itself just off the Mozambique frontier 50 miles from Limbe. I left the car at Hendersons' forestry depot on the lower slope, and the climb up was a bad three hours.

It's worth it though. I had two Africans to carry my blankets and victuals and cameras, and now they've sneaked out into the grass to eat *ufa* and sleep with some natives that live out there and they won't show up till I roar about tomorrow afternoon when I'm ready to go down, and I'm all by myself. I don't mind except for you not being here. For supper I had a shot of whiskey, (the first breaking in of the flask) and a hardboiled egg and a tomato and a piece of cheese and a bread-and-butter sandwich and a chocolate bar and a cup of coffee; and then I caught 3 frogs.

The frogs are starting to cry in their sack and I'm going to put them outside so they won't keep me awake.

Kiss Mimi and Choco and Steve and Bucho and young David—if you can catch him. I'm counting the days now instead of weeks.

I love you. A.

Limbe
September 9, 1952

Dear heart: We leave at 10 tomorrow morning. I don't truly realize it even now. I may see you before you get this. I'll never leave you again.

I went over to Blantyre yesterday morning to see Mitchell, the only real naturalist in Nyasaland, and to ask advice about taking my dwarf chameleon home alive when in strides an African with a bloody great and utterly gorgeous giant chameleon—the shield-necked kind—on a stick. Mitchell didn't want it so I paid the bloke a bob for it and am now provided with a veterinary certificate and export permit and a basketful of four elegant chameleons whose excess weight has been assessed and paid all the way to Gainesville. By Sir Wm. by God! They're really lovely.

Yesterday in the afternoon we went over to Zomba to spend the night with Dr. MacKenzie, the DMS. We drove up onto Zomba plateau to have tea with Mrs. MacKenzie and the kids who are holidaying there, the doctor going up from their house below when he has a spell off to trout fish. The plateau house is surely one of the most fetching dwellings I ever saw. It was built long ago by Scottish missionaries, and still belongs to the Mission. It's made of stone, gray granite crusted with lichens; low, perched at the very gasping brink of the empty scarp and nestled among huge gray boulders crusted too with lichens which go up the gray trunks of the gnarled Brachystegias and their twisted limbs. The trees are like Japanese dwarfed trees grown oversize but still not too big to stay among the gray rocks and gray house, and with their flat-swept tops shading from red of new leaves through a dozen shades of gray and green and brown of old leaves and pods. On the scarp side, if you lean over, holding on, you may look down on Government House and the King's African Rifles and all the rest of Zomba, said by many to be the most attractive colonial capital in the Empire, sloping down in terraced stages from the mountain foot out to the edge of the Shirwa plain. Looking the other way you see through the grayed tones on the near rocks and trees, the plateau meadow and winding trout stream with soft opulent cloud forest and outlying mushroom-like treeferns at the head of the stream and across it the steep rise of the far ridge planted to a dozen kinds of exotic conifers that show a whole new series of deep green shades in the hazy distance.

After tea we walked down through the meadow and along the cold creek and looked for trout and saw some.

Then we walked back and drove down the mountain to the town house, where all the medical staff was invited to meet us and get raving boiled.

Today we spent giving away old clothes to Wilson and piddling things like that. In the late PM we went out to old Richards, and his virgin daughters, to farewell tea.

And tomorrow we leave the hotel at 8:15 AM and the airport at 10. Nairobi in the late afternoon.

I love you. A.

In flight
Friday, September 12, 1952

Dearest: I'm writing this over a bit of the Mediterranean that you cross between the island of Elbe, which we just passed over, and Genoa, on the course from Rome, which we left an hour ago after breakfasting there, and Paris, where we'll be in another hour-and-a-half or so.

We left Blantyre day before yesterday about ten o'clock. We crossed so many datelines that I won't try to tell you the exact schedule of our trip, but only the itinerary. From Blantyre to Dar es Salaam, for an hour, then over Zanzibar to Nairobi, about 4 PM to spend the night. Next morning we checked in at Air France, to which we changed for the Nairobi to Paris flight, and got a couple of their overnight bags to go shopping for simpleminded Zanzibar curios. At ten I went to the Coryudon Museum, to which Loveridge went first in 1912 (!) and looked at their sea turtles and chameleons (the latter to check against my trio of Mlange dwarfs) and met old Copely who *was* the Museum when Loveridge got there. Then I had a long talk with the Fish Warden who's the only person I ever saw who could tell me anything about the turtles of the East African coast, and I learned some good things.

Left Nairobi about 4 PM, passed over a herd of elephants or buffalo, I couldn't quite decide which, and lots of other game (giraffes are easy to tell from 4000 ft) and then over the vast Lake Rudolph—the headwaters of the Nile—the Blue Nile, a chunk of the Sudan, a lot of Ethiopia which looks more like Honduras than anything I've seen yet, and into the dark there. (The pilot just announced we were over Genoa and I looked down and there it is.) Got to Cairo about 11 PM. Had beer, sandwiches and coffee there (after an Air France dinner with aperitif, champagne and liquor well padded out) and left about 1:30 AM. Passed over Alexandria—a spectacle, strung out in a vast delta of lights on the shore—and then slept a bit till a bump woke me up and I looked down on Crete and scattered light. From then on to Rome nothing of note. I've been talking French steadily, but not well. We're on the Madagascar to Paris plane and English is foreign to most of the crew and all the passengers. Now we're getting into the Alps and there is much more snow in the Alps this time. Most magnificent scenery of my career. At 9:30 AM we are smack over Mon Blanc, superb under glaciers spreading in all directions.

I love you. A week! Tell the young I spent the night across the aisle from 4 little French pods.

I love you. A.

Paris
September 14, 1952, Sunday

My dearest: We just left Bourget Airport and are heading

for London. The flight shouldn't be more than an hour or so.

The Paris spree was marvelous, the weather fine 'tho coolish mornings, my French better than I thought when it came to the pinches and dinner last night at Chez Vincent, a Provencal place, that I located, where we had for 2000 Francs each an aperitif, bouillabaisse of the most noble, a dry white wine, huge red raspberries and thick cream and the finest coffee in individual drip cups. I wanted you there so bad it almost blurred the victuals— but not quite. After that we went to the Ballets de Amérique Latina of Joaquim Perez Fernandes at the Théâtro de Paris which was our only shameful indulgence. The night before we went to the Follies Bergère like any dopey gringos and most of the rest of the time we spent likewise on the things you have to see: Notre Dame, Place de la Concorde, Place de la Opéra, Jardin de las Plantes, the Louvre and the Tuileries, a boat trip on the Seine around the Ile de la Cité and up to the Bois de Boulogne etc., etc.

We had a cute little hotel near Sefarino right in the middle of everything, for 1000 francs a night (the two of us). We had to miss Versailles but then we missed all of France outside the center of Paris, and you and me are going to see it some time by God. I like the French people better than any I know. They know how to have fun and don't let anybody tell you the war ruined them.

Tell our young I spent an hour watching French kids sail boats in the Tuileries fountain. Surely I'll see you before this gets there.

I love you. A.

LONDON VIA FRENCH 15-1208
MARGIE CARR   MICANOPY FLA
MEET EASTERN AIR FLIGHT JACKSONVILLE
FRIDAY SIX PM
ARCHIE

1993 Preface to the 1963 Letters

ARCHIE'S increasing interest in sea turtles and his search for answers to an increasing number of questions about their lives took him several times to Africa in the years following the 1952 *ulendo* in Tanganyka. There follows his correspondence from a short trip in 1963. These trips reinforced his belief that if wilderness is to be saved it will have to be done for motives other than more meat for man. And events have proved him to be right. The question is will the developing environmental ethic reach significant proportions in time to save the lovely landscapes and spectacular assemblages of wildlife on this earth.

Marjorie Harris Carr

Letters from Archie Carr to Marjorie Harris Carr, 1963

The May Fair Hotel, Berkeley Square, London, W.1
September 2, 1963

Dearest: Got here at 8 AM yesterday, Saturday, which was really 2 AM by gut time. Very sleepy. Slept. Then went to see *Six Characters in Search of an Author* at May Fair theater, which is in this hotel. Went to bed at 11 PM. Woke up at 3 AM, as if never to sleep again. Tossed and slept again, solid until 3 PM, just now. Going to showing of Armand Denis' film of African fauna at Royal Festival Hall at 7:30—for the Wildlife Fund. Tomorrow going to Sir Wm. Halcrow's in AM and the British Museum in PM. Leave for Nairobi 8 PM tomorrow. Get there about 8 AM Nairobi time.

Was having coffee downstairs a while ago, and a huge black man sat by me and had coffee too. Sonny Liston. Fighting exhibitions around England. Not as mean looking as pictured, but big.

I don't know why Mr. Masson [the travel agent] sent me here, but it's pretty elegant. Had green turtle soup at the Chateaubriand—which is *also* in this hotel. Wish you were here. I love you. A.

Airport, Benghazi
September 4, 1963

Dearest: Had a hectic time in London getting away. The Kenya government is suddenly a lot more strict about entrance documents than before. I had to stay over in London an extra day to get mine. The damndest thing, though. Yesterday when I thought I was leaving and weighed in at the terminal in town they reckoned I had $30. excess baggage. When I had to cancel the flight they refunded the cash, and today when I weighed in there was no charge at all. I didn't ask why.

I spent most of the extra day going between the British Passport Office, the Uganda House, and the East African Tourist Office. I got lost quite a lot, though, and once I stumbled into Westminster Abbey, and stayed to give it a looking at. It's a very imposing bit of work. Had to rent some soft shoes to go into one room—don't recall what it is called, but maybe you will—and saw there very ancient murals and a floor of tiles like in Lloyd Haberly's book. Recollect?

I got out of my visa difficulty only by changing my destination from Nairobi to Entebbe (Uganda). I was going there anyway day after tomorrow though—for the Murchison and Queen Elizabeth Park tours—so it didn't make much difference. My one disappointment was that I was going to get out of the plane at Nairobi and into a taxi and make it take me straight-away (as we say in the U.K.) on a 16 mile safari. Getting to Entebbe, or Kampala really, I don't know for sure whether I'll have a hotel room but guess I can find something.

Had a long talk with Colin Pennyquick at Cambridge. We see eye to eye, I think, about the impossibility of a beast finding its longitude in the open sea. Also had a good visit with Miss Grandison, and found no ridley at all from the whole East Coast of Africa in the British Museum. This is a very significant thing but you won't know why and I shan't explain just now.

P.S. This was written aboard East African Airways flight 715 departing London 9:30 AM for Entebbe, via Rome and Benghazi. Writing done between London and Rome. Mailing, only God knows. I love you. Love also to Mimi, Chuck, Steve, Tom and David. A.

Benghazi, Lybia
September 4, 1963

On taking off here at 2 AM a hideous sound was heard. The trouble turned out to be a motor with a stone from the runway in it. We're stuck here for nobody knows how long—till a new plane can be sent from London or Nairobi. Very hot. Pretty good hotel. Camels and asses standing about. Don't know whether we'll make the Uganda deadline tomorrow. Some august IUCN figures in the stricken passenger list though, and the departure for the parks might be held up for us.

Benghazi, Lybia
September 4, 1963 7:30 PM

The damndest thing. Just heard we'll be here till 4 PM *tomorrow*. BOAC has taken on the schedules of South African Airways, which isn't allowed to land in the East African countries. This ties up so many planes they can't bail us out. There are about 50 of us stuck here. If I leave at 4 as planned I'll get to Kampala before midnight and the tour starts at 6 AM the next day. Love to you and the young. A.

The Oceanic, Mombasa, Kenya
September 13, 1963

Dearest: Never did such wild tearing about. Just off for trip up the coast. Beautiful coast. They use remoras [a small fish with a sucking disk on the top of its head] for catching turtles, but weather too windy to go out. Bad luck there.

But the US Albatross [seaplane] just arrived to establish first air communication with Seychelles. It's to supply one of our missile tracking stations. If I should wheedle them into taking me I'd get home a bit late. I love you all. Wish you were here. A.

P.S. I'll be back in Nairobi, Sunday, 15th Sept.

Malindi, Kenya
[postcard of ancient city of Gedi, Malindi]
September 15, 1963

Walking the beach after turtle tracks opposite these ruins, I came upon crystal pools among stacks and tidal islands of limestone where mudskippers and a small skink were obviously parcelling out the basking and foraging space among themselves. Imagine! A marvelous rapprochement of reptiles and fish. No? What hath God wrought! Found Bajun people; talked with chief. Too windy to remora-fish. Love, A.

Hotel Sindbad, Malindi, Kenya

Dearest: I have by dint of great annoyance to all local persons zeroed in on a colony of Bajun islanders, the Arab-likes who catch sea turtles with sucker-fish. I'm going to commune with them in the morning with a good resourceful Swahili to tell me what they say. It's too windy to go out turtling, but I'm going to commune.

This morning I went out on the reef at Turtle Bay just south of an ancient, elaborate Arab town at Gedi. Dates from 1200 and strangling figs envelope the masonry. Imposing, right?

I like this coast. No turtle nesting but a good coast. Sucker-fishing and all. Wish you were here. I love you. A.

New Stanley Hotel, Nairobi, Kenya

Dearest: Your letter of Sept. 8 just reached me today, back in Nairobi after a small snoop along the coast north of Mombasa.

Got a lot of good turtle dope, found the Bajun remora turtlers, but was most impressed by lizards and mudskippers scurrying up rocks to escape me, from around little tide pools.

I miss you a lot, and, except when viewing animals, wish badly I was back there, or somewhere with you. Love to all. I love you. A.

P.S. Two genial Swedes here have read *The Windward Road* in Swedish and wax complimentary.

Got some swell black and white pictures at Murchison Falls and Queen Elizabeth Parks.

Tananarine, Madagascar
[postcard of Imerina, paysage des plateaux]
October 5, 1963

This is just to be sure you see what the countryside here is like. My photos are only of lemurs and cloud forest.

Be home before this gets there and am glad. Love, A.

Index

Afrikaans, ix
Akeley, Carl, 233
Alachua Lake, 160
American egret, 184, 220–1
American isthmus, 25
American Museum of Natural History, 142
Americans, 7, 17, 18, 22
American Scholar, The, 100
anhinga, 178
Arabs, 66, 70
Ariano, Captain, 16, 27–59, 102
Ascension Island, xi
Athi Plain, 5, 10
Auffenberg, Walter, 230, 231
Auk, The, 210
Australia, 122, 125

baboons, 6
Bantu, 23
Bantus, 18
Barbour, Thomas, 103
Barbus, 107
Bartram, William, 161
bataleur eagle, 6
Bates, Marston, 100, 101
Beira, 16, 17, 31
Belkin, Dan, 212–16
bell bird, 220
Bermuda, 210

Berner, Lewis, ix, **x, 18–20,** 103, 141, 158, 187, 224
bilharzia snails, 166
Bishop Laws, 64, 65
Bishop Mackenzie, 16
bison, 232
black bass, 130
black-breasted **buzzard, 197**
black vultures, 187–92
blanco, 54
Blantyre, 99, 109
boa, 142
Boadzulu, 73–8
Borassus, 169
Brazil, xi, 210
Britannia, 12
British Museum, **107**
Brycon, 54
buffalo, 28

Cakchiqueles, 26
Cape Town, 224
capitao, 126–9
Caribbean, 23
Caribs, 24
Carr, Marjorie, 130–1
Catacamas, Honduras, **190**
catfish, 58, 117
cattle egret, 165–225
Central America, 22–4, 118, 128, 129

chambo, 105–39
Chaoborus, 79–104
Chapin, James, 209
Chevrolet, 32
Chidiamperi Island, 76–8
Chinal Jul, 22
Chinyanja, ix, 27, 62, 113, 118
Chiromo, 16, 17, 20, 26, 27, 30
Chiyao, 51, 118
Cichlidae, 58, 105–39
cichlids, 58, 105–39
Clewiston, Florida, 210
Coal Tit, 198
Coban, Guatemala, 190
Coca-Cola, 153, 154
Coleridge, 161
common egret, 184, 220, 221
Conservation Foundation, 234
Corethra, 79–104
cormorants, 73–8, 167–9, 178
corn, 14, 15, 18, 59
cowbirds, 129
Cretaceous, 223
crocodile, 115, 116
cuckoo, European, 129

Darling, Fraser, 234, 237
Darwin, Charles, 122
Dedza, 61
District Commissioner, 170, 173
Ditmars, Raymond, 142
Dona Ana, 176, 177

East African Standard, 247
Ecuador, 190
Eersterivier, 225
Egypt, 209
Elephant Marsh, 18
elephants, 14–59, 247
elephant-snout fish, 87, 117
Emlen, John, 238
Empress, 30, 55
Enfield rifle, 43

Entomological Research Center, 93
Eoff, Kay, 213
Escuela Agrícola Panamericana, 188–92
Expedition to the Zambezi, 68

fire, 242–5
fish eagles, 178
Florida, 73, 74, 88, 148, 159–64, 181–5, 193, 199, 208, 210–18, 220, 223, 224, 228, 231, 235, 236, 242
Florida State Board of Health, 93
Fort Johnston, 51, 72, 108
francolins, 6
Fryer, Geoffrey, 125, 132, 135, 137

Gainesville, Florida, 160
Galapagos Islands, 122, 196–7
Game Management, xi
gazelles, 6, 217
geese, 178, 179
Georgia, 22, 244
German East Africa, 70
Ghana, 255
giant tortoises, 232
Goa, 11
Goanese, 7
Golfo Dulce, 23
Grand Marimba, 21
Grand Savanna Life, xii
Grant's gazelle, 219
great blue heron, 185
Great Tit, 198
great white heron, 220
green turtle, xi
Guanacaste, 190, 191
guapi, 145
guapote, 106
Guatemala, 21–4
Guatemala City, 24

Index

Guatemalan Indians, 23
Guendolen, 70-2

Haplochromis, 105-39
hartebeest, 217
Hemingway, Ernest, 40
Hermann von Wissman, 70-2
Hindu, 7
Hindustani, 11
hippopotamus, 173-6
hippopotamus dance, 173-6
Hogaboom, Henry, 189-90
"Holiday Bus," 7, 11
Honduras, 153, 188-92
Humber, 51
Humber Super Snipe, 103
Hydrocyon, 53
hyena, 4
hyrax, 250

Ice Age, 223
Ichtucknee Springs, 228
Ilala, 61, 64, 65, 70, 79, 80, 90, 95, 97
impala, 9, 10, 219
Indian corn, 14
Indian girls, 7
Indian Ocean, 14, 16
International Union for the Conservation of Nature, 234

jackals, 6
Johannesburg, 12
Jonah's Pond, 235
Jordan's Law, 122
Juday, Chancey, 87

Kampala, 237
Kansas, 14
Kariba Dam, 234
Kenya, 3-13, 217
Kenyatta, Jomo, 255
Khartoum, 220

khoka, 119
Kilimanjaro, 258
King, Wayne, 213
kingfishers, 178
Kipling, Rudyard, 141
Komodo dragon, 73
kongoni, 6, 217
Kota Kota, 61, 62, 65
Kruger National Park, 9, 10, 239, 247
Kubla Khan, 161
kudu, 232
kungu flies, 61, 72, 79-104

Lake Alice, 209, 235
Lake Edward, 124
Lake Eola, 193
Lake Managua, 106
Lake Mendota, 87
lake mullet, 117
Lake Nyasa, 16, 60-104, 105-39
Lake Pátzcuaro, 119
lake salmon, 117
Lake Shirwa, 76-8
Lake Tanganyika, 124
Lake Victoria, 87, 88, 124
Land Rover, 103, 165, 169
Laurenço Marques, 51
Leopold, Aldo, xi, xii
Limbe, 19, 103
lions, 3-13, 34, 37, 38, 226, 241, 242
Lisbon, 51
little blue heron, 184, 220
little green heron, 193-5
Livingstone, David, 23, 63, 64, 67, 68, 79, 80, 103, 205, 224
Longfellow, H. W., 51
Louisiana heron, 184-5
Lovell, Harvey, 193-5
Loveridge, Arthur, 142
Lowe, Rosemary, 107
Lower Shire River, 19

Maine, 210
maize, 14, 15, 18, 22, 59
Makerere College, 237
mammoth, 230
maribou storks, 167–9
marimba, 20–4
Ma Robert, 63, 224
Masai, 6
mastodon, 229
Matope, 70
Mau Mau, 7
Mauritania, 209
Maya, 22
Megaza, 164, 175, 179
Mexico, 21
Middle Shire River, 30
Mikindani, 64
Miocene, 132
Miskitos, 24
Mitchell, B. L., 19–20, 76
Mlanje Mountain, 31
Mlozi, Chief, 70
monitor lizards, 73–8
Morrambala, 207
Morris Minor, 4, 5
mosquitoes, 18, 19
Mozambique, 14–59, 62, 84, 88, 94, 164
Murchison Rapids, 16, 65
Mutarara, 177

Nairobi, 4, 5, 10, 220
Nairobi National Park, 3–13, 239, 247
National Parks, 245, 246
Nature Conservancy, 236
New York Zoological Society, 234
Nicaragua, 106
Nielsen, Erik T., 97
North America, 223–4
Ntundu, 143
Nuffield Unit of Tropical Animal Ecology, 237

nyala, 20
Nyanjas, 26, 66–70, 99, 140
Nyasaland, ix, x, 16, 17, 19, 45, 51, 60–78, 105–39, 140–58, 165–75, 178
Nyasaland Journal, 70–2
Nyerere, Julius K., 255

Ocala Scrub, 148
Okeechobee, Florida, 210
Oliver, James A., 142, 148, 149
Ol Tukai, 258
Orange Lake, 160
Orlando, Florida, 193

Paynes Prairie, 159–64, 205
pelicans, 167–9, 178
Petrides, George, 237
piranha, 54
Piri Piri, 164, 166, 169, 175–80, 187, 205, 207
Pleistocene, xii, 6, 187, 231, 236
plover, 6
poaching, 248–53
Port Herald, 165–75, 178
Portuguese, 18, 23, 118
Portuguese East Africa, 14–59, 81
Prince Philip, 234
Project Noah, 234
pronghorns, 232
Provost, Maurice, 93
Puerto Rico, 210
python, 140–58
python preserve, 73, 78
pythons, 73–8

Raphia palm, 145
rhinoceros, 248
Rice, Dale, 210, 211
Ridley turtle, x
Rift, Great African, 63, 132
Río Dulce, 24
Rocky Mountain National Park, 6

Index

Rogers, J. Speed, 83–6
Roosevelt, Theodore, 39, 233
Ruo River, 16–18, 27

St. Croix, 210
Sanderson, Meredith, 71–2
San Josè, Costa Rica, 190
sávalo, 54
savanna fauna, 231, 232
Savannah, 26
sea turtles, x, xi
Sena, 22, 51
Senas, 169–73
Serengeti, 248, 249
Shire Country, 18
Shire River, x, 16, 26, 52–5, 62, 64, 65, 70, 140–58, 165, 175, 178, 224
Shire Valley, x, 99, 153
Simon, Noel, 234
Sir William Halcrow and Partners, x
Skukuza, 9
slaving, 65–70
snails, 18
Snake Key, 73, 74
snowy egret, 159–225
South Africa, 210
South Carolina, 210
Spain, 24
Sphinxhaven, 70
Stellenbosch, 224
Stoddard, Herbert, 244
stump-knocker, 131
Suwannee bass, 230
Swahili, 11, 118

Tanganyika, 70, 142, 255
Tenghadzi, 58
Texas, 40, 41
tiger fish, 52, 53, 58
Tilapia, 105–39

Times, The, 72
tits, 198–9
Treichel, George, 234
Trewavas, Ethelwynn, 118
Tsavo National Park, 247

ufa, 99
Umatilla, Florida, 199
Universities Mission, 16
University of Florida, ix, 83, 209, 212, 235
usipa, 119, 120
Varanus niloticus, 73–8
Vipya, 63
von Wissman, Major Hermann, 70

Wallace, H. K., 199
wart hog, 155
waterbuck, 34, 232
Wayne, John, 40
wildebeest, 6, 217, 232
Wilson, ix, 17, 18, 26, 109–15, 118, 169
Wilson Bulletin, The, 193
Windward Road, The, x
woodpecker finch, 196, 197
World War I, 70
World Wildlife Fund, 234

Yao, 53, 109
Yaos, 66
Young, Edward, 64, 65, 95

Zambezi, The, 23
Zambezi fauna, 58
Zambezi River, 16, 23, 63–5, 164–6, 176–81
Zanzibar, 67
Zea mays, 15
zebra, 6, 219, 232
Zomba, 76